Janice

Thanks for all of your love & support.
Enjoy the book!

Derrick E.

The Challenge of Blackness

SOUTHERN DISSENT

UNIVERSITY PRESS OF FLORIDA

Florida A&M University, Tallahassee
Florida Atlantic University, Boca Raton
Florida Gulf Coast University, Ft. Myers
Florida International University, Miami
Florida State University, Tallahassee
New College of Florida, Sarasota
University of Central Florida, Orlando
University of Florida, Gainesville
University of North Florida, Jacksonville
University of South Florida, Tampa
University of West Florida, Pensacola

THE CHALLENGE OF BLACKNESS

The Institute of the Black World and Political Activism in the 1970s

Derrick E. White

Foreword by Stanley Harrold and Randall M. Miller

University Press of Florida
Gainesville · Tallahassee · Tampa · Boca Raton
Pensacola · Orlando · Miami · Jacksonville · Ft. Myers · Sarasota

16 15 14 13 12 11   6 5 4 3 2 1

Library of Congress Cataloging-in-Publication Data
White, Derrick E.
The challenge of blackness : the Institute of the Black World and political
activism in the 1970s / Derrick E. White ; foreword by Stanley Harrold and
Randall M. Miller.
p. cm.—(Southern dissent)
Includes bibliographical references and index.
ISBN 978-0-8130-3735-6 (alk. paper)
1. Institute of the Black World—History. 2. African Americans—Study and
teaching—History—20th century. 3. Blacks—Study and teaching—History—
20th century. 4. African American intellectuals—History—20th century.
5. African Americans—Intellectual life—20th century. 6. African
Americans—Social conditions—20th century. I. Title.
E184.7.W44   2011
305.896'073—dc22
2011011175

The University Press of Florida is the scholarly publishing agency for the
State University System of Florida, comprising Florida A&M University,
Florida Atlantic University, Florida Gulf Coast University, Florida
International University, Florida State University, New College of Florida,
University of Central Florida, University of Florida, University of North
Florida, University of South Florida, and University of West Florida.

University Press of Florida
15 Northwest 15th Street
Gainesville, FL 32611-2079
http://www.upf.com

This work is dedicated to my inner circle, my mother and father,
Joyce and H. E. White, my brother, Jerome,
and my loving wife, Stephanie.
Your love and support gave me the perseverance to write this book.

Contents

Illustrations

Abbreviations

6-PAC	Sixth Pan-African Congress
ALD	African Liberation Day
ALSC	African Liberation Support Committee
AUC	Atlanta University Center
BAN	Black Agenda Network
BEOs	Black Elected Officials
BERC	Black Economic Research Center
BPP	Black Panther Party
BSU	Black Student Union
CAP	Congress of African People
CBC	Congressional Black Caucus
COINTELPRO	FBI's Counterintelligence Program
HBCUs	Historically Black Colleges and Universities
IBW	Institute of the Black World
LDP	Library Documentation Project
MFDP	Mississippi Freedom Democratic Party
NAACP	National Association for the Advancement of Colored People
NSM	Northern Student Movement
SCLC	Southern Christian Leadership Conference
SNCC	Student Nonviolent Coordinating Committee
SRS '71	1971 Summer Research Symposium
SRS '74	1974 Summer Research Symposium
SLA	Symbionese Liberation Army
VB	Venceremos Brigade

Foreword

Scholars, politicians, activists, and the general American public view the civil rights movement from multiple perspectives. On one extreme is the story of black persistence and success in fulfilling a promise of opportunity and equal rights born during Reconstruction but denied for a century. It emphasizes an effort on behalf of black equality centered on the South and led by Martin Luther King Jr. As the story goes, King and his associates relied on nonviolent civil disobedience, mass protest, and eloquent oratory to secure racial integration and black advancement. Congress ratified their efforts in the Civil Rights Act of 1964 and the Voting Rights Act of 1965. The Civil Rights Act opened avenues for long-denied employment, legal and social justice, and advancement. The number of black college students, for example, rose from less than a quarter million in 1960 to over a million by 1977. The Voting Rights Act led to a great surge in black voter registration and to an astounding increase in the number of black elected officials—especially in the South.

On the other extreme is the story of a civil rights movement in fragments by 1968, when King died from an assassin's bullet. It was a movement destined to be ineffective during the 1970s. Amid a white backlash centered on the issue of court-ordered busing for the purpose of school desegregation and white flight from urban neighborhoods, the majority of African Americans became poorer and more isolated. In 1970, nearly twenty-seven percent of black families earned less than ten thousand dollars annually. By 1986, that figure had risen to over thirty percent, and poverty continued to afflict black communities thereafter. Just as they had earlier, most black children attended segregated schools in underfunded districts. Most black families lived in dangerous, crime-infested neighborhoods, with little prospect of upward mobility.

Partially as a result of these conflicting narratives, black leadership splintered during the 1970s among integrationist-leaning politicians, nationalists, and Marxists. As political scientist Ronald Walters of Howard University put it, a "new group of black elected officials joined the civil rights leaders and became a new leadership class, but there was sort of a conflict outlook between them and the more indigenous, social, grassroots-oriented nationalist movement."

In *The Challenge of Blackness: The Institute of the Black World and Political Activism in the 1970s*, Derrick E. White carefully analyzes the role of a group of black intellectuals during these turbulent times. In 1969, at the start of what White calls the "long seventies," black historian and theologian Vincent Harding led in the establishment of the Institute of the Black World at Atlanta University. The institute is best known for its role in defining and promoting an effort, begun during the 1960s by black college students, to establish black studies programs and departments at predominantly white colleges and universities.

White shows that the chronically underfunded institute did a great deal more than promote black studies. It advocated a practical black nationalism and mediated among ideologically diverse groups. As the nationalists, Marxists, and "traditional civil rights organizations, such as the NAACP" presented conflicting programs, the institute sought a "middle ground." It strove for a "synthesis of leading ideas and ideologies," and "consensus" through "collective scholarship." It also translated ideas into action by encouraging scholarship that served social justice.

White portrays the institute as assembling "the greatest roster of Black intellectuals, activists, and artists . . . in post–World War II American history." Its leaders included (besides Harding) Stephen Henderson and William Strickland. Its supporters included actor Ossie Davis, politicians John Conyers and Maynard Jackson, and historians Lerone Bennet Jr., Walter Rodney, and Sterling Stuckey. The institute attempted to provide a social analysis that combined a black nationalist perspective with an American pragmatism. This was no easy undertaking, and White describes the factors that led to the institute's termination in 1983. That it lasted as long as it did reflects Harding's belief that "those determined not to be moved, who know, against all odds, that they will overcome, will continue to create a more perfect union, [and] a more compassionate world."

That the Institute of the Black World's story has not been told until now reflects a historiography biased toward narratives of direct action, as opposed to those of people engaged in studied analyses of social problems. *The Challenge of Blackness* is corrective. It shows how dissent encourages intellectual contests over the direction and meaning of identity and interest. It is a welcome addition to the Southern Dissent series.

Stanley Harrold and Randall M. Miller
Series Editors

Acknowledgments

The idea for this project began with discussions of Black intellectual history in the office of Leslie Alexander, my former colleague. Several graduate students and I had almost daily conversations about history, culture, sports, and life. Leslie insisted that I read Vincent Harding's *Beyond Chaos*, planting the first seeds of this book. The seeds of this project grew out of my time at the Ohio State University. I want to thank the Department of African American and African Studies for their confidence in me. My professors at OSU have been tremendous role models and mentors. I especially want to thank William E. Nelson Jr., Demetrius Eudell (now at Wesleyan University), H. Ike Okafor-Newsum, James Upton, William Theodore McDaniel, and Ahmad Sikainga. I also want to thank my mentors in the department of history, Alexander, Warren Van Tine, and Hasan Jeffries. I am grateful for the friends that I met and who kept me sane at OSU—Javonne Paul Stewart, Jelani Favors, Ernest Perry, and everyone involved in the Black Graduate and Professional Student Caucus. Thank you.

I have received tremendous support from numerous scholars who have taken time to support this book. My colleagues at Florida Atlantic University have supported me as I have completed this project. I am thankful to Stephen Engle, Clevis Headley, Maria Banchetti, Ken Osgood, Patricia Kollander, Mark Rose, and Chris Strain for their advice and comments on my proposals and manuscripts. I also want to thank Anna Lawrence, Kenneth Holloway, and Sika Dagbovie for their friendship. I would like to thank my scholars and friends at the University of California–Santa Barbara for their help. Will Hughes, Chris McAuley, Mireille Miller-Young, and Cedric Robinson, each of you made my experiences in California memorable. In my time in the profession I have met tremendous friends and colleagues. I would like to thank Hasan Jeffries, Paul Ortiz, Pero Dagbovie, Jeffrey Ogbar, Michelle Scott, Scot Brown Stephen Ward, Fanon Che Wilkins, and Maurice Hobson. Thanks for great conversation, advice, and friendship.

Any research project needs financial backing. I would like to thank Florida Atlantic University's College of Arts and Letters and the Department of History for the financial support that allowed me to complete research and writing.

In any project, you incur many debts, and I want to acknowledge these institutions and people for their support. The Schomburg Center for Research in Black Culture Manuscripts, Archives, and Rare Books Division's support was irreplaceable. I want to thank the staff—Andre Elizee, Steven G. Fullwood, Judy Holder, Diana Lachatanere, and Nurah-Rosalie Teter—for without their help I would never have gained access to the Institute of the Black World Papers. I would like to thank Mary Yearwood and the entire Photographs and Print Division staff for access to the pictures in this book. In addition, I would like to thank Pat Clark at Emory University's Woodruff Library, who provided access to the Vincent Harding Papers. A special thanks goes to Karen Jefferson, Andrea Jackson, and the archives and special collection staff at Atlanta University's Woodruff Library.

I want to thank Meredith Morris-Babb, Stanley Harrold, Randall M. Miller, and the entire University Press of Florida staff for their support, advice, and ensuring that this project moved along at a good pace. I would like to thank the anonymous reviewers whose comments made this a stronger book. Thank you.

This project could not have been completed without the support of former members of the Institute of the Black World. I want to thank William Strickland, who always answered any question that I had. I would like to thank Vincent Harding, Robert Hill, Howard Dodson, Jualynne Dodson, Abdul Alkalimat, and Sharon Burke for sharing their experiences with me. It should also be noted that I received tremendous encouragement from scholars and activists who heard I was researching IBW, including James Turner, Ronald Walters, Mary Frances Berry, Maulana Karenga, Sylvia Wynter, Al Colon, and others. These formal and informal conversations were invaluable and reminded me of the importance of this project.

Finally, I want to thank my friends and family. This project is as much for you as it is for me. Behailu and Lisa Dagnatchew, David and Tamiko Hubbard, Alvin and Zykia Lee, Lee and Leslie Meggett, and the rest of

New Reign, thanks for your support, allowing me to sleep on your couches and in your guest rooms, and reminding me to have fun. It's a celebration. I am especially grateful for my brother Jerome White, his wife, Jenell, my nephew Nicholas, and my aunt Lenora. Thanks for your support. To my parents, Howard and Joyce White, thank you for your unceasing love. I probably do not say it enough, but I love you. I want to say thanks to family members who did not get a chance to see the completion of this book. To my grandmother, Mattie, uncles Aaron and Larry, and my mother-in-law Marcella, thank you for supporting me in life and watching over me. Last but not least, thanks to my wife, Stephanie. Without your love and support, this project would never have been completed. You believed in me when I doubted myself. I want to thank you for reading the manuscript when I knew that you did not want to. I love you.

The Challenge of Blackness

Introduction

Where Do We Go From Here?

The Long Seventies

Our course of action must lie neither in passively relying on persuasion nor actively succumbing to violent rebellion, but in a higher synthesis that reconciles the truths of these two opposites while avoiding the inadequacies and ineffectiveness of both.

> Martin Luther King Jr., *Where Do We Go From Here? Chaos or Community*

All political power presents itself to the world in a certain framework of ideas. It is fatal to ignore this in any estimate of social forces in political action.

> C.L.R. James, "Myth of African Inferiority" in *Education and Black Struggle*

In the Memphis dusk of early April 1968, James Earl Ray assassinated Martin Luther King Jr., and with this crushing blow, the decade of the seventies began. The civil rights leader's murder elicited anger, sadness, and confusion about the future direction of the civil rights movement, specifically how to achieve true equality. King prophetically anticipated the multitude of responses to his assassination when he asked, "Where do we go from here?" King's question about the future reflected the divergent realities engulfing the civil rights movement after the passage of the 1964 Civil Rights Act and the 1965 Voting Rights Act. His opposition to the Vietnam War in 1967 and his plans for a Poor People's March in 1968 strained relations with old allies such as Bayard Rustin, while his criticisms of violent Black Power rhetoric distanced the civil rights leader from an emerging cadre of Black Nationalists. King suggested that reconciliation among the various segments of the movement needed a "higher synthesis," not ideological and analytical rigidity. In the 1970s, as activists contemplated continuing the Black Freedom Struggle, the longer struggle for racial and economic justice and equality, some accepted King's challenge to reconcile the divergent threads of the freedom movement.

Into this morass of anger, disappointment, and confusion emerged the Institute of the Black World (IBW). Led primarily by historian and theologian Vincent Harding, the IBW was a collection of activist-intellectuals who analyzed the educational, political, and activist landscape to further the Black Freedom Struggle in the wake of King's assassination, specifically using their intellectual and organizational skills in an attempt to develop the synthetic analysis King sought. Fueled by King's soul-penetrating question about the future of the movement, the end of legal segregation, and the continuation of racial disparities, the intellectuals working at the IBW searched for new ideas, implemented novel organizational methodologies, and analyzed Black socioeconomic and cultural realities during the long decade of the seventies.

The Challenge of Blackness examines the history of the IBW as a means to explore how this group of activists adjusted to different ideological approaches within Black activist communities on one hand, and how the organization, and the Black Freedom Struggle, grappled with the growing conservatism of the 1970s on the other. These internal and external conflicts are evaluated by relying on three interrelated concepts: the long seventies, the IBW as an activist think tank, and associates' production of synthetic analyses. These three frameworks provide the broad context for the IBW's rise and fall, the organization's interactions with other Black activist organizations, and its legacy of activism and scholarly production.

The decade of the seventies does not evoke the nostalgia or historic memories of the fifties or the sixties for historians or cultural critics. There are obvious reasons for forgetting the seventies. It was a decade defined by crises: the murder of Jewish Olympic athletes in 1972; failure in Vietnam; the Organization of Petroleum Exporting Countries' (OPEC) control of oil and resulting embargo; growing rates of drug abuse; the worst economic environment since the Great Depression; and an American hostage situation in Iran lasting more than four hundred days. Beneath the despair, activist groups continued to push for progressive change regarding women's rights, the environment, and nuclear proliferation. Conservative groups organized to defeat what they called the excesses of the sixties, setting the stage for a conservative political revolution. The scholarship on the seventies, however, typically marginalizes Black activism during the decade, preferring to deify the nonviolent direct-action civil rights movement and demonize the Black Power era.[1]

For Black activists, the long seventies began with King's assassination in 1968 and lasted until Ronald Reagan's election in 1980. A defining feature of the decade was the increasing ideological rigidity in the form of Black Nationalism, Marxism, or integrationism. Three distinct phases of Black activism shape the long seventies. From King's assassination in 1968 through the first African Liberation Day in May 1972, Black activism witnessed tremendous, albeit temporary, unity among activists who held various ideological perspectives. The highlights of this short-lived unity were the creation and support for Black Studies programs and the 1972 National Black Political Convention in Gary, Indiana. The IBW thrived during this period of temporary unity, providing intellectual support for both Black Studies and the Gary Convention. The second phase of the decade ran from approximately mid-1972 through the 1976 presidential election and was marked by growing dissension. The main source of disagreement among Black activists was the race versus class ideological debate, and it destroyed the ephemeral unity. Black elected officials and traditional civil rights organizations such as the NAACP distanced themselves from the increasingly esoteric rhetoric of Black Nationalism and Marxism. Among grassroots activists, elected officials, and civil rights organizations, unity frayed due to ideological difference and personal ambitions. In the third phase, which ran from the mid-seventies through Reagan's election, Black activists, organizations, and elected officials simply tried to survive the growing White backlash, specifically increasing conservatism, police intervention, and the socioeconomic effects of stagflation and drug abuse. In this phase, activist organizations struggled with the weight of financial instability, police harassment, and declining influence. Black elected officials, often in demographically safe districts, manipulated grassroots activism during election campaigns but remained aloof when it came to accountability. Activists with an academic background often transitioned into professors in Black Studies programs. These programs were one of the few safe places for former progressive activists. The IBW's organizational trajectory reflects these three phases of Black activism during the seventies: fleeting unity, dissension, and survival.

By the seventies, the ideas, strategies, organizations, and aims of Black Power were central to any discussion of continuing the Black Freedom Struggle. Although Black Power's antecedents stretch back into 1950s radicalism and Black Nationalism, Stokely Carmichael synthesized and popularized these ideas into a simple slogan that spread like wildfire, requiring activists and organizations to explain, denounce, or celebrate the term. Early civil rights movement scholars were initially reluctant to study Black Power activists and organizations. More often, scholars of civil rights blamed Black Power activists for the end of the movement. For example, Clayborne Carson's *In Struggle* describes the Student Non-violent Coordinating Committee's (SNCC) shift to Black Nationalism and Black Power as the "falling apart" of the organization.[2] While this may explain some of SNCC's decline, Carson fails to systematically investigate if SNCC had reached a logical conclusion under the intellectual framework of the "beloved community" and integrationism. Historian Peniel E. Joseph accurately describes Carson's and other scholars' approaches to the emergence of Black Power as promoting the "notion that the Black Power movement destroyed the more pragmatic Civil Rights movement."[3]

Still, the very idea of a "Black Power movement" obscures tremendous organizational and ideological diversity as much as it reveals opposition to civil rights tenets. The activists, organizations, strategies, and ideologies that fell under the slogan "Black Power" were extremely diverse and sometimes contradictory.[4] Slowly scholars have begun to dissect the movement, revealing successes and failures and outlining areas of convergence and divergence between organizations. Scholars have reevaluated activists such as Robert F. Williams, Maulana Karenga, Amiri Baraka, and the Black Panther Party.[5] Scholars have examined self-defense as well as ideologies of nationalism, Marxism, and liberalism.[6] Black Power has been studied in its urban and rural contexts.[7] Recent scholarship has examined the effects of Black Power on art, elected officials, universities, and athletes.[8] The new scholarship reveals a complex narrative of Black Power activism that left an indelible mark on American society and culture. However, the scholarship on the Black Power era has not fully revealed the contours of Black activism during the long seventies, as most studies stop in the early part of the decade.[9] The long seventies accounts for the tremendous amount of Black activism, the growing dissension, and organizations' attempts at mere survival.

From the ashes of King's assassination and from the seeds of the early Black Power movement emerged a variety of new Black activist organizations that Peniel E. Joseph has described as the "second wave of Black Power."[10] Among these organizations was the IBW. Under Harding's leadership, the IBW's associates announced that they wanted to use their minds "in the service of the Black community."[11] The Institute carved out a unique role amid these manifold organizations as an activist think tank and a common source for social, economic, political, and cultural information among Black intellectuals, grassroots activists, Black elected officials, and traditional civil rights organizations. The IBW reflected a new type of think tank that emerged during the seventies, one designed to facilitate the transition to a post–civil rights era while maintaining a certain accountability to grassroots organizations.

Twentieth-century think tanks emerged in three phases. The first phase reflected the Progressive era's emphasis on technical expertise and a belief that science could solve modern problems. Leading philanthropists such as Russell Sage, Robert Brookings, and Andrew Carnegie funded institutes run by technocrats that conducted medium- and long-term policy studies. Although not value-neutral, these think tanks, like the Brookings Institute (1907), stressed objectivity. The second wave of think tanks began after World War II and focused on defense and foreign policy. The federal government funded many of these institutes, like the RAND Corporation (1948). Driven by Cold War logic, think tanks of this era often worked closely with government officials to develop policy initiatives. The IBW's founding and decision to become a think tank coincided with what scholars have called the "third wave" of think tanks. Institutes established from the early 1970s through the late 1980s differed from those created in the two previous periods because they directly marketed ideas to the public instead of to policy officials. These advocacy institutes, according to political scientist Donald E. Abelson, placed more emphasis on short policy briefs than on book-length manuscripts. Moreover, "to influence public opinion and public policy, these types of institutes placed a high premium on gaining access to the media." Radical, liberal, and conservative think tanks all tried to shape public consciousness about policy issues with the intention of transforming political norms. In the wake of the 1960s, there was a battle over which set of ideas would shape the remainder of the century.[12]

In becoming an activist think tank that developed strategies and analyses of cultural and policy issues designed to build consensus among various strands of Black activism, the IBW differentiated itself from contemporary Black research organizations such as the interracial Metropolitan Applied Research Center (MARC), which was founded in 1967 as a "pure think tank" that avoided activism or advocacy, and the Joint Center for Political and Economic Studies, founded in 1970 as an integrated research organization with moderate racial analysis that avoided activism. The primary audience for traditional think tanks like MARC and the Joint Center was the growing number of Black elected officials (BEOs). The IBW, on the other hand, had three different audiences. First, it targeted Black scholars developing Black Studies programs. The IBW's associates devoted their initial and last years to theorizing and analyzing the nature, need, and direction of Black Studies as an academic discipline. University Black Studies programs were the IBW's foundation throughout its existence. The IBW's second audience was BEOs. In particular, the IBW played an important and valuable role during the 1972 Gary Convention and in helping Maynard Jackson become the first Black mayor of Atlanta in 1972. The final audience for the IBW's advocacy was grassroots organizations. The IBW targeted these organizations through direct mailings, a newspaper column, and articles in numerous magazines, such as *Ebony* and *Negro Digest/Black World*. The IBW used these publications to promote the organization's perspective on social, political, and cultural issues. More importantly, when Black activist organizations vehemently disagreed on the appropriate ideological perspective regarding race or class, the IBW used their publications to mediate these growing divisions by promoting a synthetic analysis of issues designed to generate consensus among Black progressives. These three audiences were also essential because they financially supported the IBW in its decade-long struggle to keep its doors open. In many ways, the IBW could be seen as a poorly funded counterbalance to the conservative Heritage Foundation, a group founded in 1973 which influenced politicians with its conservative policy papers and galvanized citizens with its direct-mail campaign.[13]

As a think tank, the IBW's associates needed to produce scholarly analyses of contemporary issues facing Black communities that benefited each of its three distinctive constituencies. To complete this analytical work, the IBW's associates applied Martin Luther King Jr.'s dictum in the epigraph calling for the synthesis of leading ideas and ideologies. The IBW's members produced synthetic analysis, meaning that their scholarly production accounted for and incorporated a variety of ideological perspectives with the desire to analyze problems in such a way as to generate consensus among Black activists, elected officials, and communities. To develop a synthetic Black analysis resulting from a variety of perspectives, the IBW applied an operational methodology that it called "collective scholarship." The IBW's associates used the varying ideas held by members and supporters dialectically to reach a consensus, which became the organization's, not the individual's, analytical perspective on a particular subject. In the IBW's more than ten years of existence it constantly reconciled competing definitions, strategies, and ideologies on leading political, economic, social, and cultural issues facing Black communities.

To complete the difficult task of generating a higher synthesis, the IBW assembled possibly the greatest roster of Black intellectuals, activists, and artists reflecting a variety of ideological and political viewpoints in post–World War II American history. The IBW's roll of associates, contributors, supporters, and donors was a who's who of Black activist-intellectuals. Supporters included artists such as famed dancer and choreographer Katherine Dunham, painter and sculptor Elizabeth Catlett, actor Ossie Davis, and novelist Chinua Achebe. The IBW worked with prolific writers and teachers such as Margaret Walker Alexander, author of the award-winning poem "For My People" and the novel *Jubilee* (1966), and St. Clair Drake, coauthor of *Black Metropolis* (1946). The IBW valued the ideas of nationalists such as John Henrik Clark and Julius Lester, and integrationists such as SCLC's C. T. Vivian. The Institute worked with politicians, including Michigan congressman John Conyers and Atlanta's Maynard Jackson. There was also strong participation from Caribbean scholars. C.L.R. James, Marxist theorist and author of the seminal book on the Haitian Revolution *The Black Jacobins* (1938), Sylvia Wynter, cultural theorist and author of the novel *The Hills of Hebron* (1962), historian Robert Hill, editor of *The Marcus Garvey and Universal Negro Improvement Association Papers* (1983), Walter Rodney, Marxist historian and author of *How Europe Underdeveloped Africa* (1972), and economists George Beckford and Norman Girvan all contributed to the IBW's analysis, often spending weeks in Atlanta. Many of these men and women supported the IBW from afar as organizational consultants, donors, and by attending key programs. Some scholars moved to Atlanta, becoming the lifeblood of the organization as "senior associates." The IBW's initial list of senior associates included historian Lerone Bennett Jr., editor of *Ebony* magazine and author of *Before the Mayflower* (1963), historian Sterling Stuckey, author of *Slave Culture* (1983), economist Robert S. Browne, editor of *The Review of Black Political Economy* and head of the Black Economic Research Center, and sociologist Joyce Ladner, author of *Tomorrow's Tomorrow: The Black Woman* (1971) and editor of *The Death of White Sociology* (1973).

Despite the array of ideological viewpoints held by the IBW's members, associates, and supporters, the organization's broad ideological perspective is best described as pragmatic Black Nationalism, the belief that carefully constructed social, political, and economic goals designed to generate consensus in Black communities were more important than ideological pronouncements, conformity, and rigidity. The IBW's pragmatic nationalism differed from the cultural nationalism promoted by Maulana Karenga, Amiri Baraka, and others. Black cultural nationalism suggests that the African diaspora has a "distinct aesthetic, sense of values, and communal ethos emerging from either, or both their contemporary folkways and continental African heritage."[14] It also differs slightly from the political or revolutionary nationalism of the era, which James Smethurst effectively defines as an "open engagement with Marxism" regarding the political economy.[15] The IBW's pragmatic nationalism was rooted in specific issues such as Black Studies or the creation of a black political agenda for the seventies; thus, its pragmatism critically engaged and employed the best practices from a variety of ideological perspectives, including cultural and political nationalism, as well as integration. Literary critic and IBW supporter Addison Gayle Jr. summarized this pragmatism in a 1972 interview.

> An appreciation for a rational approach to problems. Look, our situation in this country is so serious that we can't afford to deal with problems anymore from that shoot-from-the-hip kind of approach. Problems have to be analyzed and solutions have to be found.
>
> The primary thesis from which to approach every problems is, "Is it good for Black people?" We need people for whom this will be a major preoccupation. I think the Institute of the Black World has begun a fundamental, *pragmatic* approach to the problems that confront us. We certainly need an institution of that sort. And for all the endeavors that we become engaged in, the question should be, "Is it good for Black people?"[16]

The use of the word "pragmatism" calls on both the philosophical and popular connotations. Philosophical pragmatism originated after the shock and awe of the Civil War. Scholars such as Charles S. Pierce, William James, and John Dewey developed pragmatism to contest the philosophical absolutes they believed supported the sectional divide. The first generation of pragmatists, Pierce, James, Dewey, and others emphasized the practicality of thought over philosophical universal truths.[17] As William James noted, "The ultimate test for us of what a truth means is indeed the conduct it dictates or inspires. . . . The effective meaning of any philosophic proposition can always be brought down to some particular consequence."[18] Recently, scholars such as Tommie Shelby and Eddie S. Glaude Jr. have applied the philosophical insights of pragmatism to Black activism. The IBW was a tangible example of the possibilities of applying pragmatism to Black activism.[19]

Why did so many scholar-activists volunteer their time, energy, and money to the IBW? Associates and supporters believed that an answer was needed to King's question about the future of the struggle. The defeat of legal segregation was not the end of the Black Freedom Struggle, only of the civil rights movement. The longer-term movement demanded not just the removal of racial obstacles, but what King described as "realization of equality." The IBW recognized, as did King, that true equality would require structural changes to political, economic, and cultural institutions. The analytical framework of civil rights was less applicable in a post–Jim Crow America, signaling a need for alternative institutions and new ideas. In the process, the IBW became the most radical Black think tank in 1970s America.[20]

The IBW's leadership was a group of advanced scholars—including onsite members and off-site colleagues—referred to in the organizational hierarchy as senior associates. The senior associates regularly contributed to the life and direction of the IBW, keeping the organization financially afloat with their donations and sacrifices. Although dozens of scholars held the title of senior associate, three in particular—Vincent Harding, Stephen Henderson, and William Strickland—played instrumental roles in founding, establishing, and stabilizing the IBW. Harding and Henderson, professors at Spelman and Morehouse Colleges, developed the idea of an Institute from personal discussions of King's legacy, Black Studies, and Black Power.

Before cofounding the IBW, Harding spent his adult life blending intellectualism with activism. Born to West Indian parents in Harlem, New York, in 1931, Harding grew up in the Seventh-Day Adventist messianic tradition. He graduated from City College of New York with a bachelor's degree in history in 1953 and obtained a master's degree from Columbia School of Journalism the following year. After graduation, Harding spent two years in the U.S. Army, where the violence he witnessed led him to become a conscientious objector. He moved to the University of Chicago to continue his "spiritual quest," studying intellectual history and theology, eventually earning his doctorate in 1965 with a dissertation entitled, "Lyman Beecher and the Transformation of American Protestantism, 1775–1863." During Harding's graduate education, the dynamism of the civil rights movement pulled him toward activism.[21]

After finishing his master's degree in history from the University of Chicago in 1956, Harding could not remain a passive and distant observer of the growing civil rights and antiwar movements. The pacifism of Woodlawn Mennonite Church prompted Harding to become a member, and in 1958 he drove through the South as part of an interracial church group, meeting King in Montgomery. He and his wife, Rosemarie, went south again in 1961 as representatives of the Mennonite Central Committee. On this visit they established the Mennonite House in Atlanta, an experiment testing the "possibility that [in] the South, Blacks and Whites could live together under the same roof." The project served as an experiment in interracial living and a respite for activists. The Mennonite House was near Auburn Avenue, the Black historic district of Atlanta, and around the corner from Martin Luther King Jr.'s home. The proximity between the Kings and the Hardings led to a close relationship between the two families. The Hardings briefly returned to Chicago to recuperate from their activism and for Vincent to complete his doctorate. Vincent and Rosemarie returned to Atlanta in 1965 when he accepted a faculty position at Spelman College. Upon his return to Atlanta, Vincent Harding became increasingly involved in the evolving civil rights movement. Shortly after being arrested in the 1965 Selma protests, Harding announced his opposition to the Vietnam War. He was troubled by the escalation of the conflict beginning in January 1965, and he spent the summer researching its history. Harding concluded that more Black organizations and activists should oppose the war. His research eventually became the blueprint for Martin Luther King Jr.'s antiwar speech in April 1967. When James Earl Ray assassinated King one year later, Harding believed that "certain things happened . . . largely because of what I wrote."[22] These experiences—being Black in America, coming from a nonconformist church, and getting involved in the Freedom Movement—formed the foundation of Harding's activism in the seventies.[23]

Shortly after he prepared the Vietnam essay for Martin Luther King Jr. in 1967, Harding advanced a religious Black Nationalism. In a 1967 speech, "The Gift of Blackness," Harding promoted an interpretation of Black consciousness that was similar to W.E.B. Du Bois' concept of double consciousness.[24] Harding argued that Blackness was a blessing that provided faith, perception, and prophecy, and that it could be used to oppose American White nationalism: "Our position as black people in American society gives us a perspective on this society and on this world that makes it possible for us to be free from the deadly narrowness of white American nationalism and self-righteousness."[25] Harding later expanded this view, suggesting that the narrative of American history, with its systematic exclusion of Black life and simultaneous promotion of American progress, functioned to obscure a "truer" and more humane history through which "American society might be transformed."[26] Harding's view of history connected the conceptions of the past with present social realities; it was an interpretation grounded in the Black experience. As he noted, any potential personal or scholarly transformation must begin with "the least of these."[27] Emotionally and mentally stunned by King's assassination, Harding began discussing plans with Stephen Henderson, fellow faculty member at Morehouse College, for an institution that could connect some of King's ideas about poverty, peace, and protest to the reevaluation of Black identity unleashed by Black Power.

Henderson, in contrast to Harding, operated on the periphery in the Black Freedom Struggle. After two years in the U.S. Army at the end of World War II, the Key West, Florida, native attended Morehouse College in the 1940s contemporaneously with Martin Luther King Jr. Henderson did not know the younger King, but he was a classmate and close friend of Lerone Bennett Jr., the future editor of *Ebony* magazine and an IBW senior associate. Henderson earned his master's degree (1950) and doctorate (1959) from the University of Wisconsin, completing the latter with a dissertation titled, "Study of Visualized Detail in the Poetry of Tennyson, Rossetti, and Morris." Like Harding and many other Blacks who earned doctoral degrees before the seventies, Henderson's research on White poets reflected an assumption in graduate education that Black scholarship was unworthy of study. Upon graduation, Henderson rectified this oversight and turned his full attention to Black literature. After teaching at Virginia Union College (now "University") for three years, he returned to teach at Morehouse College in 1962.

By the mid-sixties, Henderson began to examine, with the aid of his students, the need for courses about the Black experience. These courses mirrored Henderson's research on the theory of a Black aesthetic. As Henderson asserted at a 1968 literary conference, "The real revolution in America is the Black Consciousness Movement, the transfiguration of blackness, a necessary first stage in the liberation of black people, and conceivably of all Americans." Henderson's exploration of the Black aesthetic and Harding's examination of Black history neatly coincided with the push for a Black Studies curriculum on the Atlanta University Center campuses and beyond.[28]

Each of the three key associates of the IBW followed a different philosophical and activist path to the organization. Harding began with the Beloved Community of the interracial Mennonites and moved toward the "gift of Blackness," while Henderson explored the Black aesthetic. William Strickland's path consistently engaged in a more political Black Nationalist project. Strickland was not a founder of the IBW, but he played a crucial role as a policy analyst and served as a key stabilizing figure throughout the organization's existence. Younger than his two colleagues, the Boston native spent two years in the U.S. Marine Corps before graduating from Harvard College in 1961. Strickland then enrolled in the doctoral program at Harvard University, but devoted considerable time to the Northern Student Movement (NSM). Founded in 1961 by Peter Countryman, a White college student, NSM's initial purpose was to provide "moral, physical, and financial" support to the Southern movement. Soon, NSM realized that its support of the Southern movement was limited at best, and NSM activists began to work in Northern urban communities, conducting a series of after-school and summer tutorial programs. NSM eventually expanded their activities by establishing neighborhood councils for health and welfare. When Countryman returned to Yale University in 1963 to finish his doctorate and the organization's members decided they needed a Black director, Strickland accepted the position of executive director. During his tenure as director, he shifted NSM toward becoming an all-Black organization by encouraging Whites to work for change in their communities instead of in predominantly Black ones.[29]

Strickland became increasingly involved in the growing Black Power movement. Strickland's rise to director of NSM led to other opportunities, such as becoming the New York chairman of the Mississippi Freedom Democratic Party (MFDP) when the organization challenged the seating of the regular Mississippi Democrats at the 1964 Democratic National Convention in Atlantic City, New Jersey. The MFDP's rejection of future vice-president Hubert Humphrey's compromise of two nonvoting seats at the convention further fueled Black activists' frustration with racial liberalism and expanded Black Power as an alternative to liberalism. Strickland understood the MFDP's challenge as one to "racist institutions," rather than "civil rights." He concluded, "We the Northern Student Movement support the Mississippi challenge because it has taken on the institutional inequities and the institutional deprivation which tie Mississippi and Harlem together in history and in blood."[30] In addition, Strickland's personal relationship with fellow Bostonian and 1967 Black Power Conference organizer Nathan Wright led him to accept a position as deputy director of the conference. The Black Power Conference incompletely addressed the challenges posed by Black Power. Strickland did not agree with some of the conference's conclusions, and began exploring ways to transmit the political and cultural potential of Black Power through alternative and independent institutions. For example, Strickland worked with Harding in developing the *Black Heritage* television series, which consisted of more than one hundred episodes devoted to Black history and culture. As Strickland remembered, "When Vincent said, 'Let's rethink the world,' I said, 'Yeah, baby, let's do that!'"[31] This working relationship led Strickland initially to commute to Atlanta, where he discussed the ideas surrounding the notion of a Black curriculum with Harding and Henderson.[32]

Malcolm X also influenced Strickland's commitment to establishing independent institutions. Strickland first met Malcolm Little through a cousin who "ran" with the then-gangster. Later, while teaching a class on race relations at Harvard in 1961, Strickland invited Minister Malcolm X to give a lecture in his class. The two stayed in touch until Malcolm's assassination in 1965. Strickland maintains that Malcolm provided the foremost critique of American racism, declaring "I'll be a Malcolmite until I die."[33]

Harding, Henderson, and Strickland each had a different approach toward Black activism and scholarship (religious-historical, aesthetical, and political), and their ability to work together exemplifies the IBW's commitment to generating a synthetic Black analysis and to collective scholarship. The Institute's legacy centers on its ability to facilitate and generate cooperation among differing components of the Black academic, political, and activist communities.

The IBW engaged in pragmatic relations with Black Power–era organizations during the long seventies. The IBW contributed to three critical areas of the Black Freedom Struggle in the seventies—Black Studies, Black politics, and Black ideology. At the beginning of the decade, there was considerable agreement among Black activist communities about the need for Black Studies, a Black political agenda, and a redefined ideological perspective. Despite the initial unity, dissension emerged over the details. The IBW tried to reconcile the various viewpoints into a higher synthesis. Thus, in each area, the IBW's research associates were critical of the prevailing ideologies of Black Nationalism, Liberalism, and Marxism. The IBW hoped its criticisms would make each aspect of activism during the long seventies stronger. The IBW not only critiqued, but also supplied alternative solutions to these problems—solutions that strengthened the vestiges of the Black Freedom Struggle in the seventies, thereby demonstrating its credo of analysis over ideology.

The Challenge of Blackness explores the IBW associates' desire to create pragmatic and synthetic analyses for post-1968 America and to generate a coherent attack against systemic social, political, and economic inequality. The IBW's noble goal of formulating a programmatic racial solidarity faced numerous obstacles. The IBW associates were experienced enough to realize that it would be difficult transcending ideological, class, and structural divisions inside Black communities, yet they held firmly a belief that synthetic analyses would induce a workable consensus among civil rights leaders, Black Power activists, politicians, and Black communities. What emerges from the IBW's history is a dialectic interpretation between the goal of unity and a tension-filled reality. As an intellectual organization, the IBW operated in the space between unity and tension; between solidarity and disunity. In general, the IBW's history is a metaphor for difficulties faced by the entire Black Freedom Struggle during the long seventies. The organization's successes and failures suggest an incomplete victory for the Black Freedom Struggle, meaning the IBW and other organizations realized the need for a new synthetic analysis capable of describing and interpreting a post–Jim Crow America and a postcolonial world, as well as prescribing potential solutions designed to eliminate the vestiges of centuries of racial oppression. Unfortunately, for financial, ideological, and political reasons, the IBW's associates could not complete this ambitious goal, leaving Black activism without a key location to think and to research. With the IBW in serious decline by the mid-to-late seventies, there was no counterweight to a growing conservative onslaught that sought to roll back some of the gains of the civil rights movement and to limit any future expansion of racial equality.

Looking back on the decade, Harding observed, "scattered all around the landscape of the 1970s, we have seen the needy, broken, often wasted lives of our own people, facing a future in which new issues, new questions, new threats, and new problems are constantly emerging, matters that go beyond the best conservative, liberal, or radical thinking we have known."[34] *The Challenge of Blackness* examines how one organization developed synthetic political, cultural, and economic analysis in order to address the changing circumstances of the Black Freedom Struggle in the seventies. Each chapter explores how the IBW's pragmatism mollified oppositional forces, how the organization used every available means to simply survive, and the effects that pragmatism had on the IBW and the freedom movement at large.

Chapter 1 examines demands for Black Studies programs emerging from Historically Black Colleges and Universities (HBCUs), which served as the intellectual basis for the Institute's origins and an institutional foundation throughout the organization's existence. The chapter chronicles Harding and Henderson's contributions to the national debates on Black Studies in the pages of leading magazines and journals. Following the debates, Harding and Henderson developed plans for establishing Black Studies at the Atlanta campuses, forming the W.E.B. Du Bois Institute for Advanced Afro-American Studies, a precursor to the IBW and a component of the Martin Luther King Center. With these experiences, Harding and other associates at the Atlanta University Center began to formulate what I call a Black university perspective: they emphasized intellectual opposition to the normative methodological and epistemological approaches to racial analysis, structural autonomy, and relevance to Black communities. The IBW organized a Black Studies Directors Conference in November 1969, which served as an end to the more than two years of intellectual work on Black Studies and exemplified the organization's belief in collective scholarship, critical support, and pragmatic engagement.

Chapter 2 chronicles the eventual separation between the IBW and the Martin Luther King Center, which resulted from differing visions of the IBW's purpose and opposing perspectives on the future direction of the Black Freedom Struggle. The IBW's first encounter with the significant dissension that would overwhelm Black activism came from within. The King Center's rigid adherence to liberalism and its protection of King's legacy meant it could not comprehend the IBW's pragmatic nationalism. Thus, while the IBW was promoting a synthetic analysis generated from a diversity of perspectives, the King Center leadership only saw this as a narrow Black Nationalist agenda that threatened to sully King's legacy. The chapter also explores the IBW's post-separation approach to its finances and organizational structure by examining the group's philosophy toward funding and its 1971 Summer Research Symposium, which further developed the organization's identity as a think tank. The symposium highlighted this shift, as the IBW received intellectual insights and instructions from C.L.R. James, St. Clair Drake, and others on how to enhance its analysis of structural racism. The IBW's leadership determined that becoming a think tank would foster internal unity, make the organization useful to a wider constituency of Black organizations, and ensure survival without the King Center's patronage.

Chapter 3 explores the IBW's political analyses through its creation of a Black Agenda Network (BAN), its work during the Gary Convention, and associates' assistance of Maynard Jackson's bid for mayor of Atlanta. Theoretically, the IBW shifted from its Black university perspective and began promoting a broader "Black perspective," one that focused more on structural racism than on curricular concerns. The IBW's policy work highlighted the temporary unity among various segments of the Black activist community, but periodic frustrations reveal the emerging fissures in the movement.

Chapter 4 examines the dissemination of the IBW's synthetic analysis by investigating essays in the IBW publications, *Monthly Report* and *Black World View*. These publications reveal how the IBW moved beyond ideological sectarianism and growing dissension between Black Nationalists and Marxists to produce systemic analysis designed to forge a racial consensus on pressing issues. Moreover, these publications were the

IBW's direct link to grassroots organizations. After the 1974 Summer Research Symposium and the influence of Walter Rodney, the IBW's analysis became more radical, promoting a racialized political economy as a synthetic analytical frame. This position was a dialectic response to the sectarian race/class debate between Black Nationalists and Marxists during the mid-seventies.

The final chapter outlines the decline of the IBW and its attempts to simply survive the conservative backlash against Black activism and radicalism. The chapter examines the vicious break-ins and harassment by police forces. This terrorism further crippled the financially struggling organization. In addition, this chapter recaps the financial woes that the IBW faced during its existence. In the end, the break-ins and financial problems forced the IBW to close its doors shortly after its tenth anniversary. Because the conservative movement's ascendancy was in full swing at the time of the IBW's demise, the loss of this intellectual space and its synthetic analyses meant there was no Black progressive counterbalance for conservative ideas about civil rights, racism, and racial policies such as affirmative action. Indeed, the loss of an arena where radical ideas could be debated in a dialectical manner compounded the growth of racial conservatism.

The epilogue explores the IBW's legacies and the impact of its closing by briefly evaluating the organization's contributions to Black Studies, a Black political agenda, and its use of collective scholarship. Ultimately, the IBW was an example of the Black radical tradition during the seventies and serves as a model for twenty-first century organizations.

A Note on Style

Throughout the book I have chosen to capitalize "Black" and "White." Not only was this style preferred in the seventies, but the terms are nouns that reflect population groups, not colors. As Benedict Anderson reminds us all, communities are imagined; thus, "Black" is no less real than American. I recognize that neither population group was homogeneous and I examine Black and White critics and supporters of IBW. Moreover, I prefer the term "Black" to "African-American" because the latter expression is based on a cultural narrative with immigration at its center. New World Blacks did not immigrate. The hyphenated nomenclature represents a cultural narrative that belies the empirical history of Blacks and American Indians. Moreover, the immigrant paradigm is an epistemological narrative that was instituted during the seventies to limit civil rights gains. In fact, some of the IBW's associates argued against this immigrant narrative; thus, capitalizing "Black" and "White" is both a professional and personal decision.[35]

1

"The Challenge of Blackness"

The IBW and the Black Studies Movement

"We are building / up a new world / We are building / up a new world / We are building / up a new world / Black Folks / Must stay strong."
Opening of the IBW's Black Studies Directors Conference Hymn, November 1969.

At the IBW's Black Studies Directors Conference in November 1969, Vincent Harding led thirty-five scholars in this hymn set to the old Black spiritual "We Are Climbing Jacob's Ladder." The IBW had invited the scholars to Atlanta to develop and assess the burgeoning field of Black Studies. By the 1969 fall semester, dozens of colleges instituted Black Studies programs. In the year before the conference, the IBW associates proposed and debated the field's structural and theoretical bases in leading journals and magazines. As Atlanta University Center (AUC) faculty members, Vincent Harding, Stephen Henderson, and Gerald McWorter were leading commentators on the national dialogue about Black Studies programs, and each scholar applied their ideas in developing a Black Studies program at the AUC. From their experiences in theorizing the field of Black Studies and in trying to establish such a program on a historically Black college campus, the IBW associates promoted a Black University perspective that emphasized intellectual opposition to racial analytical norms, insisted that Black colleges and Black Studies programs become more relevant to Black communities, and stressed that these programs and colleges obtain structural autonomy from White financial and political influence. Harding, Henderson, and McWorter's development of a Black University analytical perspective generated consensus between competing approaches to Black Studies. More importantly, their belief in the need for structural autonomy led them to establish the Institute of the Black World. Although the IBW evolved into a think tank for Black activism, its origins and foundations were rooted in the Black Studies movement that emerged from Black college campuses.

The opening song set the tone for the conference, as did the keynote speech by *Ebony* editor and IBW associate Lerone Bennett Jr. The three-day conference consisted of intense discussions about the nature, needs, and future of Black Studies programs. Bennett captured the importance of the seminar and the IBW in his speech, "The Challenge of Blackness," which described the IBW as "a center for defining, defending, and illustrating blackness." For Bennett, the Black experience was at the center of the human experience: "We of the Institute of the Black World believe that the black man is the truth or close to the truth, that blackness constitutes the truth of the truth, and that Black Studies is the revelation of that truth and the search for the true meaning of blackness."[1]

Bennett's speech summarized the IBW's purpose and identified a Black University perspective, which stressed intellectual opposition to contemporary racial scholarship, called for a renewed commitment from the university to Black communities, and emphasized structural autonomy. The Black University perspective was the product of IBW associates' attempts to theorize the field of Black Studies and their efforts to start a Black Studies program at the six colleges—Spelman College, Morehouse College, Clark College, Morris Brown College, Interdenominational Theological Center, and Atlanta University—that collectively formed the Atlanta University Center (AUC). Bennett reiterated the IBW's belief that a Black scholar must "define and control blackness." Bennett anticipated that the "Challenge of Blackness" would lead the IBW to redefine the American experience "in order to remake American society."[2] Bennett's speech justified the IBW's purpose, provided a broad framework for Black Studies, and shaped the organization's trajectory in the 1970s.

The IBW's founding was inextricably tied to the Black Studies movement that swept across college campuses in the late 1960s. The IBW's supporters and associates fulfilled three simultaneous roles. First, IBW members furthered national discussions on Black Studies programs in leading magazines and journals such as *Negro Digest*, *Ebony*, and other periodicals. By 1969, the cohort of scholars at the AUC were leading commentators on the emerging field. The IBW particularly focused on the development of Black Studies programs at HBCUs. Second, at the local level, the IBW—initially named the W.E.B. Du Bois Institute for Advanced Afro-American Studies—tried to create a Black Studies curriculum at the AUC, where Harding, Henderson, and Gerald McWorter were faculty members. Harding and Henderson envisioned the Du Bois Institute as a quasi-independent Black research association that was affiliated with the newly formed Martin Luther King Center and the AUC colleges. At the AUC, Black Studies scholars put their ideas into praxis, but the results were uneven. When the IBW associates supported a student protest calling for the AUC to become a "Black university," the IBW's relationship with the AUC soured. Third, the IBW, now separated from the AUC, shifted its focus to become an outside evaluator of Black Studies programs. The IBW's assessment of Black Studies concluded with the Black Studies Directors Conference. In all three instances, IBW associates relied on collective scholarship to generate a synthetic analysis of the purpose and potential of Black Studies. Collective scholarship was a democratic process that both allowed for multiple voices and viewpoints on the subject of Black Studies and, through dialectical debates, created a Black university perspective, a theoretical synthesis of the field. At every stage, the associates' intellectual work in shaping Black Studies faced criticism both locally and nationally, thus demonstrating the heterogeneity of Black thought and the difficulty of generating theoretical synthesis and operational consensus. These tensions foreshadowed the hostility over ideological perspectives that engulfed the Black Freedom Struggle in the mid-seventies. Led by Vincent Harding, the IBW associates suggested a pragmatic response, the Black university perspective, as a means to overcome these tensions.

Black Studies on Campus

Between 1968 and 1970, dozens of universities, beginning with San Francisco State University, founded Black Studies programs or departments. The protests that established the first Black Studies program at San Francisco State University were the product of student activists connecting with established Black Power organizations. Former SNCC member Jimmy Garrett transformed the San Francisco State University Black Student Union (BSU) from a purely campus organization into one that connected with other Bay-area organizations. These organizations included the Black Panther Party and the Black House, a Black cultural nationalism group in San Francisco's Fillmore district led by writers Marvin X, Ed Bullins, and Eldridge Cleaver. The San Francisco State University BSU also joined with other minority-led campus organizations, including the Latin American Students Organization, the Filipino-American Students Organization, and El Renacimiento (a Mexican student organization), to form the Third World Liberation Front in March 1968. The student organizations led a series of protests in 1968 that led to the creation of the first Black Studies Department and the first Ethnic Studies Department the following year. Colleges across the country, from Cornell University to Brandeis University, from The Ohio State University to the University of South Carolina, faced similar demands for Black Studies programs—demands which often ran against conservative administrators and verged on violent confrontations. Most notably, Black Cornell University students led an armed occupation of a campus building in the spring of 1969. These and other student-led protests engulfed campuses during the late 1960s and early 1970s.[3]

Faculty and student protests for Black Studies programs simply codified decades of Black scholar-activists' opposition to the popular and scholarly interpretations of Black life and culture as inferior. Carter G. Woodson founded the Association for the Study of Negro Life and History (ASNLH) in 1915 and the *Journal of Negro History* in 1916 to illuminate the "truth" about Black history.[4] While Woodson provided an institutional basis for challenging the governing assumption of Black inferiority, W.E.B. Du Bois used a variety of roles—academic, editor, novelist, journalist, and propagandist—to counter scholarly and popular discourse of Black inferiority. In his classic *Black Reconstruction* (1935), for example, Du Bois outlined the need for Black scholars to respond to the White scholarly record. Du Bois argued, "We shall never have a science of history until we have in our college men who regard the truth as more important than the defense of the white race, and who will not . . . Support a prejudice or buttress a lie."[5] The early Black history movement was often premised on the idea of history as an objective science, thus Black scholars needed to provide the "truth" of Black history and culture.[6]

By World War II, most scholarship on Black life rejected blatant assertions of racial inferiority. Still, well-meaning scholarship on race relations contained anti-Black bias. Gunnar Myrdal's pioneering work on race relations *An American Dilemma* (1944) exemplified the academic marginalization of Black culture. Myrdal asserted, *"In practically all of its divergences, American Negro culture is not something independent of general American culture. It is a distorted development or a pathological condition, of the general American culture."*[7] This perspective came under fire during the civil rights movement, which grew in the fifties and sixties backed by the strength of Black religious culture.

Despite the challenge posed by the civil rights movement, Black culture was often still defined as abnormal. The *Moynihan Report* (1965) infuriated scholars and activists when it asserted that the "deterioration of the Negro family," and not the vestiges of slavery and Jim Crow, was the biggest obstacle to full integration. Although Daniel Patrick Moynihan's claims reflected the research of leading Black scholars such as E. Franklin Frazier and Kenneth Clark, the civil rights community harshly criticized the report. Bayard Rustin believed the report was incomplete and "exaggerated the negative," while equating poverty with Blackness.[8] One task of Black Studies programs was to problematize these scholarly interpretations, especially considering the effects that the dominant representations had on public policy. Black Studies programs' intellectual oppositional role had broad support in Black communities.

By the early seventies, there was tremendous agreement in Black America on the need for and importance of Black Studies. A 1970 Time-Louis Harris poll found 85 percent of Blacks polled supported Black Studies in high schools and colleges, as "an important sign of Black identity and pride."[9] Between 1969 and 1974 approximately 120 Black Studies programs were started at universities nationwide.[10] Yet the overwhelming support obscured areas of ideological, structural, and programmatic strain in the field. Despite its challenge to normative education and its emergence from the freedom movement, Black Studies, as a discipline, lacked self-definition, and instead reflected the various interests and directions of the professors in specific departments. As a result of Black Studies' interdisciplinarity, emerging departments used existing personnel to develop courses, which often overemphasized professors' specific disciplines (history, sociology, political science, and so forth). Therefore, many Black Studies departments in the seventies only covered aspects of a Black Studies curriculum without theorizing the entire field of study.[11] To combat the bias in traditional disciplines, scholars theorized on the scope, purpose, and methodology of Black Studies in journals and at conferences. Harding, Henderson, McWorter, and other future IBW associates situated the organization to play a major role in these conversations.

Toward a Black University

The explosive growth of Black Studies programs provided Harding, Henderson, and other colleagues an opportunity to evaluate the emerging field. They judged Black Studies from the perspective of working at HBCUs, where they theorized an idea for a Black university—a broader, university-wide design for implementing Black Studies. This was the IBW founders' initial interaction with others developing Black Studies programs.

While student protests at predominantly White colleges like San Francisco State, Cornell, and Columbia University grabbed headlines, students' demands at Black colleges often failed to register on the national radar. The demands for Black Studies were similar, but the context and history of HBCUs meant students and faculty members' protests were also broader in their demands and implications. Framed in terms of creating a "Black university," demands at HBCUs referred not to the racial demographics of the student population, the faculty, or the administration, but instead hinged on claims of autonomy from White ideological, political, and financial resources, along with the need for HBCUs to redouble their efforts to become relevant to the local Black communities that surrounded them.

In a March 1967 issue of *Negro Digest*, political scientist Charles V. Hamilton introduced the idea of a Black University in his lead essay, "The Place of the Black College in the Human Rights Struggle." Hamilton asserted that "Negro" colleges had a "prevailing ethos" stemming from the Black experience (or the experience of Blackness), and that this experience should influence its curriculum, faculty members, and administrators.[12] He believed that the "Negro College" had shunned this ethos to its own detriment. Hamilton proposed that these colleges "turn to Black people . . . to find out what their insights tell us about what kind of college we should have." His solution called for the creation of a revolutionary Black college or university that would be "relevant to the *lives* of the students and *their* expectations." The new university would tackle community problems and introduce racial pride and militancy. Although Hamilton called for militancy, he still prioritized academic study. Academics would, however, "reject the shibboleths of 'objectivity' and 'aloofness'" and "pose the hard questions, to challenge established myths." Hamilton's essay captured the tone of informal discussions about how HBCUs should reorient their mission considering the emergence of Black Studies and looming desegregation.[13]

Whether HBCU students were fully aware of Hamilton's essay or not, their protests embodied Hamilton's conceptual framework. Students not only asked for Black Studies programs, but also called for a transformation of the entire Black college structure, especially the composition of the trustees and the sources of funding. For example, at Howard University in March 1967, students protested a lecture by Lieutenant General Lewis B. Hershey, director of the selective service during the Vietnam War. In response, Hershey urged local draft boards to punish college protesters by revoking their deferments.[14] Black students understood the connections between racism at home and on the battlefront, where Black soldiers were overrepresented on the front lines and underrepresented as officers. Student and faculty protestors at Howard University viewed Hershey's presence on campus as antagonistic to the needs of Black students as well as to the local Washington, D.C., Black community. For protestors, Hershey's invitation constituted a case where Howard University did not represent the best interest of its constituents and instead capitulated to the needs of the federal government, which held the university's purse strings.[15] Given the diversity of opinions on Black Studies programs and the creation of a Black University, Harding, Henderson, and other colleagues sought to develop a broad evaluative framework.

Black University Perspective

As Black Studies programs emerged, the varying objectives of students, faculty members, university administrations, and civil rights organizations hindered the creation of a unified academic discipline. Acclaimed Black historian John Hope Franklin even admitted, "I don't know what black studies is."[16] In addition to the confusion created by academic interdisciplinarity, another source of instability in Black Studies was the development of two different approaches to the field. Sociologist Fabio Rojas notes that there were tensions between Black Studies programs that emphasized "community education," and academic Black Studies.

Supporters of the community education perspective "aimed at providing training for individuals who would teach or do social work in the African American community," and emphasized the need for Black Studies to be "relevant" to Black communities. Academic Black Studies stressed strong interdisciplinary scholarship from the social sciences and the humanities. Supporters of this view accentuated the need to counter or oppose the dominant scholarly assumptions.[17] Although these two approaches were not mutually exclusive, local implementation tended to rely on one or the other.

Harding, Henderson, and McWorter mediated the tensions between the two perspectives by finding a pragmatic intellectual framework for the field. They developed a "Black University" perspective or approach to Black Studies. This perspective promoted opposition to the dominant racial analysis, relevance to Black communities, and autonomy from White political, economic, and intellectual control. The Black University perspective was pragmatic, as it deemphasized traditional disciplines and ideologies in favor of a vision of Black Studies that met the various and often-conflicting needs of the university and the community. More importantly, this perspective, derived from Harding and Henderson's experiences at HBCUs, placed a premium on structural autonomy. The AUC faculty members believed autonomy was the mechanism to fulfill the needs of both the academic and community education approaches to Black Studies. Harding, Henderson, and McWorter expressed this perspective in various publications.

In the years following these initial demands for Black Studies, scholars discussed the attributes, feasibility, and purpose of the proposed academic discipline. Dialogues about the possibilities and implementation of Black Studies occurred in a variety of forums in which future members of the IBW prominently participated. Essays in leading journals, especially *Negro Digest,* echoed student claims that in order for the "Negro" University to become relevant to the life and needs of Black communities, faculty members and students had to transform it into a Black University.[18]

Negro Digest was the first publication from John H. Johnson, publisher of *Ebony* and *Jet* magazines. Johnson initially modeled *Negro Digest* on *Reader's Digest*, publishing reprints of articles on Blacks. In 1961, Hoyt Fuller took over the editorial duties, shifting the magazine's content from article reprints to original scholarly essays. Under Fuller, *Negro Digest,* renamed *Black World* in 1970, became the leading publication shaping the discourse on Black aesthetics, Black consciousness, and the Black University. On the pages of *Negro Digest*, IBW associates Harding, Henderson, and McWorter sketched out the framework of a Black University perspective.[19]

Intellectual Opposition

Student protest activities that led to the creation of Black Studies programs often obscured the field's intellectual rationale. Unlike other academic social science and humanities disciplines instituted in the late nineteenth and early twentieth centuries, Black Studies emerged as students and faculty members incorporated the ideas of the Black Freedom Struggle within their academic institutions and confronted the inherent biases in Western education.[20] Whereas traditional disciplines appeared in the context of the dominant ideologies, Black Studies challenged the inherent assumption in Western education that Blackness (and non-Whiteness and non-maleness) was negative and pathological when compared to White middle-class norms.[21]

The IBW's Black University perspective opposed the dominant racial theories and connected the epistemological challenge of Black Studies to programmatic concerns. Black Studies assumed that there was a link "between the epistemology of knowledge and the liberation of people."[22] The IBW associates believed that Black Studies needed to articulate a theoretical framework countering the dominant epistemology, or knowledge systems, operating in colleges, Black and White, that defined Black culture as pathological and its intellectual production as inferior. As a result of this reigning ideology, the university definition of success often came at the expense of Black communities and culture.[23] The belief in Black cultural pathology functioned as the basis of racial policy for nearly three centuries. In this skewed framework, many scholars and activists asserted that assimilation and integration were the only political and cultural choices for Black Americans.

Supporters of Black Studies rejected the idea of Black cultural pathology. Black Studies scholars and supporters identified biased academic scholarship, such as Myrdal's *An American Dilemma*, as a source of this flawed assumption that was the basis of racialized public policy.[24] Although primarily identified as AUC faculty members, the IBW associates were at the forefront of theorizing the necessity of intellectual opposition to normalized racial theories. For example, Gerald McWorter, a Spellman

College sociologist and rising star in his field during the late 1960s, captured the importance of this intellectual opposition in a 1968 *Negro Digest* essay. He wrote that the university must have an "ideology grounded in an uncompromising goal of psychological independence from the oppressor (and his oppressive system)."[25] Harding added that the Black University would "attempt to place the rise of the West in proper historical perspective, refusing either to do homage to—or to be terrified by—what may well prove to be no more than a hyper-active aberration in the context of mankind's long, essentially non-Western pilgrimage."[26] McWorter and Harding understood that Black Studies must challenge racial theories that devalued Blackness. Racial inequality went beyond legal segregation—racial theories that implied Black cultural inferiority were equally effective when connected to public policy. The IBW associates continued the mantra of Carter G. Woodson, the father of Black history, which stated, "When you control a man's thinking, you do not have to worry about his actions."[27] Thus, any conception of Black liberation or equality required a new system of knowledge, which at the beginning of the long 1970s it seemed only Black Studies was capable of providing.

Community Relevance

Faculty members and students at HBCUs who wanted a Black University envisioned more than just an academic Black Studies program. They expected their colleges to become more attuned to the needs of Black communities. The civil rights movement, especially the creation of freedom schools, raised expectations and, for many, altered notions of success by making service to Black communities paramount to middle-class status. Hoyt Fuller suggested that the Black University had to go beyond the traditional university and be "community-oriented," designed to help communities achieve self-determination.[28] McWorter envisioned a Black University based on an ethic of "communalism," as opposed to individualism. He wrote, "This means that instead of hoping for social progress through the individual merits of its students or faculty *qua* individuals, progress is to be viewed as a social process through which the community is uplifted with the aid of its contributing people." In this vision of a Black University, community organizers were equals with faculty members and administrators. For McWorter, the goal of a Black University was "service to the community."[29]

Associates also defined the Black community diasporically. Harding proposed that the Black University address the African diaspora by inviting "representatives of the anti-colonial forces, members of Liberation Fronts, religious and educational leaders from the re-borning nations of the world . . . in order to give deeper meaning to the searching. Such a university might well become a sanctuary of sorts for some of the world's revolutionaries."[30] McWorter insisted that any concept of a Black University include a center for international study. Associates' evolving Black University perspective called for relevancy to national and international Black communities.

Structural Autonomy

The fundamental component of the IBW associates' Black University perspective was the insistence on structural autonomy. McWorter asserted that a Black University needed not just "as much structural independence as necessary to survive in the world, but to prosper." Behind the call for structural autonomy was the legacy of financial dependence that plagued HBCUs for most of the twentieth century. After Booker T. Washington's 1895 Atlanta compromise speech, the Wizard of Tuskegee used his accommodationist strategy to enhance his position with White philanthropy. By the early twentieth century, Washington was the gatekeeper for the philanthropic funding so desperately needed by HBCUs. For HBCUs to unlock these revenue streams, their administrations had to adhere to industrial education. Therefore, the historic Washington versus Du Bois debate about the proper educational strategy—industrial or classical education—initially favored Washington because his relationship with philanthropy forced desperate HBCUs to implement or enhance industrial education. By the 1960s, HBCUs had become so dependent on outside or state funding that some Black college presidents prohibited their students from protesting segregation. The legacy of accommodation by HBCUs was a principal reason that Harding, Henderson, and McWorter called for structural autonomy.[31]

When students and faculty members called for a Black University, they understood the need for structural autonomy. For example, Atlanta University Center students insisted on "independence from . . . the colonial influence of foundations like Ford and Rockefeller."[32] Institute of the Black World associate Stephen Henderson approached structural autonomy from a different angle by recognizing the inherent limitations of HBCUs as freestanding, single institutions. To counter the financial weaknesses that many HBCUs faced, he suggested that the Black University could be accomplished by establishing regional centers in areas with large Black populations, such as Atlanta, Washington D.C./Baltimore, and Raleigh/ Durham. These regional centers would improve the finances of the colleges and provide greater assistance to large Black communities. He also called for the sharing of resources, faculty and student exchange among universities, and the hiring of "Specialists in Blackness." These adjustments would make the Black University a center for Black culture. The results, according to Henderson, would be "a new structure, a new balance, and, one hopes, a new man—a new vision of what it means to be a man."[33] Structural autonomy was essential if the idea of a Black University was to materialize.

Harding and Henderson summarized the Black University perspective in two 1970 *Ebony* articles titled, "Toward the Black University." Harding called for a reconceptualized Black University to "break the long-established familiar patterns of white domination and control over black higher education." To complete this task, he and Henderson theorized the need "to understand economic, sociological, political, and artistic theories and categories but they will all be reshaped and joined in new ways to illuminate the meaning of [Black] experiences, problems, and directions." A Black University would need to be guided by "service to the black community on every technical and personal level." To complete the intellectual and community goals of a Black University, new funding sources that allowed for autonomy needed to be found. These two essays summarized the associates' Black University perspective, which emerged from their participation in debates and conferences on the subject.

Black Studies or a Black University

The conversations in leading journals and magazines on Black Studies and the Black University reveal broad points of agreement. Supporters were adamant that Black Studies programs at predominately White colleges and the potential Black University at HBCUs had to develop and promote intellectual opposition to mainstream racial theories. Social scientists had spent decades demonstrating the numerous ways in which Blacks were supposedly inferior to Whites. Even among liberal scholars, who believed that Blacks could become equal to Whites, the only perceived solution was assimilation or integration. The civil rights movement defined segregation as psychologically and culturally damaging to Blacks. Black Studies programs' intellectual opposition posited that the scholarly and political notions of a damaged Black psyche and the associated imagery were racist and paternalistic. Such intellectual opposition and calls for relevancy pointed out that scholarly literature on the damaged Black psyche set up an unbalanced equation in which Blacks could never achieve equality. The American cultural system was premised on Black exclusion, thus, integrating into a broken system would only produce broken results. The logical solution from a Black Studies point of view was to create a new system—one that recognized the relationship between epistemology and liberation. Advocates of Black Studies and the Black University who believed in this connection insisted on prioritizing relevancy to Black communities. This effort was not just an attempt to bridge the town and gown gap, but also represented a belief that Black liberation, or what Harding called a new humanity, emanated from the dissemination of new ideas.[34]

Theoretical agreement notwithstanding, the creation of Black Studies programs at predominately White colleges and universities initially caused personnel problems for HBCUs. The newly formed programs strained the small Black professoriate, who mostly worked at HBCUs because of the legacy of segregation. Many HBCU faculty members were concerned about the effect that emerging Black Studies programs at White colleges would have on Black colleges. Student and faculty proponents of Black Studies at White colleges believed, and often demanded, that Black professors should lead these departments, programs, and classes. Advocates at HBCUs argued that Black Studies at White colleges created a brain drain from Black colleges, as leading Black professors were lured to White colleges by lighter teaching loads, higher salaries, and, at times, greater prestige. Harding declared, "Now every black Ph.D. who has his name mentioned twice, or published in the slightest review, is besieged by Northern as well as Southern white institutions—most often in response to militant, urgent and often threatening demands by their black students."[35] The desire for Black professors outpaced the limited pool of candidates because of the small number of Blacks holding doctoral degrees in 1970 (about 1 percent of all professors). The demand for professors acutely affected HBCUs because in 1970 nearly 85 percent of Black professors worked at such institutions.[36] For example, Miles College, a small HBCU outside of Birmingham, Alabama, had to replace forty-five of its sixty-one faculty members between 1967 and 1969.[37] Other HBCUs faced similar challenges. Moreover, the logic of integration made HBCUs seem like less desirable locations to earn a degree or work than their integrated counterparts. Harding addressed a painful contradiction between integration and Black Studies.

Harding's *Negro Digest* essay, "New Creation or Familiar Death? An Open Letter to Black Students in the North," argued that demands for Black Studies programs and concomitant demands for increased numbers of Black students and faculty members had "appeared to encourage the destruction of those colleges and universities . . . in the South." Specifically, Harding believed that Northern White universities' demands for a Black presence on their campuses came at the expense of HBCUs in the South. Harding compared the brain drain to the colonial position held by European metropoles in Africa. Northern White universities' ability to offer scholarships to promising Black students as well as to offer faculty salaries considerably higher than those afforded by Black colleges made Harding wonder if many were "tempted to sell out the Black colleges of the South." However, he did not insist that White universities' practice of recruiting Black faculty members and students absolutely end. Harding's letter was "not meant to stifle debate"; rather, he wanted the conflicting implications to spark a discussion. His goal was to promote a dialogue "in the spirit of black ecumenical concern as we move toward a new humanity." Out of the debate, Harding sought a cooperative solution with Northern Black Studies programs.[38]

Although personnel issues remained an underlying tension between supporters of Black Studies programs at White universities and Black University supporters working at HBCUs, both groups understood the need for structural autonomy, and the difficulty of obtaining such independence. Both groups faced opposition from scholars, such as Harvard professor Martin Kilson Jr., who believed that many "proposals for black studies programs . . . [are] of dubious value."[39] Because promoters of a Black University envisioned autonomy from funding sources at the university level, supporters' claims were met with stiff resistance. Black college administrators were concerned with personnel, financing, and "policy-making."[40] Therefore, in the late 1960s, structural autonomy was difficult for a Black university to establish or maintain, because of the scope of the Black University idea and the financial realities of HBCUs.

Black Studies programs at White colleges struggled with autonomy too. However, there were no expectations for Black Studies programs at White universities to change the entire university system, though advocates and supporters expected to control their programs. Thus, autonomy here meant attaining departmental status, which included the ability to develop curriculum, hire faculty members, and grant tenure. Departmental status provided a measure of autonomy and secured Black Studies' position in the university.[41] The differences between creating an autonomous Black University and a Black Studies department became readily apparent when Harding, Henderson, and McWorter shifted from theory to praxis and tried to transform the AUC into a Black University. As a result, the IBW and its Black University perspective emerged not simply from theoretical contemplation, but from the dialectic process of activism.

Black Studies at the AUC

Theory met praxis when McWorter, Harding, and other faculty members became embroiled in a student protest that engulfed the AUC campuses. The events in a speech class at Spelman College in early November 1968 affected the IBW, leading its founders to seek out as much autonomy as possible. When a White speech instructor named Justine Gianetti shouted "JACKASS!" at a particularly unruly female student, she momentarily hushed the awed classroom. The students were taken aback by the audacity of this ill-composed instructor and, as class was dismissed, they refused to sit idly by and be disrespected. Reflecting a tradition of activism that had swept across the South since the 1950s, the students used tactics of the civil rights movement and the language of Black Power to make a clear statement against Gianetti. Their actions garnered support from Harding, McWorter, and other AUC faculty members. Student protests merged with plans for the W.E.B. Du Bois Institute for Advanced Afro-American Studies (the original name of the IBW). As student and faculty protests grew more confrontational, they created problems, both internal and external, for the newly formed Du Bois Institute and for Harding, who was held partly responsible by the Martin Luther King Center and by the AUC.[42]

Two days after the "jackass" incident, on Wednesday, November 6, students arrived for Gianetti's 1:00 p.m. class prepared to make a statement to her and to the entire Atlanta University Center. In almost military formation, students, some of whom were not enrolled in the class, entered the room, encircling Gianetti. By 1:15 p.m., the students had informed her that they were removing her from the classroom because of her outburst in the previous session. "Your statement was indicative of your racist attitude; and we do not intend for you to teach here, anymore," said one of the students. Gianetti refused to leave and tried to regain control of the antagonistic situation, but the students were adamant, taking her by the arms and escorting her from the Fine Arts Building. As soon as the instructor was outside, students swiftly moved shoulder-to-shoulder to block the three entrances into the building, blocking Gianetti's attempts to reenter.[43]

The students passed out a one-page handbill explaining their actions. The document, which had "Student Called a Jackass" scrawled across the top, stated:

On November 4, at Spelman College, a white instructor of public speaking clearly displayed her natural inability to relate to Black students, when she referred to a member of her class as a "jackass." This incident clearly reflects the racist and oppressive character of our institutions. For some strange reason, our administrations are unable and/or unwilling to deal with this situation.
DO OUR ADMINISTRATORS REALLY RESPECT US AS BLACK STUDENTS? IF SO, WHY DO THEY ALLOW RACISM TO CONTINUE TO EXIST ON OUR CAMPUSES?[44]

When AUC security officers tried to talk with the students about returning to class, they were accused of being "traitor[s] to the race." The students echoed Malcolm X, stating that they would "use any means necessary" to prevent Gianetti from reentering the building. At 1:48 p.m., the speech instructor left the area. Students held their positions until it was clear that the teacher was not returning. One hour from its start, the protest was over and the student movement at the Atlanta University Center was off to a dramatic start. "This was purely a racial thing," said one of the students, "We don't believe that all white instructors are racists, but there are some others around here with whom we may have to deal with the same way." With the expulsion of Gianetti, the Black Studies movement appeared to have begun at the AUC campuses.[45]

The protests against Gianetti resulted from the convergence of several factors: the legacy of student activism at the AUC, a rebellion against social conservatism on campus, and the development of Black Studies there. The escalating protests ensnared the IBW in controversy. Student protests were not unusual on the AUC campuses. In the 1920s, students were inspired by the spirit of the New Negro and rebelled against social prescriptions at Black colleges that presumed Black immorality. Amid a growing civil rights movement, AUC students, including Julian Bond, published "An Appeal for Human Rights" in local Atlanta newspapers and in the *New York Times* to outline grievances of the Black community in 1960. Students then led desegregation campaigns against local stores and restaurants. By the late 1960s, Bond, Ruby Doris Smith-Robinson, and other former AUC student activists had become legends and role models for their activism and courage. Atlanta University Center students also rebelled against social prescriptions in the late 1960s. Inspired by broader conceptions of freedom resulting from the civil rights movement, the AUC students, especially those in the Student Government Association at Spelman College, lobbied the administration to loosen the rules that governed campus morality. Relying on a legacy of protest activities, students merged their protest against Gianetti with a push for a reduction in campus rules and calls for a Black Studies curriculum.[46]

Before the various protests against Gianetti and social norms, Harding and Henderson planned to develop Black Studies on the AUC campuses. Students and faculty members' desires for Black Studies conflicted with the traditionally conservative values of the institutions. In 1965, Spelman College only had one course devoted to the Black experience. Despite this conservatism, Harding, Henderson, and others believed that the AUC was an ideal location for developing Black Studies and creating a Black University. The AUC fit the profile outlined in the *Negro Digest* articles of an ideal location for a Black University, because it was a large urban area with a significant Black population and a diverse Black faculty that not only included Harding, Henderson, and McWorter, but also political scientist Mack H. Jones, historian Melvin Drimmer, cultural critic Richard Long, and others.[47]

Harding and other faculty members developed a pragmatic strategy to create a Black Studies program that fixed the glaring omissions in the AUC curriculum and reinforced Harding, Henderson, and McWorter as national spokespersons on the subject. Months before protests began against Gianetti, Harding, Henderson, McWorter, A. B. Spellman, and Councill Taylor proposed the creation of the W.E.B. Du Bois Institute for Advanced Afro-American Studies. The proposal recognized that the AUC had responded to student, faculty, administration, and community pressure by expanding and increasing course offerings to more than thirty separate classes. However, the authors did not believe that this was enough, and further asserted that a core of teachers needed to be established at every level of the discipline. Echoing Henderson's suggestion in *Negro Digest* for regional centers, they suggested that the AUC was an excellent location "to institutionalize the present surge of interest in the Black world."[48]

Faculty members saw the Du Bois Institute as a vehicle to combine academic and community approaches to Black Studies, and therefore sought a connection with the AUC and the Martin Luther King Center. Academically, the institute wanted to produce research similar to the Atlanta University publications on Blacks led by Du Bois from 1897 to 1910.[49] Furthermore, the institute planned to offer additional courses in order to establish a bachelor's and master's degree in Black Studies. The creators of the Du Bois Institute conceived an enhanced research program that included community members, faculty, international scholars, and doctoral candidates as research fellows. Moreover, they planned for the institute to provide the AUC and the Atlanta community with seminars, colloquia, and lectures in Black Studies. They also envisioned the institute as having a close connection with the Atlanta University Library and the Martin Luther King Center. Overall, proponents believed the proposed connection between the Du Bois Institute, the King Center, and the AUC would allow the HBCUs to "leap into an internationally celebrated status of preeminence and distinction, for having responded creatively and vigorously to the greatest domestic crisis of our nation in recent history."[50]

The Du Bois Institute demonstrated its potential to the AUC by adding new courses taught by high-profile faculty affiliated with the institute. The institute sought "the most creative scholars, writers, and artists" in the fields of Black Studies. It was hoped that these scholars, in conjunction with the Du Bois Institute, might "uncover and review neglected or unknown data on the Afro-American experience, create through their research, writing and performances new knowledge and works, and disseminate these materials to the Atlanta University Center Institutions, to the adjacent communities and other educational institutions."[51] The institute gave the AUC a preview of the curricular possibilities when it detailed the new courses in Black Studies that would be offered the following year. For the fall 1969 semester, the institute's associates offered a variety of Black Studies courses: Lerone Bennett Jr.'s "Black Reconstruction in America;" Chester Davis's "Building Black Curriculum in Public Schools;" Stephen Henderson's "Blues, Soul and Black Identity;" Joyce Ladner's "The Socialization of the Black Child;" and William Strickland's "Racism and American Social Analysis."[52] Harding and Henderson saw the proposed Du Bois Institute as "a base where black people could become the primary interpreters of the Black Studies experience."[53]

In addition to a proposed connection with the AUC, Harding and colleagues outlined plans for the Du Bois Institute to combine with, yet remain independent of, the forthcoming Martin Luther King Jr. Memorial Center. In the initial plans for the King Center, Harding was named director of the center's Library Documentation Project. Although the Du Bois Institute planned to provide significant services to the AUC, the King Center, and the Atlanta community, it wanted to remain independent, with its own "Advisory Board of Directors." Therefore, the founders of the Du Bois Institute planned that it would "be incorporated as a separate entity and administer its own fiscal affairs." In affiliating with the AUC and King Center, the Du Bois Institute anticipated becoming "a focal point for Afro-American Studies in the United States."[54]

The decision to connect the Du Bois Institute with the AUC and the King Center was essentially a pragmatic way to start the organization. The prestige of Morehouse College, Spelman College, and Atlanta University would further enhance the Du Bois Institute's profile, allowing it to serve as an alternative model to Black Studies programs elsewhere. The Du Bois Institute's ties to the AUC were provisional and tenuous, as each university in the system responded to the demands for Black Studies in a cautious manner. However, the institute's links to the King Center were stronger and initially more permanent than those with the AUC, in part as a result of Harding's role at the King Center and the personal relationship he had with the King family. When Coretta Scott King officially announced plans for the King Center, it included a monument at King's tomb, the restoration of his birthplace, a library, a park, a museum, and two academic institutes, one of which was the Du Bois Institute. Coretta King said, "What we see beginning now is no dead monument, but a living memorial filled with all the vitality that was his life, a center of human endeavor, committed to the causes for which he lived and died." The Du Bois Institute believed that its mission to shape the discipline of Black Studies merged with the directives of the King Center.[55]

While Harding, Henderson, McWorter, and the other AUC faculty members were developing plans for the Du Bois Institute, students formed an organization to help create a Black Studies program on the campuses. One month prior to Gianetti's ejection, students formed the Ad Hoc Committee for a Black University and presented a list of proposals to the AUC presidents demanding changes to "the racist American educational system, but even more specifically in the Atlanta University Center." The committee called for a more relevant curriculum, one that replaced the European framework with a program focused on Black and African cultures. The Ad Hoc Committee declared,

> European culture has crushed all but life from blacks from the time it appeared on African soil to this very day! Slavery ended 100 years ago! But, it is completely apparent to all of us that a more subtle form of slavery has continued to exist. The so-called "Negro College," with the Atlanta University system high on the list, continues to function as one of the main tools used by our oppressors to perpetuate the cruel colonization of Africans in America. In essence, our sincere desire for growth, truth, and a relevant education has been used against us.[56]

In addition to a relevant curriculum, the committee demanded majority student representation on all university committees, the disarming of the Atlanta University Security Patrol Force, the end to cultural events not related to Black culture (such as the Atlanta Symphony Orchestra), and automatic college admission for anyone involved in the Black Freedom Struggle. The students' demands reinforced certain changes supported by some faculty members. However, both student and faculty plans were delayed after Gianetti's expulsion, as the students' demands forced an immediate reaction.

All of the AUC administrations responded to the expulsion of the speech instructor. The universities issued a joint press release insisting on academic freedom and reminding students that violence and physical coercion would not be tolerated. Subsequently, the administrations introduced small, incremental changes that addressed initial student concerns about social prescriptions. After an all-night vigil, Morris Brown College president John Middleton abolished curfews for women, compulsory dress codes, and compulsory class attendance. Clark College followed with similar changes. At Spelman College, President Albert E. Manley suspended classes for two days to hold a "Speak Out" on the topics raised by the student committee. On the first day, discussions paralleled those at Morris Brown and Clark College, with a focus on social restrictions. The second day emphasized the idea of Black-oriented curriculum. Manley supported the idea of "increased emphasis upon curricular and extracurricular experiences and courses in Afro-American culture and greater involvement in community programs," as long as the program was not racially exclusive or caustic to non-Black faculty and students. The changes in social restrictions, nominal support for Black Studies, and the Thanksgiving and Christmas holidays resolved much of the immediate tension. Spelman College Student Government Association president Betty Ann Childers commented to *Jet* magazine in November 1968, saying that students "were satisfied with the *direction*" of Black Studies courses. However, students eventually grew impatient with the slow pace of institutional change concerning Black Studies.[57]

Atlanta University Center administrators relaxed social restrictions, but they were cautious in establishing Black Studies. Some believed that their school's existence as a Black college adequately addressed the needs for a positive Black identity. Many HBCUs offered a few courses on Black history and literature, but administrators believed the "second curriculum," the presence of Black faculty and staff, represented the main alternative without resorting to a formal program of study.[58] In addition, normal bureaucracy slowed the implementation of Black Studies at HBCUs. The AUC created a task force composed of students and faculty members to examine the curriculum and recommend areas of change. In spite of student activism, the above-mentioned factors slowed the development of formal Black Studies programs at the AUC and other HBCUs.[59]

Faculty members supported student complaints, but they also had their own grievances against the AUC administrations. They bristled at the administrations' authoritarian leadership and complained of a lack of communication between the presidents' offices and themselves. Relations between Black faculty members and college administrators often depended on both internal and external factors, including the educational philosophy of the president and board of trustees, the school's public or private status, the size of the endowment, and the college president's ability to withstand external pressures.[60] During his years in Atlanta, Harding worked to change the faculty's relationship with the administration. He participated in the community condemnation of Spelman College's firing of Staughton Lynd and Howard Zinn because of their support of SNCC in the early 1960s, and he believed that he and other young faculty had changed the culture of the Department of History and Sociology because "the curriculum began to respond to the changing needs and mood of the students." Harding used these experiences to support student desires for a Black curriculum.[61]

Students reciprocated support when faculty members challenged the administration's seemingly authoritarian decisions. In January 1969, for example, Morehouse College decided to not rehire professor A. B. Spellman because of his support for the previous semester's student protest and his broad support for Black Power, the Black arts movement, and Black Studies. Spellman, like many faculty members at Black colleges, was on an annual contract, which may have made him a target for dismissal at any sign of radicalism.[62] Although the AUC was more progressive than many rural and Southern Black colleges, it still faced internal and external pressures to eliminate troublesome faculty members. Spellman's research supported calls for Black Studies and its corollary, the Black arts movement, and his involvement with the Du Bois Institute made him an easy target for administrative action. Morehouse College president Hugh M. Gloster heightened the animosity by publicly defaming Spellman's character. In front of the entire student body, Gloster alleged that Spellman had misled students because he had taken a temporary teaching position at Emory University. The president implied that Spellman had a greater commitment to the "Lilly white school" than he had to Morehouse, and that his "often-stated commitment to black curriculum in the A. U. center was entirely jive." In an open letter, Spellman defended his character and stated that Gloster was using the issue as a smokescreen to avoid developing a Black curriculum. He explained that he took the job at Emory because Morehouse refused to offer him more than a one-year contract.

Students rallied on Spellman's behalf. The student-produced *Atlanta University Black Paper* stated,

Being Black students, we are all concerned about the kind of treatment afforded Mr. Spellman, but we all realize that this isn't the real issue. This is just another incident in the struggle to subjugate Black People. This is another show of authoritative, sophisticated force to squelch the thrust of the educational revolution. This is but another attempt to deny Black students their identity.

We all know that the real issue involves around . . . to whom are Black Colleges responsible? Are they responsible to white donors and the system that denies Black People, or are they responsive to Black College students and the Black Community? You see, this question surpasses the question of Black Curriculum, because if a college is responsive to the Black Community a Black Curriculum is a must. . . . If education for Black People is to become a reality then Spelman, Morehouse and other Black Colleges must change their commitments. The interests of the Rockefellers, Fords, DuPonts, and Harrimans conflict with the interests of Black People. . . . THIS IS THE REAL TRUTH.[63]

Students supported Spellman by invoking the Black University perspective. In applying this analytical frame to the AUC, students concluded that the universities were not operating in the Black community's best interests and that changes were necessary. After the Spellman incident, more dramatic student confrontations strained the cooperative venture between the Du Bois Institute, the AUC, and the King Center.[64]

Students pushed the AUC to implement a Black Studies program and alter its relationship to White philanthropy in order to become more relevant to the Black community. After the January incident involving Spellman, student activists, along with former SNCC workers Willie Ricks (Mukasa Dada) and Cleveland Sellers, planned a student takeover. The action was foiled, however, when students opposed to the idea informed the Morehouse College president.[65] In early April 1969, several students requested a meeting with the AUC Board of Trustees later in the month, demanding that the university come under Black control, change its name, and implement a Black Studies program. The board ignored the request. On April 17, 1969, a group of students crashed an Atlanta University trustees' dinner, issuing an ultimatum that called for White trustees to resign. The writers of the document insisted that the Black community should control the educational system and establish a "new process of control" for the Atlanta University Center.[66] No trustee signed the "Black Power in education" document, which intensified the students' later response.

The following day, April 18, ten students, including James Early and Samuel L. Jackson, and two professors, McWorter and Spellman, entered a Morehouse Board of Trustees meeting demanding an immediate hearing. They chained the doors shut from the inside. In what would be known as the Harkness Hall Incident, a group of between fifty and seventy-five students guarded the door from the outside as the students and faculty members inside made their demands. The group refused to release the imprisoned trustees until three demands were met. First, the board had to accept that the name of the AUC be changed to Martin Luther King University. Second, Black trustees would manage the AUC. Finally, all six institutions needed to be merged into a single university; trustees would have to persuade the other five institutions to accept the merger. After nearly thirty hours of captivity, the trustees agreed in principle to promote a merger of the institutions and to increase the number of Black members on the board. As far as the name change, Martin Luther King Sr., a Morehouse trustee, stated that the King family did not wish the name to be changed and that the activists were exploiting King's name and legacy. Following the coercive meeting, Morehouse president Gloster tendered his resignation. However, students led by Student Government Association president Nelson Taylor, who opposed the protest, persuaded Gloster to remain in his position. In the end, the students' actions led to increased Black and student representation on the Morehouse College Board of Trustees. Atlanta University agreed to establish Black Studies in the fall 1969 semester under the leadership of literature professor Richard Long. Despite making these concessions, the trustees expelled several students and threatened the careers of the faculty members involved.[67]

Although Harding, Henderson, and others proposed the original plan for Black Studies at the AUC, their involvement in establishing Black Studies there was minimal. McWorter and Spellman's roles as leaders in the Harkness Hall incident created a backlash against the entire Du Bois Institute project. The King Center leadership was not pleased, especially because two members of its board of directors, Martin Luther King Sr. and Benjamin E. Mays, had been detained in the protest. In addition, the AUC was upset that faculty members had encouraged students and had led a coercive and potentially violent protest that disrupted the schools. The AUC administrations believed that Harding was the "mastermind" behind the protest, despite the fact that he had not been on campus the day of the takeover. In a move to alleviate the pressure on the Du Bois Institute's plans, Harding reluctantly agreed with the King Center Board's decision to force McWorter and Spellman to resign from the institute's planning committee. McWorter remembered agreeing to these terms because he felt the King family wanted to eliminate the radicalism of the Du Bois Institute, a position which Harding accepted to protect the institute. Spelman and Morehouse Colleges both refused to rehire the two faculty members. McWorter and Spellman's support of the student takeover strained the relationship between the Du Bois Institute and the AUC.[68] By the summer of 1969, Harding and his associates had reconsidered future plans for working with the AUC, only agreeing to teach the seminar courses in the fall 1969 term. By eliminating the possibility of a formal connection with the AUC, Harding made the Du Bois Institute an exclusive component of the King Center.

The Du Bois Institute backpedaled from its formal connection to the AUC, because the events surrounding the Gianetti and Harkness Hall protests highlighted the lack of autonomy the institute would have in its relationship with the universities. Despite some concerns, Harding believed that the King Center provided the type of autonomy the institute needed to flourish. The semiautonomous institute had a multilayered structure. The senior research associates, led by Harding and Henderson, coordinated the day-to-day operations and the programmatic elements of the organization. The initial senior associates were Bennett, the senior editor of *Ebony* and author of *Before the Mayflower*; Joyce Ladner, a sociologist, former SNCC member, and the lone female associate; Chester Davis, an education specialist; and Sterling Stuckey, a historian. The next level was composed of an administrative staff that managed the institute's office, helped the senior associates with their research, and organized the institute's library of documents.[69] Outside of the organization, a network of colleagues actively supported the institute as collaborators, participants in fund-raising, and "sounding boards and critics."[70] Finally, the governing council, which included scholars John Henrik Clarke, St. Clair Drake, William Strickland, actor Ossie Davis, famed dancer Katherine Dunham, and others, was the liaison between the group and the King Center. It was the governing council, along with the senior associates, of the Du Bois Institute that renamed the organization the Institute of the Black World, because it was "more descriptive of [the] purpose."[71] Associates believed that they were creating an organization with the goal of "experimenting with the degree to which the varieties of opinions within the Black experience could be brought together in a real unity of work and commitment."[72] With the name change, the Institute of the Black World was ready to announce its purpose to the nation.

In the "Statement of Purpose and Program," IBW associates declared, "the gifts of their minds are meant to be fully used in the service of the black community." Their purpose was to produce "scholarship in the context of struggle." The IBW had ten areas of focus. The associates planned to define and refine Black Studies, create a Consortium for Black Education, conduct academic research, support Black artists, develop new teaching materials, craft a Black policy studies center, connect with intellectuals and scholars across the Black diaspora, prepare a "new cadre" of intellectuals "fully committed to the struggles of the black world," sponsor summer seminars and workshops, and develop a publishing program.[73]

The protests at the AUC affected the IBW and its associates. By supporting the student protests, the associates threatened the IBW's existence before it could even open. It further cost McWorter and Spellman their jobs in the AUC and at the IBW. AUC administrators also expelled or suspended student leaders Early, Jackson, and others for their role in the protests. The IBW survived because Harding was not directly involved in the protest, although administrators and King Center trustees believed he was the mastermind behind the plot. The entire event demonstrated to the IBW associates that they needed as much structural autonomy as possible. Both the AUC and the IBW mutually agreed to end any discussion of a formal relationship. The protests and reactions signaled that achieving a synthesis on Black Studies and a Black University would be difficult. Finally, the protests convinced associates to move beyond theoretical discussions of Black Studies and the Black University to more detailed analyses of the programs. By investigating the curriculum and philosophy of Black Studies programs, the IBW associates hoped to identify the strongest ones—those on which they could model future programs. Harding and Henderson believed this examination of programs would stabilize Black Studies departments by providing a model for departmental development. All in all, the associates' theoretical and practical work in Black Studies made evaluating the emerging discipline a logical first initiative for the IBW.

The IBW and Evaluating Black Studies Programs

The IBW's soured relations with the AUC over the student protests may have destroyed the organization's opportunity to build a Black Studies program at prestigious Atlanta HBCUs, but it did not alter the organization's commitment to Black Studies. Harding, Henderson, and now William Strickland believed the IBW could help emerging Black Studies programs. The shift from building an actual program to collecting data and analyzing other academic programs marks an important but subtle change in the organization's history that signaled its beginnings as a think tank. The institute wanted to become "an international center for Black Studies." Consequently, the IBW associates evaluated Black Studies programs to understand the "context" in which they were developing. To accomplish this task, associates examined Black Studies programs' "relationship to the surrounding Black community, their sense of self-definition and direction, and the political struggles—of every kind—surrounding them."

The IBW approached the academic field with five assumptions. First, Black Studies was not fully established, thus, there was no clear understanding of the "ways in which a profound mining of the black experience challenges and transforms the basic educational structure of the nation." Second, the process of defining Black Studies was "logically . . . a task and a challenge for black people in America and elsewhere." Next, the IBW and the King Center wanted to play an important role in defining Black Studies and creating curricular models that linked the variety of perspectives on the academic field. Fourth, the IBW believed that Black Studies should be interdisciplinary, meaning it wanted to explore how such programs integrated multiple disciplinary perspectives of the humanities and social sciences. Finally, the associates believed Black Studies would take years, not months, to build. They wanted to expose makeshift programs while promoting and supporting strong, well-conceived ones. With these explicit goals, the senior associates, led by Harding, sought to build an organization that systematically lent critical support to Black Studies and to move beyond the haphazard development of the academic field. By analyzing Black Studies programs, the IBW associates understood that opened themselves to criticism. Nonetheless, associates believed a pragmatic model derived from empirical analysis, not ideology, would accommodate differing approaches to the field of Black Studies.[74]

In the summer of 1969, associates altered the IBW's identity, and the organization made its initial attempt to become a think tank as it sought to analyze developing Black Studies programs. The IBW evaluated Black Studies programs and departments by surveying hundreds of them, asking questions about curriculum, philosophy, faculty statistics, and pedagogy. As the IBW defined them, these research questions explored Black Studies on the White campus, Black Studies on the "Negro" campus, Black curriculum programs in public and independent elementary and secondary schools, and critiques of Black Studies. At the National Association of Afro-American Education Conference in Atlanta later that summer, the IBW introduced some of its preliminary results.[75] They concluded that many of the programs on White campuses were "unfocused in terms of content, structure, and ideology," and neglected areas such as Black philosophy, the Caribbean, and Latin America. The data on programs on Black campuses was imprecise. However, Black Studies on both White and Black campuses had little "effect on the total life of the campus." The data collected on independent public primary and secondary schools was, at the time, too small to generalize. Despite the noncontroversial nature of the IBW's analysis, it drew criticism during the summer conference.[76]

Former colleague Gerald McWorter harshly criticized the IBW's analysis of Black Studies. During the conference, McWorter, who at this point had changed his name to Abdul Alkalimat, led a group that opposed the developmental trajectory that the field of Black Studies was taking as well as the IBW's role in facilitating that progress. Members of the Alkalimat-led group produced an essay, "Kweli," (Swahili for "truth") outlining their concerns with the conception of Black Studies and the IBW. The group opposed "the chain of enslavement of African people in this alien land in the guise of Black Studies." They believed that the funding of Black Studies by White resources ensured that the field could not "develop a counter program which speaks against it [White funding sources]." The lack of "self-determined" and autonomous funding meant Black Studies reinforced the status quo and was a form of neo-colonization. The group also identified the IBW as part of the problem. They stated that both the desire for integration exemplified by the civil rights movement as well as the creation of parallel institutions that replicated dominant values represented choices between colonialism and neo-colonialism. The oppositional group believed that their position "invalidates the very institute sponsoring it," namely, the IBW.[77] Alkalimat later saw his criticism of the IBW as related to Harding's ambiguous relationship with radicalism. According to Alkalimat, "This was in keeping with the practice to love Black radicals when they help move resources into the control of the Black middle class, but when it serves their purpose they dump the radicals." The Alkalimat-led group's criticism also reflected fallout from the Harkness Hall incident, after which Harding agreed to remove Alkalimat and Spelling from the organization in an attempt to save the IBW.[78]

Alkalimat's critique raised important questions about the relationship between funding and independent intellectual work. On the surface, Alkalimat's criticisms of Black Studies and the IBW appeared to be a reaction to his expulsion from the AUC and the IBW. It is clear that his opposition to Black Studies was temporary, because he later developed a successful Black Studies program at Fisk College (now University), published an introductory text to Black Studies, and has spent more than forty years promoting the discipline, especially in connection to technological innovations.[79] Despite the temporary nature of his opposition to Black Studies, the issues he highlighted about the conflicts between funding and intellectual perspective troubled the IBW throughout its existence. At the height of the Black Studies movement, Alkalimat's criticisms about funding sources were troubling, but did not alter the IBW's analysis of Black Studies programs or its plans for the directors conference. At this point in the organization's history, the IBW believed its principal funding source, the King Center, respected its goals. Alkalimat suggested that the IBW's independence was a mirage, but Harding disagreed and continued to promote the November conference on Black Studies.

In November 1969, the IBW hosted "The Black Studies Directors Seminar." At the seminar, more than thirty-five directors of Black Studies programs discussed and dissected the research collected during the summer.[80] The attending scholars "attempted to identify that very small segment [of Black Studies programs] which seemed to hold some clear promise as possible models on which the thousands of Black students in northern schools could build in their movements toward an education appropriate to our struggle."[81] Joyce Ladner acknowledged the seminar's significance and the importance of the IBW in her opening remarks.

I think it is very important that you understand why we are here. Each of us could be any place else in these United States, but we are here because we intend to build an Institution that does not exist any place today. We are committed to building that Institution almost at all costs. I think the thing that distinguishes us from groups of black people who are scattered about elsewhere . . . is that as a group of black scholars . . . we are building that Institution together even if we have to take care of ourselves, even if we have to experiment with various forms of communal living.[82]

The IBW associates believed that the seminar would begin to shape the field of Black Studies. The intellectuals at the IBW agreed that an ostensibly color-blind universal curriculum was discriminatory toward the contributions of Blacks. According to historian Sterling Stuckey, "our role . . . is to summon forth and cast out manifold white mythologies, to scatter the building blocks of the white American fantasy." The scholars concluded that they needed a theoretical perspective to analyze and understand the calls for Black Studies and Black Power in general. During the sessions, scholars emphasized the Black University perspective, intellectual opposition to the dominant racial theories, relevancy to Black communities, and structural autonomy.[83]

The panel discussions helped the scholars in charge of Black Studies programs to understand the challenges that lay ahead. Bennett moderated the first panel, which included Armstead Robinson, the head of the Black Student Alliance at Yale, and sociologist Basil Matthews of Talladega College. Robinson argued that Black Studies did not exist and that "Brothers and Sisters—students and faculty—are pimping Black Studies." He claimed that students wanted A's without studying, and faculty wanted paychecks without presenting "innovative approaches to the study of the Black experience." He continued by saying that the only chance for Black Studies' survival was committed directors. Matthews promoted diasporic study in order to "gain some insights into African culture" and what happened after slavery. Subsequent panels explored the problems that directors of Black Studies programs faced, including issues of staffing, curriculum, funding, and autonomy. The discussion revealed an unexpected problem in the field: Black students did not take the courses seriously. "Directors, almost universally, reported that students were refusing to study using the rationale of 'that's the white man's thing.'" Black students' demands for Black Studies and subsequent behavior, according to the directors, were a contradiction that many believed "could stifle and kill Black Studies and seriously impede the struggle for Black liberation." At the conclusion of the symposium, the IBW deemed the conference "fruit-ful" and asserted that "every participant left stronger."[84]

The IBW's Black Studies Directors Conference was the culmination of nearly two years of examination of and participation in the Black Studies movement. The conference furthered the Black University perspective by emphasizing intellectual opposition to dominant racial ideologies, the need for structural autonomy, and relevancy to the Black community. Associates advanced this viewpoint by using the IBW's methodology of collective scholarship. They used the conference not to dictate how Black Studies programs should be administered, but rather to develop strategies on curriculum, faculty, and administration. The IBW's conference marked the organization's shift from being a site for Black Studies to an activist think tank. This change is significant because the IBW's trajectory moved away from Black Studies and education to analyze broader problems facing Black communities. Finally, the IBW facilitated the stabilization of Black Studies programs and gave young directors, like Cornell University's James Turner and Brandeis University's Ronald Walters, a sense of direction and support.

Conclusion

The August 1970 issue of *Ebony* magazine asked, "Which Way Black America? Separation? Integration? Liberation?" The issue contained essays from multiple perspectives. National Association for the Advancement of Colored People chairman Roy Wilkins wrote on integration, suggesting "the siren call of separatism has repeatedly failed." Institute of the Black World associate and *Ebony* editor Lerone Bennett Jr. promoted liberation against the "false choice" of integration or separation. In his piece "Toward the Black University," Harding asserted that the Black University "has nothing to do with separation or integration." Instead, the "deepest concern within the black community today—beyond issues of survival—is to find pathways toward unity and solidarity, toward inner strength and communal wisdom." Harding summarized the basis of unity through the Black University perspective and called on supporters to reject imposed definitions of "a still arrogant white world." He believed the Black University would be concerned with the Black community and would be an "advocate and major intellectual resource . . . to move with its surrounding community toward the radical change that is necessary."

Harding proclaimed that the IBW was not a Black University, but a "research center" that would "create the content, direction, and materials for those re-ordered institutions." The essay summarized the IBW associates' two years of work on Black Studies and the Black University. Harding's essay positioned the IBW outside of formal programs, yet placed it as a key contributor to those programs.[85]

The IBW emerged from the Black Studies movement as a key evaluator of it. Henderson described the institute's objective as giving "direction to the Black Studies Movement." He added that the IBW was "acting as a catalyst, a kind of obstetrician to a new way of thinking which wasn't really all that new on reflection. A new way of thinking about integration, of art, humanities and political struggle."[86] As leading theoreticians on the Black Studies movement, IBW associates Harding, Henderson, McWorter (Alkalimat), and Bennett collectively promoted the Black University perspective of intellectual opposition, structural autonomy, and research relevant to the needs of Black communities. In essence, the Black University perspective was a first step in facing the challenge of Blackness during the long 1970s.

Associates' plans for Black Studies faced criticism and opposition. Although the critiques led to clearer, better-articulated justifications for Black Studies, the opposition posed by Black college administrators as well as radical and liberal organizations forced the IBW to deal with another major theme of Black Studies and Black Power in general—structural autonomy. The Harkness Hall takeover and the AUC and the King Center's subsequent demand for the removal of McWorter and Spellman from the institute's planning committee made Harding realize that the institute's structural autonomy was tenuous at best. The IBW made the pragmatic decision to become an activist think tank, believing it had found the necessary balance between intellectual independence and structural autonomy through its exclusive affiliation with the King Center. Harding believed that the connection with the King Center provided enough political, intellectual, and financial space for the IBW to move from Black Studies to other parts of its ambitious program. However, the security and autonomy provided by the King Center would prove to be a mirage.

Figure 1. Headquarters of the Institute of the Black World at Chestnut and Beckwith Streets, Atlanta, Georgia. Institute of the Black World Photograph Collection. Photographs and Prints Division, Schomburg Center for Research in Black Culture, the New York Public Library, Astor, Lenox, and Tilden Foundations.

Figure 2. Attendees at Institute of the Black World Conference. Institute of the Black World Photograph Collection. Photographs and Prints Division, Schomburg Center for Research in Black Culture, the New York Public Library, Astor, Lenox, and Tilden Foundations.

Figure 3. C.L.R. James delivering a public lecture during Institute of the Black World Summer Research Symposium, June 16, 1971. Photo by: Phillip A. Ghee. Institute of the Black World Photograph Collection. Photographs and Prints Division, Schomburg Center for Research in Black Culture, the New York Public Library, Astor, Lenox, and Tilden Foundations.

Figure 4. Vincent Harding and St. Clair Drake at Institute of the Black World Summer Research Symposium, June 16, 1971. Photo by: Phillip A. Ghee. Institute of the Black World Photograph Collection. Photographs and Prints Division, Schomburg Center for Research in Black Culture, the New York Public Library, Astor, Lenox, and Tilden Foundations.

Figure 5. Vincent Harding (left) and William Strickland (right) at the Summer Research Symposium, August 19, 1971. Institute of the Black World Photograph Collection. Photographs and Prints Division, Schomburg Center for Research in Black Culture, the New York Public Library, Astor, Lenox, and Tilden Foundations.

Figure 6. Walter Rodney speaking at the Institute of the Black World Summer Research Symposium 1974. Institute of the Black World Photograph Collection. Photographs and Prints Division, Schomburg Center for Research in Black Culture, the New York Public Library, Astor, Lenox, and Tilden Foundations.

Figure 7. IBW panelist Mack Jones and Janet Douglass. Institute of the Black World Photograph Collection. Photographs and Prints Division, Schomburg Center for Research in Black Culture, the New York Public Library, Astor, Lenox, and Tilden Foundations.

Figure 8. Howard Dodson introducing speakers; panelist Grace Lee Boggs, right. Institute of the Black World Photograph Collection. Photographs and Prints Division, Schomburg Center for Research in Black Culture, the New York Public Library, Astor, Lenox, and Tilden Foundations.

2

"Liberated Grounds"

The IBW's Independence and Reorganization

The Black Studies Directors Seminar was the springboard for the IBW and the King Center's official openings in January 1970. The program, "A Celebration of Blackness," announced the Institute of the Black World with flair. The five-hour event took attendees on an artistic trek through Black history. Katherine Dunham's dance troupe began with African dance, Margaret Walker Alexander recited poetry from the Harlem Renaissance, and Don L. Lee (Haki Madhubuti) ended the program with his Black Power poetry. Approximately five hundred people attended the opening ceremony, and many toured the IBW offices, which were located in W.E.B. Du Bois' old home at the edge of the AUC campuses. Coretta Scott King, outfitted in African clothing, welcomed the audience and posed for pictures with Vincent Harding, Lerone Bennett Jr., and other attendees.[1] Days later, the King Center also officially opened with the first public celebration of Martin Luther King Jr.'s birthday and the move of his remains to an Auburn Avenue tomb engraved "Free At Last, Free at Last, Thank God Almighty I'm Free At Last."[2] Harding, who headed both the Library Documentation Project and the IBW components inside the King Center, noted that the meaning of freedom on King's tombstone was ambiguous. He wondered whether Blacks could only achieve freedom through death, or if freedom had already been attained. For Harding and the IBW's network of associates, the immediate meaning of freedom depended on the organization's ability to produce synthetic analyses of a post-King America that could generate a consensus on the next steps in the Black Freedom Struggle.[3]

From its opening, the IBW embarked on a broad program, one that ended with Harding and other associates asserting that the organization was an activist think tank. The institute shifted away from Black Studies, implementing other parts of its program during its first year of existence. By embracing its expanded program, the IBW set out to accomplish its diverse goals in areas of research publications, lectures, and meetings with Black intellectuals who held "varieties of opinions."[4] The IBW's role as a think tank reflected Harding's desire to facilitate cooperation among the different activist communities through honest dialogue in hopes of continuing a unified movement into the seventies.

The King Center initially provided the structural autonomy for the IBW, which its associates used to accomplish an expanding agenda. When the King Center officially opened in January 1970, along with the tomb, the Library Documentation Project (LDP), and the IBW, it had distinct advantages in fundraising and overall support. The center benefited from the outpouring of sympathy for King's murder as well as from people's fear of violent outbreaks, like those that occurred in hundreds of cities after the assassination. In contradistinction to the private colleges in the AUC, which were dependent on White philanthropy and needed to maintain a positive, non-radical image, the King Center possessed considerable leverage in terms of public relations. However, as the IBW associates worked on their programs, the sympathy for King and fear of violence failed to translate into financial stability. The IBW's first major confrontation with the ideological dissension that eventually swept over most of the Black activist community came from the King Center. When the King Center's funding was threatened, the IBW's structural autonomy, as a component of the center, evaporated. The relationship between the center and the IBW deteriorated, leading to a contentious separation that strained longstanding friendships between Harding and the King family. The separation also forced the IBW to rethink its finances, its identity, and its leadership structure.

The IBW's separation from the King Center occurred because the latter insisted on a narrow racial liberalism from all of its components, reflecting its larger goal of becoming the official interpreter of King's life and legacy. The King Center provided the IBW with physical space, but over the course of 1970, its board of directors also demanded strict ideological adherence to civil rights liberalism. The IBW and the King Center's differences reflect larger issues regarding the interpretation of King's life and legacy. After his assassination, a variety of groups sought to explain the significance of King's life and activism. The mainstream press emphasized his "dream" and nonviolent action against the backdrop of urban rebellions and Black Power militancy. The SCLC stressed King's aggressive nonviolent activism, which they continued in a variety of campaigns after his death. Harding approached King's life from a nuanced perspective, one that accepted his religious ecumenism and his radicalism in terms of peace, poverty, and racial pride. These somewhat conflicting interpretations formed the basis of a contested historical memory. The King Center, under Coretta Scott King's leadership, sought to be the official voice and interpreter of King. In this process, the center and its commitment to commemoration were essential. The center echoed the mainstream media's interpretation by focusing on King's belief in nonviolence and by making the March on Washington the centerpiece of the historical narrative. This decision, rooted in ideology and memory, reduced or eliminated King's ideas on poverty, militarism, and racial pride. King's views expressed in *Where do We Go From Here: Chaos or Community?*—such as a guaranteed income, universal health care, and the importance of racial pride—were, perhaps deliberately, marginalized for the sake of a broadly approved and supported memorial.[5]

The center's board required a narrow, King-centered historical interpretation of the civil rights movement. Any King Center component that deviated from this narrative faced intense scrutiny and, ultimately, contraction. The center's version of King's legacy stifled any radicalism or any alternative historical narratives. Harding later described the effect of the narrow historical interpretations behind the commemoration of King as having "frozen the frame of the smiling, victorious hero, locked in the magnificent voice proclaiming the compelling dream."[6] When the Harding-led divisions, the LDP and the IBW, failed to follow the tenets of civil rights liberalism and countered the official historical narrative of King, the center's board displayed a form of sectarianism often associated with Black Power. Moreover, the center's opposition to the IBW represented a hegemonic civil rights liberalism, where traditional civil rights organizations like the King Center and the NAACP set the racial agenda. The IBW's first major experience with the dissension that dominated protest communities during the mid-seventies came from the King Center. The IBW's pragmatism, synthetic analyses, and Harding's ecumenical spirit could not reconcile the differences between the King Center and the IBW.

The events leading up to the IBW's separation from the King Center in September 1970 exhibited how problems of ideology, historical memory, and intellectual perspective threatened the IBW's existence. In the end, Harding recognized that "an embattled, colonized people need liberated grounds on which to gather, to reflect, to learn, to publish, to move towards self-definition and self-determination." The IBW associates initially believed that a connection with the King Center would provide "liberated grounds," a location of intellectual autonomy providing critical support for Black activists.[7] Associates analyzed the movements of the 1970s, identifying examples, strategies, and ideologies that could create a fuller understanding of how to achieve Black equality in post–Jim Crow America. The IBW's belief in collective scholarship and synthetic analyses meant that Harding and other associates critically engaged with a wide array of activists who held different ideologies and believed in diverse tactics. Through this conception of collective scholarship, the IBW allied with individuals and organizations incompatible with the King Center's understanding of the future of the movement or its narrow version of the past. Instead, the IBW sought synthetic analyses that would generate a broad consensus among Black activists. Unfortunately, the ramification of these goals was a collision course that some people had anticipated when the organization's name became the IBW.

The IBW's First Year

After its official opening, the IBW started a program of publishing, a lecture series, and established connections with other Black intellectuals and activists. Each activity increasingly drew the ire of the King Center Board of Directors, who believed the IBW's goals were antithetical to the center's.

Publishing

The institute spent the better part of its first year trying to accomplish its extensive goals, especially publishing associates' research. The IBW's initial publishing goals were met primarily through a cooperative publishing agreement with Don L. Lee's Third World Press to produce the "Black Papers," a pamphlet series written by associates examining how "contemporary political, economic, and social policies shape the life of the black community."[8] Bennett's Challenge of Blackness speech, delivered at the Black Studies Directors Conference, became the first "Black Paper" published by the IBW, a significant accomplishment considering the organization's meager finances.

Harding's *Beyond Chaos* (1970), the second in the IBW's series, argued that a new historiographical tradition had emerged in the wake of the civil rights movement. Harding used the shift from "Negro History to Black History" as a metaphor for the political change from racial liberalism to Black Power. In his interpretation, Negro history attempted "to reveal the 'contributions' of blacks to the American saga; its emphasis on black heroism in the wars; its call for racial pride and for continued struggle to enter the mainstream of American life; its claim to be primarily interested in objective truth, while writing history through tears." Harding asserted that Negro History did not challenge the basic values and assumptions of White America. In contrast, he argued, Black history did not want to be a part of the American narrative; rather, its "emphasis is on exposure, disclosure, on reinterpretation of the entire American past." According to Harding, such a reinterpretation was more than an academic exercise; it was political as well because "it recognizes that all histories of peoples participate in politics and are shaped by political and ideological views."

The goal of Harding and other's publications was to "affect black power aspirations and programs."[9] Bennett's *The Challenge of Blackness* and Harding's *Beyond Chaos* became guiding principles for the institute in its programming and political work. It was clear from the initial publications that despite its connection to the King Center, the IBW, under Harding's leadership, would not simply promote civil rights liberalism. Harding was willing to converse with proponents of alternatives to the liberal framework as well as with staunch believers in it. The IBW associates believed that the work to which King had dedicated his life was incomplete. Furthermore, they approached the possibility that the problems of poverty, institutionalized racism, and psychological inferiority in the Black community that King had identified in his last years could not be solved within the framework of liberalism, but instead needed synthetic analyses that included contributions from nationalist and Marxist thought.[10]

As the IBW was publishing its series of "Black Papers," some associates used publishing opportunities outside the IBW/Third World Press imprint to challenge scholarly assumptions about Black life and culture. Joyce Ladner and Stephen Henderson contested the dominant intellectual assumptions held by social science and literature, respectively. Looking back at her early years affiliated with the IBW, Ladner remembered it as the "single most productive year of my academic career."[11] Her *Tomorrow's Tomorrow: The Black Woman* attempted to "reconceptualize the 'deviant/pathology' model of black family life and black women."[12] She viewed inner-city Black women as powerful for their ability to "cope and adapt." Ladner further argued that the pathology model reflected the "inherent bias of the social sciences." Whereas the traditional social sciences asserted that Black culture was a problem, and hence deviant from White culture, Ladner identified the problem as institutional racism. This shift in perspective allowed her to reevaluate the Black family and its women as strong, a characteristic demonstrated by their ability to survive a hostile reality. As Ladner asserted, "it has been the overt and covert malignancy of institutional racism which has produced the alleged deviance and pathology. . . . It was the institutional racism which caused the so-called family disorganization, matriarchal society, high rates of juvenile delinquency, 'illegitimacy,' violence and homicide." Ladner called for the social sciences to redefine the alleged problem of Black culture and women. Facing the social problems of the seventies—inadequate wages, substandard housing, poverty, disease, and drugs—Ladner believed that Black women had to rely on the historical legacy of survival strategies that emerged from an autonomous Black culture.[13]

While Ladner addressed flawed assumptions in the social sciences, Stephen Henderson theorized a Black aesthetic. Henderson's introduction to *Understanding the New Black Poetry* attempted to theorize "the continuity and wholeness of the Black poetic tradition in the United States." Believing Black poetry was widely misunderstood, Henderson identified theme, structure, and saturation as the basis for analyzing a "Black" poem. For Henderson, a poem was thematically Black if it examined "the idea of Liberation," which included an array of definitions, concepts, and political strategies translated into a poetic form. Moreover, a Black theme contained a spiritual dimension, "liberated from the temporal, the societal, and the political." The combination of the search for spiritual and temporal liberation was a necessary theme in a Black poem. The structure of Black poetry, admitted Henderson, was the most difficult to explain. He concluded that Black poetry must derive its structure from either Black speech or Black music. Finally, he described saturation as the "communication of Blackness" and an attachment to the "truth of the Black experience." Henderson used the concept of saturation to theorize the emotive feeling of Black experiences—the joys and pains of not being fully incorporated into America and the survival strategies that created a distinctive culture. He did not expect this framework to be the definitive analytical frame for Black poetry, but he designed the theory, in line with the spirit of the IBW, to "facilitate discussion."[14]

The IBW, through these publications, made significant contributions to the developing research in Black Studies. They countered the dominant academic paradigms that had failed to explain or adequately theorize the Black experience in America. Each publication pointed out the inherent biases in mainstream scholarship and offered an alternative theory. These theories reflected pragmatic nationalist scholarship designed to challenge the epistemological assumptions produced in the university, which filtered, as Ladner's researched showed, down to the everyday lived experience of Black people as institutional norms. Scholarship by IBW associates stabilized Black Studies by providing it with a strong academic basis. Moreover, the publications indicated the institute's larger concerns of transforming the contemporary system of knowledge regarding the Black past and providing usable analysis for activists trying to alter contemporary America.

The King Center leadership did not believe the scholarship produced by the IBW associates was reflective of King's ideas and legacy. By March 1970, people affiliated with the King Center began to describe the IBW as a "racist-oriented" organization whose objective was "militant racial action rather than seeking truth through education." These early opinions of the IBW only hardened after the IBW began its lecture series.[15]

Lecture Series

In addition to publishing academic-oriented texts, the IBW organized a lecture series that showed a commitment to exploring the different ideological viewpoints of intellectuals and activists. The IBW invited C.L.R. James, Robert Hill, Stokely Carmichael, Horace Cayton Jr., Margaret Walker Alexander, and Robert Brisbane for its initial lectures. This collection of scholars reflected two organizational goals. First, as the IBW's "Statement of Purpose" declared, "Persons and organizations representing the full spectrum of ideological thought in the black community will be brought together periodically for unpublicized encounters outside of the polemical arena." James was a noted Leninist scholar who wrote the classic history of the Haitian Revolution, *Black Jacobins*, and who had formed several small socialist organizations in the United States, including the

Johnson-Forest Tendency. Hill was a noted Jamaican scholar of Marcus Garvey. Carmichael was a former leader of SNCC and the leading personality surrounding Black Power. Cayton, the grandson of the first Black United States senator Hiram Revels, had coauthored *Black Metropolis*, a pioneering work in Black urban sociology, with St. Clair Drake. Alexander wrote the award-winning novel *Jubilee*. Brisbane authored two books on Black activism in the twentieth century.[16] The lecturers presented the Atlanta community with varying perspectives on and scholarly approaches to the Black Freedom Struggle. Second, the IBW also wanted to establish "creative links" with Black scholars across the diaspora.[17] The presence of James and Hill connected the IBW to a broader world of radical intellectual activism in both the Caribbean and Europe. The lecture series accomplished both objectives, but caused apprehension outside of the King Center.

The IBW's decision to consult a wide spectrum of Black ideological thought garnered attention from the FBI's Atlanta Field Office. Founded in 1956, the FBI's Counterintelligence Program (COINTELPRO) was an investigative initiative designed to disrupt dissident political organizations. It began by investigating the Communist Party and the Ku Klux Klan, but as the civil rights, antiwar, and feminist movements took off, COINTELPRO targeted progressive organizations, often using illegal means. Some of the most intense investigative and destabilizing activities were aimed at what the FBI called "Black Nationalist Hate Groups," like the Black Panther Party. The bureau opened a file on the IBW because of its role in Black Studies, especially its support of Malcolm X Liberation University (MXLU), an experimental, independent college in North Carolina.[18] Although the connection between the IBW and MXLU was tenuous at best, the FBI, per J. Edgar Hoover's directives for COINTELPRO, lumped the IBW with other so-called Black Nationalist Hate Groups and opened a file in 1969.[19] Through an informant most likely affiliated with the King Center, the FBI learned of the brewing internal conflict between the IBW and the King Center over the differing interpretations of King's legacy. Informal discussions amongst members of the board of directors began as early as February 1970 about the IBW's differing direction and purpose. From the perspective of the King Center informant, the IBW's "Statement of Purpose" indicated that the organization was to be a "spawning place for activists" and that the institute's desires to rewrite Black history put it in "compliance with the thinking of persons believing in the most radical concepts of black supremacy." The informant kept the FBI abreast of the internal dealings, telling agents that Harding temporarily convinced the board that the Institute of the Black World was keeping with the philosophy of King.[20]

The reasons behind the individual's choice to report to the FBI cannot be fully determined without knowing the informant's identity. Nonetheless, the actions make sense given the King Center's desire to become a commemorative site, which required broad governmental and public financial support. Perhaps the informant believed he or she was placing the center in governmental favor. It is also unclear if Coretta Scott King knew about the informant, but based on the family's history with the FBI, it is unlikely that she did. The FBI illegally spied on and slandered Martin Luther King Jr. while he was alive, and they spied on his widow and advisor Stanley Levinson throughout the seventies. In any case, the FBI and its informant made a simple connection between the IBW and other Black Nationalist groups; a link the King Center reinforced with its growing distrust of Harding and the IBW. Whether King's widow agreed with the informant's activities, her actions and those of the board of directors toward Harding and the IBW confirmed the FBI's suspicions.

Out of all of the IBW's first-year activities, sponsoring an April 1970 lecture by Stokely Carmichael solidified the institute's public image as a distinct and radical component of the King Center, one truly devoted to autonomous intellectualism. The Carmichael lecture, more than any other, raised the ire of the King Center's board. Harding and Strickland had worked with Carmichael during their time in the civil rights movement, and they used their past connections to arrange the lecture. Inviting Carmichael was in some respects also a recognition of the former SNCC leader's personal intellectual and ideological growth. At the time of the 1970 lecture, Carmichael's position as a leading national Black Power spokesman and personality was in transition. Carmichael famously introduced the Black Power slogan on the civil rights landscape in June 1966. In fall 1967, Carmichael and Charles V. Hamilton's *Black Power: The Politics of Liberation in America* attempted to clarify the slogan by establishing it as a version of ethnic pluralism.[21] Also in 1967, Carmichael toured the Third World, including Cuba, Vietnam, Algeria, and Guinea, meeting with revolutionary leaders such as Fidel Castro, Ho Chi Minh, Sékou Touré, Kwame Nkrumah, and exiled Black American activists Robert F. Williams and Shirley Graham Du Bois. After returning to the United

States, he facilitated a brief merger between SNCC and the Black Panther Party. Carmichael's "flirtation" with the Panthers and his subsequent 1968 expulsion from SNCC fueled his desire to organize a Pan-African political party. Carmichael moved to Conakry, Guinea, in 1968 to study under Nkrumah and Touré. His visit to Atlanta was part of a short return to the United States in which he formally announced his new Pan-Africanist ideology and political party.[22]

Despite his fourteen-month absence from the American political scene and his evolving political philosophy, Carmichael's lecture still caused much consternation in the Atlanta community. Opponents of Carmichael and his philosophy blamed the IBW and Harding for promoting a needlessly antagonistic agenda. When Carmichael arrived in Atlanta, he excluded the press from his lecture, on the grounds that the media consistently distorted his ideas and statements. Carmichael's reputation and his requested media ban made it difficult for Harding to secure a lecture hall on the AUC campuses. To accommodate the anticipated large crowd, the IBW requested the complimentary use of Morehouse College's Archer Hall, one of the largest facilities in the AUC. However, Morehouse officials worried about having Carmichael speak there, and chose to walk a tightrope between university needs and student desires. University officials recognized that appearing to sponsor Carmichael's lecture could embarrass its board of trustees, which included Benjamin Mays and Martin Luther King Sr., men who personified civil rights liberalism. Furthermore, it could have impaired financial support from White philanthropists, the United Negro College Fund, and the American Baptists, each of which disliked any radical inclinations.[23] On the other hand, Morehouse administrators did not want to give militant students ammunition and motivation for another round of protests by refusing Carmichael the opportunity to speak, remembering the Harkness Hall incident that had engulfed the campus the previous year. The university's solution was to treat the IBW's request as a business decision. Morehouse billed the IBW three hundred dollars to rent the auditorium for the evening. Harding and Henderson believed that their faculty status should have allowed them free use of the venue, but they accepted the Morehouse decision and paid the fee. The King Center was also upset because the IBW did not notify either Coretta Scott King or the center's board of directors before planning the event. Harding's failure to notify the King Center demonstrated administrative and ideological independence from it. Harding and other associates did not wholeheartedly agree with Carmichael, but they believed his perspective was influential and worth discussing.[24] Moreover, Harding believed the IBW was the place from which such a dialogue should emerge.

Carmichael's speech addressed the problems looming between the IBW and the King Center. In front of an audience of nearly one thousand people, Carmichael tried to bridge the perceived gap between King's image and himself. Addressing the barrage of personal attacks he had faced since his departure from the Black Panthers and his expulsion from SNCC, Carmichael invoked King's legacy as a unifier and asserted his desire to emulate this characteristic. "Dr. King never attacked any black man and that's why I had a great deal of respect and admiration for him—because he cared about his people and he always sought to unify us rather than to divide us."[25] He later hinted at the underlying tensions between the IBW and the King Center and its desire to make King's life the focus of study:

> I speak before the Institute of the Black World, a forum that is trying to combine all the studies of the black world and according to it, make its focal point the writings and research of the late Dr. Martin Luther King Jr. I think most of us would agree with that. We may have some quibble about whether or not Dr. King's works should be the focal point of the Institute of the Black World, but none of us would quibble about the fact that his works must be included because he contributed a fantastic amount of knowledge, time and energy to our movement.[26]

Carmichael's words hinted at the behind-the-scenes tension between the IBW and the King Center. Carmichael presented a nuanced interpretation of King that emphasized his radical and pragmatic components. He reminded the audience that it was King who had taught confrontation, "not the Black Panthers, not Malcolm X," and that despite Black Power's intellectual and political contributions, it had been King who "taught us how to mobilize the masses." In honoring King as a unifier and revolutionary, Carmichael tried to heal the split in the movement between civil rights liberalism and Black Power. Moreover, Carmichael, like the IBW, tried to find a higher synthesis between the two perspectives. Unfortunately, the King Center felt that there was no room to compromise with what they simplistically saw as Black hatred.[27]

Although Morehouse College's administration had been apprehensive about his lecture and the King Center was irritated over Carmichael's presence, an FBI agent believed that his speech was not "the fiery type . . . normally delivered by Carmichael." Regardless of this assessment, the King Center Board of Directors remained suspicious of the IBW's purpose and goals. Coretta Scott King and others on the King Center Board wondered if the two organizations had similar objectives.[28]

Diasporic Networks

The IBW associates' interactions with radical scholars from across the African diaspora further increased tensions with the King Center. Associates purposefully consulted Black intellectuals who held an assortment of ideological perspectives. These consultations raised the IBW associates' awareness of diverse analytical perspectives and arguments beyond the simplistic dichotomy of integration and separation. Moreover, scholars like James were members of an informal, radical, diasporic intellectual network that had been disrupted by the Cold War. The United States government, in the name of the Cold War, harassed progressive Black intellectuals, seeking conformity to a domestic civil rights agenda that precluded discussions of Pan-African links and disrupted a burgeoning diasporic intellectual network that grew before World War II.[29]

The IBW became a key location for reconnecting the radical Black intellectual network neutralized by the Cold War's attack on leftists, such as C.L.R. James. After World War II and early in the Cold War, the government repressed many Blacks for their left-leaning views. Under the auspices of the House Un-American Activities Committee, Senator Joseph McCarthy and his fellow cold warriors destroyed the diaspora-based strategies developed out of the 1935 Ethiopian Crisis and the 1936 Spanish Civil War by organizations such as the Council of African Affairs, led by Paul Robeson, and James' International African Service Bureau. Historian Penny Von Eschen has pointed out that the Cold War altered political discourse on civil rights, which "left no room for the internationalism that had characterized black American politics through the mid-1940s."[30] Because of this shift in focus, domestic civil rights became the primary objective, forcing Pan-Africanists such as Robeson, Du Bois, and James out of the country or into isolation.[31] The space provided by the IBW reconnected a network that dominated the intellectual horizons during the 1940s and reflected the possibilities of Black Power intellectualism.[32]

Robert Hill's saga of joining the institute exemplifies this reconnected diasporic network. According to Hill, the ordeal was "a tale to be told." During his time as a student at the University of the West Indies, Hill studied the life and political activities of Marcus Garvey. He also combined research and activism by joining the Jamaican Black Power movement and working on the newspaper *Abeng*, which he and other young West Indian intellectuals, including the economist George Beckford, formed. *Abeng* had its roots in the uprising that followed the Jamaican government's refusal to allow Guyanese Marxist historian Walter Rodney to reenter the country after he left briefly for the 1968 Black Writers Conference in Montreal. Hill had organized this particular Conference of Black Writers, and the conference panelists included notable West Indian intellectuals, Rodney, novelist George Lamming, theorist C.L.R. James, sociologist Orlando Patterson, economist Norman Girvan, and veteran activist Richard B. Moore. Hill and Rodney also shared the stage with Black Power activists such as Harry Edwards, James Forman, and Stokely Carmichael. Rodney and Hill coauthored "Statement of the Jamaican Situation," a paper describing the independent Black government in Jamaica as a neocolonial regime, one in which the beneficiaries of independence were "a narrow, middle-class sector."[33]

Hill supported Rodney because the Guyanese historian was a tremendous scholar committed to working-class people. Rodney's scholarship and intellectualism rejected middle-class norms, and he chose to "ground" with the Jamaican lower and working class, namely the Rastafarians. By grounding with the Rastas, Rodney demonstrated a commitment to working-class activism and an openness to an alternative interpretation of history. Rastas, who had been demonized and criminalized for their Ethiopianism, dreadlocks, and spiritual use of marijuana, had origins that were rooted in the nexus of twentieth-century Pan-Africanism. The Rastafarian movement is a Pan-African messianic theology that believes former Ethiopian emperor Hailie Selassie I was God incarnate, and that his presence fulfilled Scripture, namely Revelation 19:16 and 5:5.[34] Influenced by Marcus Garvey's movement in the 1910s and 1920s and the diasporic opposition to Italy's fascist attacks on Ethiopia in the years preceding World War II, Rastas developed a complex set of religious rituals and symbols, most notably Black pride, dreadlocks, communal living, and smoking ganja or cannabis, all of which opposed Western cultural norms. Jamaican authorities' principal explanation for such philosophies was madness, and they arrested early Rasta spokesperson Leonard Howell and placed him in a mental asylum in 1954. Rastafarians' mad discourse, language that shows the rules of exclusion, was outside of the government's tourism narrative.[35] Furthermore, Rastas represented a radical alternative to Western culture's negation of Blackness. According to Caribbean scholar Anthony Bogues, "Rastafari's ontological practice is a frontal assault against colonial and racial knowledges and practices that makes the African human a thing, a Caliban, a savage, who then becomes a problem, a pathology, a native, a nigger, a Kaffir, and at best a Negro." It was a combination of colleagues like Hill, students, and Rastas that protested Rodney's ban from Jamaica. Hill's research on Garvey and support of Rodney exemplified an evolving Pan-African analysis rooted in both Black Nationalism and Marxism during the sixties.[36]

Using *Abeng*, Hill and his colleagues analyzed the Jamaican Labor Party's (JLP) position on Rodney and examined the social problems in the country from the perspective of the Jamaican working class. They concluded that the JLP was complicit in many of the nation's social problems. According to *Abeng* cofounder George Beckford, "The political response to the JLP repression took many forms. There were various nationalist groups and organizations, many of which came together behind the Abeng [sic] newspaper. Many of these groups were formed by radical intellectuals of middle-class backgrounds. Through them, the militance of the Black Power Movement in the U.S.A. and the revolutionary slogans of the National Liberation Movements of the world, fed into mass struggle."[37] This type of analysis led the Jamaican government to harass Hill by revoking his passport. After a protracted legal struggle, he regained his passport only to be placed on a government blacklist of subversive individuals. By the end of 1969, Hill was "stranded in a real way" after losing his job as a radio commentator.[38]

It was during this difficult period that Hill first heard of the IBW and began his decade-long association with the organization. He found it interesting that he did not recall learning of the IBW from the various Black Power activists who came to Jamaica on what Hill called "political tourism," or from the local media. Rather, he learned of the IBW at Amy Jacques Garvey's home, where he read several IBW publications laying on her telephone stand, including essays from the Black Studies Directors Conference. Hill remembered Jacques Garvey for carrying on the

Garveyite tradition, which held that "We know no boundaries where the African is concerned, until all Africa is free." This tradition of diaspora and interconnectedness reflected not only Jacques Garvey's life work, but also the IBW's goals. Another veteran scholar-activist and IBW associate, St. Clair Drake, also facilitated Hill's move to the IBW. While Hill was unable to leave Jamaica, fellow students at the University of the West Indies notified him that an older man, Drake, was looking for him on campus. Drake was in Jamaica on a fellowship, and the two became close friends after Hill nursed the older scholar through a bout of malaria. At the conclusion of the fellowship, Drake encouraged Hill to come to the United States to give a series of lectures on college campuses.[39]

Hill still faced an uphill battle to enter the United States because he had been blacklisted in Jamaica. Although he regained his Jamaican passport through litigation, the United States Immigration and Naturalization Service still denied him entry into the country. The IBW and others launched an extensive letter-writing campaign to get Hill a visa, and they succeeded in the spring of 1970. Hill arrived in Atlanta to lecture on Marcus Garvey for the IBW.[40] But when Hill returned to Jamaica to accompany his family back to America, INS detained Hill at reentry and deported him. Once again, the Black intellectual network, ranging from Drake to John Henrik Clarke and the IBW, mobilized; eventually the United States granted Hill a visa, and he rejoined the institute in 1971 as a senior associate. Hill's saga reflected the IBW's desire to connect Black intellectuals from across the diaspora and generations to build a top-notch research organization. The King Center, however, did not understand how Hill's research on Marcus Garvey and activism in support of Walter Rodney fit within the framework of honoring King. Consequently, the King Center Board expressed increasing displeasure with the direction of the Harding-led component.[41]

The IBW's publications, lecture series, and connections with diasporic intellectuals point to the organization's engagement with a variety of ideological perspectives, with the goal of developing synthetic analyses. The IBW's ideological experimentation explored various perspectives ranging from liberalism to Black Nationalism to Marxism. Adding Carmichael to the lecture series antagonized the King Center Board, especially Coretta Scott King. From her perspective, Carmichael opposed her husband's vision and threatened the center's deliberate attempts to fashion a safe and heroic historical depiction of King. The IBW's ideological diversity put it on a collision course with the King Center's rigid civil rights liberalism and its associated memory construction.[42]

Separation from the King Center

While the IBW's activities disturbed some members of the King Center Board, another point of contention was the multiple posts that Harding held at the King Center and the AUC. By 1970, Harding supervised the Library Documentation Project (LDP), consulted the King Center Board on the general direction of the memorial, headed the IBW, and remained a faculty member at Spelman College. Harding's multiple positions and his activities at the IBW led to a deterioration of his relationship with the King Center Board and Coretta Scott King in particular. The King Center Board of Directors' evaluation of the components of the Memorial Center was a transparent attempt to assert control over the Harding-led components and to rein in the King Center's spiraling expenses. Harding and the board's differing visions of the goals and direction of the center led to icy exchanges that betrayed years of friendship. The latent hostility surfaced when the King Center made a concerted effort to reel in the IBW.

The center's decision to assert control over the Harding-led divisions was about ideology and the construction of historical memory. The center steadfastly supported civil rights liberalism, with a focus on fundraising and on solidifying King's historical legacy. Coretta Scott King was obviously aware of her husband's rapid descent in popularity from his 1964 apex, when he was named *Time* magazine "Man of the Year" and won the Nobel Prize, to his nadir after the 1967 anti-Vietnam speech.[43] Mrs. King envisioned the center as a means to restore her husband to the pantheon of American heroes, and she did not want this mission derailed by Black Power radicalism, no matter how pragmatic and experimental. The King Center Board of Directors evaluated the Harding-led components—the LDP and the IBW. Although regaining control of these divisions was a goal, the center presented its assessment as part of routine fiscal year planning. For the new fiscal year, both the IBW and the LDP wanted an increase to their respective $300,000 and $250,000 budgets. Considering that the center had failed to receive anticipated millions of dollars, the evaluations were deemed necessary from ideological, memory construction, and financial standpoints.[44]

Evaluating the Library Documentation Project

In May 1970, Harding prepared a report that outlined the LDP's accomplishments for the King Center Board and its evaluation panel. The library was the first element of the King Center and had its own advisory council separate from the King Center and the IBW. The LDP's purpose was three-fold. First, it gathered primary documents on the post-1954 civil rights movement, with Martin Luther King Jr.'s papers as the focal point. Second, the library had to identify and catalogue these materials. Finally, young adults received "on-the-job training" in archival work at the library. In just under two years, the LDP staff had made considerable inroads in gathering materials on the civil rights movement. The staff had traveled to Alabama, Mississippi, Michigan, Ohio, California, and Washington, D.C., to acquire civil rights documents and personal papers of James Foreman and Fred Shuttlesworth as well as the organizational records for the SCLC, SNCC, and CORE. There were over 450 audiotapes, 90 reels of microfilm, and 550 photographs that needed to be processed, and the library obtained additional archival materials daily. The report noted that these accomplishments occurred despite the library's financial problems. The LDP had accrued a $45,000 debt since opening, much of which resulted from the King Center's approval of its budget before it could be financed. The situation became so acute that $35,000 was transferred from the IBW to the library to meet payroll. According to the LDP report,

> We have thereby been involved in what might be called a tragicomedy [sic]: The Board has approved our budgets, approved our work, promised to secure funds, led us to expect them and to plan with them in mind. When these funds have not materialized we have been questioned about the level of our operations and asked whether or not we are too large, too ambitious or too inefficient in our planning.

Harding concluded that the library needed approximately $200,000 to $225,000 for each of the next two years to reach its stated goals.[45]

The King Center Evaluation Panel assessed whether the LDP was "moving in the direction that the Board intended." This innocuous phrase obscured a deliberate attempt to eliminate the presence of anyone who was affiliated with or enamored of Black Power. The evaluation panel consisted of five members: John Maguire, Dora McDonald, Randolph

Blackwell, Edythe Bagley, and Isaac Farris (chairman). This subcommittee was ostensibly neutral, as Maguire and Blackwell were part of the LDP advisory council, while McDonald, King's former secretary at the SCLC, Bagley, Coretta Scott King's sister, and Farris, King's brother-in-law, represented the King Center. However, the recommendation made it clear that the panel represented the desires of the King Center alone. The evaluation panel recommended that the King Center Board establish guidelines and procedures for making the Martin Luther King Jr. papers a priority over those of other organizations and individuals involved in the civil rights movement. The panel suggested that a room be dedicated to King's pictures and mementos. It further advised that the library's Oral History Project be "given immediate attention and consideration" in terms of documenting King's life "through persons who were close to him" or affected by him. This emphasis, according to the evaluators, should occur "at the expense of other tasks." In addition, the committee wanted specific hiring guidelines in order to control the staff's ideological perspectives.

> Guidelines should be set forth in reference to the philosophy and background of the individual. The social philosophy of a staff member should be important here: for example, we can sense the difficulty of a person immersed in the philosophy of the Black Power Movement functioning at peak efficiency in a Center built and founded around the philosophy of non-violence.[46]

The evaluators suggested, in theory, a loyalty oath in the name of nonviolence. Finally, the panel urged the LDP and the King Center to manage their finances more stringently, because the "integrity and reputation of each Board member are at stake when bills of the King Center are not paid on the dates when they are due." In order to meet financial obligations, the report suggested that staff members be laid off.[47]

At a following June meeting, the King Center Board moved to implement the panel's recommendations. The board made the Oral History Project on King's life and work the "primary emphasis." During the discussion on the specific staff qualifications, Harry Wachtel, former corporate lawyer and SCLC advisor, raised the issue of the racial composition of the library's staff.[48] The board viewed the lack of Whites working at the LDP as problematic. Their concern was one of perception rather than logistics. Harding believed the surrounding colleges in the AUC produced plenty of qualified Black applicants. He reiterated that it was not an accident that no Whites worked in the library, to which Coretta Scott King responded that "token integration" was necessary. During the meeting, the board restated the need to reduce library personnel, and it was Harding's responsibility to "eliminate those positions necessary in order to meet our financial responsibilities." Based on the marginal notes on the meeting's agenda, Harding was unsatisfied with the position of the King Center Board, and the Library Governing Council's subsequent "Plan of Implementation" reflected this disagreement.[49]

Harding and the LDP's Governing Council responded point-by-point to the evaluation. Harding explained that an oral history emphasis would require more staff rather than less, telling the King Center Board it would need to provide funds for two full-time interviewers, two full-time transcribers, and one full-time editor. The LDP Council also revealed that, despite the King Center Committee's insistence on making King's life and work central at the LDP, Coretta Scott King had not made her husband's "letters, memoirs, manuscripts, and diary, as well as his daily itinerary, reports, memos, leaflets, speeches, photographs, tape recordings, and the like" available to the library.[50] In addition, the LDP Governing Council believed that the focus on King was "to deny and diminish the tremendous influence he had on the movement as a whole." King's greatness could only be understood within the context of the larger movement.[51]

The LDP Council also provided a practical answer about the racial composition of the staff. "Our hiring policies will not be racially exclusive. In practice, we shall deliberately and systematically provide every opportunity for gainful employment and the development of skills for Blacks. . . . We anticipate no difficulty in finding Blacks for these positions in the future, as we have not in the past."[52] The Library Governing Council defended its autonomy regarding hiring and opposed any notions of reducing staff size, believing any attempt to make King's life and work the focal point needed at a minimum the existing staff. They informed the board that its micromanaging had perhaps led to the recent resignations of John Hope Franklin and Louis Starr. The LDP's Council also suggested that the departure of the two scholars was perhaps prompted by the idea of the council being "an Advisory body only rarely convened and . . . powerless to shape and direct the Library program." Finally, the letter pleaded not to sacrifice the staff to budgetary concerns.[53]

A July 26 meeting between the King Center Board of Directors and the LDP Governing Council failed to produce a resolution. At the meeting,

Harding submitted his resignation as director of the LDP, Willie Harriford Jr. was elected as acting director, and Georgia state representative and former SNCC activist Julian Bond was voted chairman of the governing council. The LDP Council, believing Harding's resignation had resolved a major source of tension, then subjected King Center representative Isaac Farris to "a series of very searching and very serious questions about the [center's] financial situation," their commitment to the library, and the willingness of their board to "delegate certain powers formally into the hands of the Governing Council."[54] Although the LDP Governing Council asserted its autonomy, Farris disagreed, believing the King Center Board should shape and control the direction of all the center's components. The following day, the King Center Board had the final word on the direction of the LDP. The board quickly dissolved the LDP's Governing Council, a committee that included Julian Bond, attorney C. B. King, educator Horace Mann Bond, Spelman College president Albert Manley, and King biographer and historian L. D. Reddick.[55]

The elimination of the governing council gave the King Center unobstructed authority to dismiss twenty-one of thirty-three LDP staff members four days later. Ostensibly, the staff's removal was due to a "tenuous financial situation," but as an internal memo pointed out, "the Library [had] been functioning from pay check to pay check for a considerable period, the staff assumed there was not money and volunteered to work full-time for half-pay." The LDP staff members offered to work for less pay, but the King Center Board rejected the proposal. Harding was disappointed at the decision because Coretta Scott King had announced at the July 27 board meeting that the King Center was getting three hundred thousand dollars from a Martin Luther King Jr. film. Harding wondered, "what has been the purpose of raising funds for the Martin Luther King Jr. Memorial if they are not going to be used in the service of black people?" To this rhetorical question there was no clear answer.[56]

The dismissed workers did not quietly accept their firing. At an August 1970 press conference announcing Dr. Julius Scott as the new King Center director, several former staffers protested their release with picket signs charging "unfair labor practices."[57] The workers maintained their removal was "inconsistent with the work of Dr. King, who was killed in the struggle for fair labor practices."[58] The staffers issued a list of demands that included rehiring the fired workers, transferring Dr. King's papers from his office and Boston University to the LDP, reinstating the governing council, outlining the responsibilities and authority of the King Center Board of Directors, and adding staff members from each King Center unit to the board.[59] In response to these demands, Coretta Scott King called a second press conference the same day to rebut the charges of unfair labor practices, reiterating that the workers were "laid off" because of the King Center's financial problems.[60]

The refusal of the board and Coretta Scott King to meet with the fired staff represented a conscious decision to place Martin Luther King Jr.'s legacy in the relative safety of civil rights liberalism. The board's decisions seem particularly askew in light of King's Poor People's Movement and his support of economic reform through a guaranteed income. The King Center's hagiography limited the scope of King's work and legacy, marginalizing his analysis of the political economy and his anti-imperialist critique.[61] Behind the scenes, several members of the King family, including Coretta Scott King, held Harding responsible for the discharged workers' actions because he did not issue a statement "condemning some or all of their statements and actions," thereby placing the King family in a "totally hostile situation."[62] Harding's role in tacitly supporting the laid-off workers' demands set the stage for a confrontation between the IBW and the center. The LDP crisis was just the beginning of the problems facing Harding and the IBW.[63]

Evaluating the IBW

The IBW similarly ran headlong into King and her advisors' conceptions of the center's purpose. At the July 27 meeting, when the King Center dismissed the LDP Governing Council, Harding also received a King Center committee's evaluation of the IBW. Harding tabled his response until August 10 so that he would have time to review the document. Shortly after the meeting, it was clear to Harding that because of the events since the Carmichael speech, "rational solutions were quickly impaired."[64]

The IBW associates observed the deteriorating relations with the King Center and questioned Harding's desire to maintain the affiliation. The IBW's formal connection to the King Center, almost from its very founding, worried some institute associates. As early as 1969, Strickland remarked on rumors that the IBW was "a front for the man" because of the King Center's ties to "the establishment."[65] By August 1970, there was a chorus of concerns. Original IBW senior associate Joyce Ladner, whose sister Dorie was one of the workers fired from the LDP, wrote from

Tanzania about the tensions in the King Center and wondered what was left to fight for "within" the center. She concluded, "There can be no reconciliation with Mrs. King. In fact, reconciliation at this point is not ideologically compatible with the thrust of the black community." In the end, she suggested independence. "A more pressing question," Ladner asked, "is what can be gained through the symbolic connection . . . with MLK than cannot be obtained through more independent means." Strickland also noted the King Center "had no perspective on the problem," as they viewed equality in terms of integration and independence as segregation. He questioned the King Center Board's interpretation of Martin Luther King Jr.'s life. "Martin stood for [a] fight against, war, poverty, racism, where does [the] board stand and how do they propose to further those fights?" These questions of independence became more acute in the fallout of the LDP protests and the evaluation of the IBW.[66]

In the King Center's evaluation, the committee, led by former Morehouse College president Benjamin Mays, criticized the IBW about three basic issues. First, the IBW had not made the work and life of Martin Luther King Jr. a priority. In particular, the report pointed to the pictures of various Black leaders, such as Malcolm X and W.E.B. Du Bois, that adorned the walls of the IBW offices.[67] Second, the institute made no public or overt commitment to nonviolence. The board's committee believed that it "was not an accident that no reference is made to the doctrine of nonviolence as a method of perfecting social change." The committee found it "difficult to understand" how in the King Memorial "there should be hesitancy and even deliberate avoidance of affirming commitments" to nonviolence. Finally, the evaluation panel chastised the IBW for excluding White scholars. Based on these three issues, the board concluded, "The Institute's purpose was not in harmony with the one adopted by the Center's Board."[68]

The IBW responded to the criticisms leveled by the King Center's committee. To the charge of not giving the work and life of Martin Luther King Jr. primacy, the IBW stated its "primary commitment and first priority must be to record, analyse [sic], and forward the larger struggles of African peoples."[69] The diasporic, pragmatic, and synthetic-analysis perspective of the IBW was beyond the King Center's "own sentimentally-oriented image of a memorial to Martin." The institute remained committed to "the stark, unromantic needs of Black struggle—today's and tomorrow's." The King Center wanted scholarship that honored the greatness of King and announced the civil rights movement's conclusion; the IBW wanted to "represent the best spirit of Martin." The IBW presented its critical perspective as one that moved beyond validating a fallen hero and instead attempted to liberate Black people across the globe.

Harding and other associates responded to the remaining accusations. Associates answered the charge that the institute lacked a commitment to King's philosophy of nonviolence by highlighting their devotion to the liberation of Blacks globally. In a letter to supporters, who had begun to hear about the internal conflict in the press or through rumor, Harding explained that the IBW "cannot base its work on and demand loyalty to any one exclusive philosophy or strategy."[70] The interactions with scholars across the diaspora during the first year reminded the institute that no one philosophy could solve the multitude of problems facing Black communities. In reaction to the final accusation of excluding White scholars, the IBW intimated to the committee that it was founded on the conception that Black people must control and define the Black experience.[71] Despite this systematic rebuttal, the King Center asserted its control over the IBW, forcing the associates led by Harding and others to conform to the new regulations or pursue independence. Unable to maintain its autonomy within the confines of the King Center, the IBW chose independence, which officially occurred on September 1, 1970. Once separated from the King Center, the IBW embarked on a path of autonomy and self-determination. But with its new independence came a stark financial reality—the IBW could no longer use the King name to raise money. The intellectual independence the IBW achieved would have been short-lived without immediate attention to fundraising.[72]

This separation shows how the King Center's narrow vision of racial liberalism created a circumscribed interpretation of King's legacy. The center's commemorative vision reiterated a heroic interpretation of King in hopes that they would attract substantial political and economic support. The family and its advisors rightfully wanted to protect King's image. By making integration and King's "I Have a Dream" speech the focus of their commemorative vision, Coretta Scott King and her advisors provided a simple and heroic narrative that meshed with American mythology. The IBW and the LDP under Harding's leadership began with the less-popular post-1965 King, who opposed the Vietnam War, grappled with the ideas of Black Power, and analyzed America's political economy.[73] Scholars have described King's later philosophies as "democratic socialist," dedicated to human rights, and demanding economic justice.[74] In the same vein as these scholarly interpretations, the IBW's understanding of King's legacy stressed that it did not announce the end of the civil rights movement, but rather it outlined ways and areas where it could continue. Harding's perspective drew on King's thoughts at the end of his life. King observed, "The Negro revolt is evolving into more than a quest for desegregation and equality. It is a challenge to a system that has created miracles of production and technology to create justice. If humanism is locked outside the system, Negroes will have revealed its inner core of despotism and a far greater struggle for liberation will unfold."[75] For its part, the King Center's "I Have a Dream" vision had one important advantage; it was slightly easier to secure financial support from White-directed philanthropy when promoting the unifying version of the legacy. The King Center's heroic narrative deified integration and announced the end of the civil rights movement, but it failed to address issues of racial inequality. Separation meant the IBW associates could begin to address the weaknesses of the King Center's interpretation of the civil rights leader and of the movement, but first associates had to address problems created by the IBW's newly independent status.

Reorganizing the IBW

In December 1970, the IBW recounted a difficult but successful first year for its expanding network of associates and donors. "The Institute was born into a national struggle over the control of the definition of the black experience. We committed ourselves immediately to that struggle, convinced that the black community had no future if it did not act responsibly to define for itself and others the nature of its own past and present." The report briefly discussed the separation from the King Center, and the IBW associates asserted they were "strengthened by the ordeals of the past, better prepared to move forward." The revised statement of purpose stressed that the IBW was an "autonomous operation" and emphasized the need for Blacks "to control the definition of our past and our present if we are to become masters of our future." Now independent, the institute believed that it could recruit the necessary scholars, those who would "use [their] skills of research and analysis to forward the struggles of the black community towards self-understanding and ultimate liberation."[76] Between fall 1970 and summer 1971, senior associates and staff members held meetings to discuss position papers on how to reorganize a newly independent IBW. The meetings and the papers written by Harding, Strickland, and Hill identified three topics—finances, identity, and leadership—as the basis of reorganization. The IBW emerged from these sessions with a plan to survive independence and prepared to influence the freedom struggle of the seventies.

Reorganizing Finances

Inadequate funding had fueled the acrimony among the King Center components. The LDP had a 1969–70 budget of nearly $250,000, and the IBW had a budget of nearly $300,000. Although, under Harding's leadership, each unit received grants to contribute to the budgetary needs, it had been assumed that the King Center would supply a substantial percentage of the money. However, the King Center never received the funding imagined at the beginning of the project, constraining both the LDP and the IBW. After the initial excitement over the opening of the King Center, donations began to dwindle, and the largest source of income came from a movie on the civil rights leader.[77] At the controversial July 27 meeting in which the King Center Board of Directors laid off LDP workers and presented a negative evaluation of the IBW, Coretta Scott King announced movie profits of approximately $300,000, with the LDP and the IBW each receiving $50,000. The meeting also signaled a shift to "brick and mortar" parts of the King Center and away from the programmatic aspects. The King Center Board believed a memorial park, which was given $150,000 of the movie proceeds, would generate more donations than the IBW or the library. It was clear, however, even before this controversial meeting, that the IBW had to secure its own funding sources.[78]

To subsidize their programs, the institute's associates debated whether to accept money from White funding sources. Senior associate Lerone Bennett Jr. circulated a memo in January 1970 that outlined his position on funding sources. He laid out five reasons why the IBW should accept money from White "liberal sources and the government." First, Bennett realized that the IBW needed money for survival and completion of its mission. Second, he argued that White money was a form of reparations. Third, Bennett believed that all White money was "stolen recently or at an early date from black, brown, and red people." Next, he argued that the IBW should accept money and be critical of the entire process of grants, claiming, "We should not only seek 'white' money but we should demand as much money (more, in fact) as white institutions and intellectuals receive. . . . I believe our goal should be black hegemony, and black hegemony should start with a demand for parity (and more) in funding." Finally, Bennett believed the IBW should accept funding from these sources because "a large proportion of the money labelled [sic] 'white money' is in fact black."[79] Although Bennett argued in favor of accepting White funding, he recognized this was not "an ideal solution." Rather, it was a pragmatic resolution to an immediate problem. Bennett alleged that there is "no such thing as pure autonomy or pure black money," meaning the question was one of "relative autonomy." He suggested to the institute that control of, rather than the source of, the money was essential. Bennett believed that the IBW could maintain control by avoiding dependency on a single source.[80]

Not all of the IBW associates agreed with Bennett's pragmatic financial perspective. Historian Sterling Stuckey issued his resignation in early 1970, in part due to the institute's stance on finances. Stuckey's disappointment began with Harding's attempt to add another associate, jazz musician Marion Brown, to the staff. Stuckey believed there was only approximately one hundred and sixty dollars in the treasury, and thus that the IBW could not meet the present senior staff salaries. After a vote amongst the senior staff, which Stuckey claims was "the first vote in the history of the Institute," Brown was not hired. According to the historian, "it was the consensus that any money received by the IBW would be used to cover existing needs and debts, not to finance Marion Brown." Despite this vote, Harding unilaterally decided to add Brown to the staff, nullifying the senior staff's vote. This disrespect for the staff and incurring of additional debt did not please Stuckey.[81] In addition, Stuckey did not agree with the IBW's philosophy of securing White funding sources. He stated, "Though I knew that some foundation money was being relied on, from the start I viewed this as a very temporary, though very serious, contradiction, never dreaming that an attempt would be made to provide a philosophical justification for its continuance, to say nothing of deepening dependence on white people for financial support."[82] Stuckey's commentary about finances marked the end of his time at the IBW as a senior associate.

Despite such reservations about funding sources, the IBW survived primarily via White financial backing. Before the separation, approximately eighty-three percent of the IBW's funding came from White sources, mostly foundations and Northern universities.[83] In late February

1970, the IBW secured a $100,000 Ford Foundation grant that ensured their survival while increasing their reliance on White foundation money. It is clear from recent scholarship on the Ford Foundation that although the money was earmarked for the IBW, it was their connection to the King Center and the foundation's perception of their liberalism that helped secure the grant. Sociologist Fabio Rojas argues that the Ford Foundation's influence on Black Studies was limited, but it did attempt "to sever connections between black studies programs and cultural nationalism."[84] The foundation granted the IBW money (which was reduced to $65,000, with the remaining $35,000 going to the LDP) because of its proximity to King and his legacy.[85] The IBW also received grants from the Cummins Engine Foundation and the Schumann Foundation for $45,000 and $10,000 respectively.[86] Northern schools starting Black Studies programs provided money as well. After student protests at Wesleyan University, the school paid the IBW $96,000 to consult in starting a Black Studies program.[87] Dartmouth College paid the IBW $10,000 to supervise students doing research on Black topics in Atlanta.[88] As Ladner reminded Harding during the crisis with the King Center, the lack of independent funding, a concern introduced earlier by Stuckey, was the "logical outcome" of "white control and/or influence."[89]

The ideological divisions that led to conflicting interpretations of King's historical legacy at the IBW and the King Center were a primary cause of the separation, but it was the financial terms of the separation that proved essential for the IBW's future success. The IBW wanted and needed a fair financial settlement out of the separation. They asked for a transitional budget and public relations capital. The IBW sought to recoup the $35,000 loan to the LDP and receive funds promised from the King film. The IBW also needed to keep its existing facilities, which were leased through the King Center. Strickland suggested an amicable break, but resented the King Center Board's "attacks on Vincent's [Harding's] integrity, [so much so] that there can be no negotiations if they persist on that course."[90] In the end, the IBW obtained most of its terms. The official date of separation was September 1, 1970, and the IBW received a $25,000 grant from the King Center and $25,000 from Howard University, money "earmarked for the work of the Institute so that a continuity of employment of the Institute staff may be facilitated." The IBW leased its furnished offices from the King Center for one dollar per year, contingent on paying the property taxes. These terms signaled the IBW's official independence from the Martin Luther King Jr. Memorial Center. Still, the IBW's survival needed outside support and a little organizational creativity.[91]

The IBW was over-reliant on foundation support, and Strickland and other associates wanted to move toward a financial base rooted in Black communities. The IBW mailed letters to supporters asking for financial donations. "We are badly in need of immediate financial assistance. . . . We have spent unimaginable energies simply waging this struggle for the right to define our own work. We have had to neglect the fund-raising task."[92] Despite the bleak financial outlook, there was a ray of hope. After the mailing, the IBW received $2000 in contributions from supporters, letting associates know that there was a constituency for the institute's work. In August, the IBW's leadership had conducted another direct mailing to more than 500 friends and associates interested in the group's work. From August 1970 to January 1971, they received approximately $10,800, an average of $20 per person. Individuals from many backgrounds offered monetary assistance. For example, political scientist Ronald W. Walters donated one hundred dollars, and anthropologist Councill Taylor pledged his continual support.[93] Strickland believed that for the IBW to survive, the organization "must strive for self-sufficiency" by getting its growing network of associates to pledge or donate money.[94]

Associates also made personal sacrifices to keep the IBW's doors open. Faced with the possibility of having the foundation and university grants stopped, associates survived by making a variety of financial decisions designed to preserve as much autonomy as possible. Strickland suggested that members of the senior staff could reduce their salaries from one-third to one-half by "retaining honoraria and advances," and by taking positions at universities if necessary. This "theory of the small organization" was the basis for the IBW's survival throughout its more than ten years of existence.[95] Strickland concluded, "discipline, productivity, seriousness—within and without, economic responsibility. Let those be our watch words of the future." With that in mind, Strickland noted that any financial plan required the IBW to transform its internal accounting procedures. He asserted that the institute needed to improve its "confused" bookkeeping. The financial inaccuracies led some supporters to become "disillusioned" and others to suggest that members of the IBW were "rip-off artists."[96] Separation put the IBW in a financial free fall, which associates tried to resolve through donations, seeking grants, and even taking other jobs. These strategies allowed the IBW to "specialize in survival."[97]

Reorganizing Identity

In addition to improving its financial status, associates also worked on improving the IBW's organizational identity by clarifying its purpose and decreasing Harding's responsibilities. Strickland believed that the IBW faced a "problem of identity." The IBW's pragmatic nationalism and synthetic analyses fostered by collective scholarship opened the door to confusion about the organization's purpose. Strickland further thought that the name "Institute of the Black World" was too broad, provided no boundaries, and opened the organization to "opportunism." For him, the institute's wide range of possible meanings became obvious when a new sign was erected. "I came back from a trip one day," Strickland recalled, "walked up the steps and there was the sign: ' . . . dedicated to the struggles of African peoples.' A fait accompli. IBW thus became formally and publicly identified with a particular ideology in a very informal and casual way. The ramifications of the ideology, its enduring relevance for black people, its historical sufficiency and analytical clarity, none of these questions was thoroughly gone into before the fact."[98] The IBW's uncritical use of the language of Blackness here symbolized how the discursive representations of Black Power had become normal. Discursive Blackness signaled unity; at the same time it cloaked cleavages in the movement, providing avenues for co-optation.[99] Strickland believed the IBW's casual use of language permitted the organization to be loosely identified with any ideological perspective regardless of its actual position. The sign minimized the actual work required in forging political consensus and downplayed the magnitude of ideological divisions. Institute of the Black World associates believed that agreements among Black activists emerged from collective scholarship generated through hard empirical data, structural analysis, and dialogue, not through slogans.[100]

Another source of confusion identified by the reorganization documents was a common belief that the IBW was a school, instead of an activist think tank that evaluated Black Studies curricula and pedagogy. Many outside observers remembered the IBW for its work in the field of Black Studies. In its initial concentration on the Black University and Black Studies, the IBW wanted to become a national evaluator of Black Studies programs. The Black Studies Directors Conference was the first step in serving this function. The separation from the King Center reduced the IBW's capability as a national evaluator. However, many scholars and activists outside of Atlanta had their first introduction to the IBW through the development of Black Studies.[101] The IBW's initial programs inextricably linked it to Black Studies. Not only did outsiders connect it with Black Studies, but many of the associates did so as well. Founding member Stephen Henderson remembered the IBW primarily for providing direction to Black Studies, and seemingly failed to recall other IBW projects, such as the *Black Agenda*, its newsletter, or the summer symposia.[102] The semester-long presence in Atlanta of students from Wesleyan University and Dartmouth College also intimated that the IBW was a school, as did its proximity to the AUC. The IBW's offices were only blocks away from the AUC campuses. The IBW continued to use AUC facilities for programs, and it cosponsored events with university organizations. To eliminate any internal confusion, Strickland declared that the IBW's job "is not to be a school but, to promote change in schools and scholars."[103]

By early 1971, the IBW clarified its identity. Strickland stated, "We are intellectuals and we do intellectual work. That is neither a cause for shame or celebration. We have a role to play in the struggle. Our duty is to ascertain that role then play it."[104] For the IBW, Black intellectuals had to describe the social, economic, cultural, and political problems facing the race, analyze these problems, and prescribe remedies. To assist associates in these goals, the IBW sought advice and consultation from leading diasporic intellectuals. The IBW made plans for a Summer Research Symposium (SRS '71) that examined the role and importance of Black intellectuals and scholarship.

In the summer of 1971, the IBW invited C.L.R. James, Edward Kamau Braithwaite, St. Clair Drake, and George Beckford to Atlanta for SRS '71. Although Walter Rodney was scheduled to attend, he canceled to complete research in East Africa. The symposium's theme was "The World of Black Scholarship—Past, Present and Future."[105] The invited scholars addressed several topics during their seminars and public lectures, including critical examinations of seminal Black scholarship, projections of future research tasks, and discussions of the role of Black scholars.[106]

Before the symposium, Strickland outlined how SRS '71 was going to refine the IBW's Black analytical perspective. "It could not mimic the racism of 'white western scholarship.'" Tradition, he maintained, functioned to defend White scholarship from questions of race and class. He believed radicals needed to prioritize race and class, unlike liberals who denied them, instead glorifying the "individual." White scholarship maintained the status quo by "giving primacy to 'great men' and elites" and ignoring the variables of race and class in favor of individualism. For Strickland, the task of Black scholarship was to "reinterpret our own history and that of our oppressor" and to define Blackness beyond its typical conventions of praising indigenous Black culture, reasserting continuities between Africa and the diaspora, and "proudful breast-beating of blackness and absolutist rejection of modernity on the grounds that it is western or white." He believed these conceptions of Blackness were "defensive," representing an attempt to prove Black humanity. In preparation for the symposium, he set forth some goals.

> Our task then, goes beyond blackness, it is not only the resurrection of black history but the reinterpretation of the West. But this is simply not an arbitrary academic task. . . . In contradistinction then to the white approach and the black fixated approach we must clarify one essential dynamic which characterizes our struggle. We must apprehend and counterpose to the individualism and materialism the movement of men and social forces, the contradictions of oppressor AND [sic] oppressed, the politics of class and mass movement, the relation between black movement and white resistance. This is the historical necessity to define the black liberation struggle and the stage in which it finds itself. It is also a precondition to glimpsing the future that lies ahead.

The symposium was an opportunity for the IBW to expand its synthetic Black social analysis.[107]

The six-week symposium consisted of seminars, research projects, and public lectures. Participants spent between nine and fifteen hours each week in seminars led by the IBW's senior associates and the invited scholars. James provided "insight into the politics and movement of the masses," and analysis relating leadership to mass action. Drake and the other scholars helped the IBW associates and staff understand "black methodology and social analysis." In addition, the attendees conducted research projects, presenting their results at the end of the summer. As the community-oriented portion of the program, the public lectures formed the basis of the IBW's audiotape lecture series, "New Concepts for a New Man," which were sold throughout the IBW's existence to raise money.[108]

There were four interrelated symposium goals: to familiarize participants with the seminal works of Black scholarship; to introduce participants to major Black scholars; to engage the participants in serious discussions of the "past, present, and future condition of Black people (intellectuals, teachers, and educators) in the process of charting a progressive Black future based on our reassessment of our past and present condition"; and to develop a theory and methodology of Black social analysis.[109] The process of collectively developing methodologies and social analysis exemplified the larger goals of the IBW. The conference served as "an integral part of the development of IBW," and was a "part of the clarifying process by which we [the IBW] grasp the essential meaning of our history and flesh out the concept of 'education for liberation.'"[110]

During the first week of the symposium, Marxist theorist and veteran Caribbean activist C.L.R. James identified the Black scholar's role as "to learn and understand and let people know what is happening," as well as "to illustrate, understand it [the Black Freedom Struggle] and he must be able to explain it in historical and social terms, otherwise the education that he has and the money he may be getting are of no use to the Black people as a whole. He has a function to perform. He does not have to teach people to go and fight as they fought in Watts . . . but you [have to] have mass support for any work . . . that you may do." James also stressed the need to write histories that represented a strong Black viewpoint. "The writers, particularly, in England," he noted, "usually tried to be . . . well balanced, but you can't write a well-balanced history of revolution because a revolution is something that creates disorder and unbalances everything. And if you are going to write on both sides, you write nothing!" Using his classic *Black Jacobins* (1938) and W.E.B. Du Bois' *Black Reconstruction* (1935) as models of revolutionary scholarship, James concluded that the works "tried to show that black people were able to make historical progress, they were able to show how a revolution was made, they were able to produce the men who could lead a revolution and write new pages in the book of history."[111]

In a similar vein, sociologist St. Clair Drake emphasized that institutions such as the IBW were a part of "intellectual tasks" as opposed to "street tasks," such as the collective self-defense of urban rebellions.[112] Drake outlined several fundamental roles for Black intellectuals: raising Black consciousness, supplying information for the movement, and creating special institutions, such as the IBW. He stressed a three-pronged approach, based on his intellectual experiences. First, intellectuals needed to contribute to a theoretical component of their academic discipline. Second, after adding to their broad field of study, intellectuals needed to become empirical experts of an aspect of the social structure. Third, Black intellectuals should "select a problem that contributed to racial advancement, as we used to call it. Today we call it Black Liberation." Black scholarship, according to Drake, had to challenge ostensibly objective scholarship and thereby supply a counter-ideology.[113]

The other scholars discussed similar themes from their disciplinary fields of study, which produced a counter analytical narrative that challenged the hegemony of White scholarship. For example, West Indian economist George Beckford emphasized linking intellectual production with the masses, and explored the economic, social, and political causes of poverty in the Caribbean. Edward Kamau Braithwaite discussed his thesis that the basis of West Indian folk society had African origins, exploring its implications for Black Americans. Harding led an analysis of Lerone Bennett Jr.'s *Confrontation: Black and White* (1965) and *Black Power, USA: The Human Side of Reconstruction, 1867–1877,* (1967). Harding also delivered lectures on "the relationship of black religion to black resistance movements." Strickland analyzed American politics through the framework developed by James Boggs' *Racism and Class Struggle: Further Pages of a Black Worker's Notebook* (1970). Finally, Robert Hill historically analyzed Pan-Africanism through the lens of Garveyism. All the scholars emphasized the need to "disenchant" the prevailing representations of Blacks, for these created the paradigms of "value and authority" and shaped the social and political actions and structures of Blacks. As C.L.R. James said later, "all political power presents itself to the world within a certain framework of ideas. It is fatal to ignore this in any estimate of social forces in political action."[114]

The presence of James, Drake, and others enhanced the IBW's analytical perspective because their research identified hegemonic structures. While the dominant scholarship privileged Whiteness, the middle class, and men, the IBW's developing perspective addressed racial and class bias in American society. Despite these insights, associates' gender analyses were nonexistent at this point, continuing a weakness often found in Black (and White) intellectual history.[115] This glaring limitation notwithstanding, the IBW's analysis moved beyond liberals' representations of race relations. The IBW's association with and study of Black intellectuals such as Du Bois, James, and Drake recognized the limits of exclusively race- or class-based analysis. The SRS '71 was a dialectical process that provided the institute with concrete examples of the radical intellectual tradition.

The symposium influenced the faculty members, as well as graduate and undergraduate student attendees. A Columbia University student described her experience as initiating a "thought and analysis process . . . that I had never encountered." In fact, when she returned to Columbia and faced "white scholarship," the analytical perspective learned at SRS '71 led to resistance in most of her classes. She concluded, "SRS '71 was a crucial experience in black education."[116] Patricia Daly, then a Livingston College professor, felt the research component of SRS '71 was exceedingly benefi-cial and allowed her to develop new classes. After the symposium, Daly moved to Atlanta and became an IBW associate and briefly a director.[117]

Reorganizing Leadership

The IBW's plans for reorganization also altered Harding's responsibilities. Its initial organizational structure, while affiliated with the King Center, included a full-time research team made up of senior associates Hard-ing, Strickland, Henderson, Davis, Ladner, Bennett, Stuckey, and Robert S. Browne, and a staff composed primarily of interns from the Southern Education Foundation. The governing council included Bond, Andrew Young, Harry Belafonte, and others who advised research associates and consulted on the institute's direction. After the separation, Stuckey, Ben-nett, Browne, and Ladner left the day-to-day operations, resigning as se-nior associates. The governing board also changed to reflect the separa-tion from the King Center, adding an array of radicals and nationalists such as Clarke, Drake, and Julius Lester. The IBW's staff fluctuated in the early years as well. While the IBW was a component of the King Center, the Southern Education Foundation paid for interns. Students from Wes-leyan and Dartmouth filled some of the staff positions. Eventually, the staff was primarily composed of local graduates and activists from the Atlanta community. Despite the number of people associated with the institute before and after the separation, the central force of the organiza-tion was Harding. Early external criticism of the IBW noted Harding's predominant position. A nameless commentator in a *Newsweek* article on the founding of the IBW believed, "Vince [Harding] wants to make the King Library the Vatican of black studies with himself as the Pope."[118] The internal review of the organization was not as hostile to Harding as the critique in *Newsweek*, but it similarly recognized his centrality as both a blessing and a potential liability.

Strickland argued that the IBW needed to redefine Harding's leadership position. He asserted that the IBW had been:

> an appendage of its major personality, Vincent [Harding]. Vincent is our major source of direction, our contact to money, and the resources and the major shaper of our program. If something were to happen to him, IBW would flounder about—lost. We would not know who he has been in contact with, or about what; what he may have committed us to, or why. This style of leadership hinders positive organizational development because it fosters dependency and insecurity in the ranks. Where one man is the ultimate arbiter, *modifications in organizational life cannot be separated from challenges to authority*.[119]

Strickland believed that reorganization must make the IBW stronger than any one person. To do this, the IBW instituted more accountability and collective decision-making.

The fall 1970 reorganization essays proposed changing the institute's structure to incorporate Harding into its inner workings. Strickland proposed four "units of labor"—education and publication, politics, administration, and an executive committee—each headed by a senior associate. Strickland suggested that Harding lead the education and publication unit, Davis direct the administration unit, and he run the politics unit. Harding added to Strickland's suggestions by calling for an additional committee on economic support that would be led by fundraising professionals. Accountability for the new units would run through an executive committee composed of Harding, Strickland, Hill, and Melvin Huell. "We have placed," said Strickland, "the strongest people in the organization on the committee to reflect the main areas of business, politics, and education and to get the best out of the individual strengths represented." Ultimately, the significance of the reorganization into smaller units was to integrate Harding into the "programmatic life of the Institute."[120]

During the IBW's reorganization, associates maintained traditional gender role allocations by naming Mayme Mitchem "political secretary" and Jualynne Dodson "administrative assistant" to support the four-person executive committee. Although reorganization subjected Harding's role to democratic oversight, the IBW's executives maintained the tendency of Black organizations not to give women leadership titles. Even without formal titles, women throughout the Black Freedom Struggle took leadership roles, and the women in the IBW were no different. Several women took the lead in numerous daily activities, a process that sociologist Belinda Robnett has described as "bridge leadership."[121]

Staff member Sharon Bourke's experiences in the IBW demonstrated the consequences of the associates' disinterest toward gender analysis and how collective scholarship kept the institute stable, despite this weakness. Bourke arrived in Atlanta from New York in 1970 with an impressive resume. She was a poet and writer who reported on the local Black art scene. Her influence on the IBW was immediate, and she forced its members to reexamine their own work. The executive committee admitted that her "style and commitment to work was a reproach to our [IBW's] own slothfulness, to our own seriousness." Moreover, she was such a "concrete model of disciplined serious work" that a member of the committee believed her qualities—"works and studies, seeks ways to further her understanding and advance the interest of the org. [sic], [h]as compatible not antagonistic concerns, utterly reliable, writes well, has selfless political perspective and enthusiasm for the struggle, honest and undevious [sic]"—should be general work criteria. Harding, Strickland, and others on the executive committee viewed her as the ultimate staff person and an equal, recommending that Bourke become assistant director of the IBW.[122]

Because of these qualities, the committee was shocked when it received a letter of resignation from Bourke, who had returned to New York during the summer of 1971. For Bourke, the return to New York provided different experiences that led her to question the institute's "principles-policy-program in a way that [she] didn't question it before." New York provided "freedom," in the sense that it allowed "the struggle to be waged in a more experimental, more questioning way than I believe IBW does." She described the IBW members as conservative on topics of class, gender, religion, and lifestyles. Although she admitted to having the same conservative viewpoints, she found it troubling that some members of the executive committee insisted that growing movements, such as "Women's Lib, Gay Lib, consumer movements, music movements, etc.," had little relation or impact to the Black struggle, for she thought them serious as well. They were not "silly, diversionary, divide-and-conquer fads, but [a] consequence of a new stage of historical development. Not a sign of decay but of something being born." Bourke felt more freedom in New York than Atlanta, because New York activists were "fighting on every possible ground."[123]

Bourke's concerns illuminated problems the IBW faced in terms of its gender analysis. Female intellectuals were notably absent from the roster of invited SRS '71 scholars, and this lack of women mirrored the marginalized role of women in the IBW. From 1969 to 1970, Joyce Ladner was the lone female senior associate. Other women inside the institute served as assistants. At the time, it seemed that the female staff members had no objections to their roles as secretarial support for Harding and the other senior associates. However, in 1970 and 1971, a new group of women joined the IBW's staff. This group included Jualynne Dodson, Jyl Hagler, Patricia Daly, Janet Douglass, Aljosie Yabarua, Mayme Mitcham, and Sharon Bourke, each an activist-intellectual in their own right. According to Dodson, none of these women were prepared to work as secretaries, and each believed she had intellectual contributions to make to the IBW. The female staff's struggle to attain active intellectual roles in the IBW highlighted that although Harding, Strickland, and Hill were committed to racial and class radicalism, this did not transfer to the question of gender.[124]

The staff, led by women, challenged the IBW's leadership, and even briefly led the organization. When the IBW's executive committee—Harding, Strickland, Hill, and Melvin Huell—demanded that the staff support its shift to a think tank, they issued stricter rules regarding organizational discipline, asserting that "the needs of the organization will consistently be placed before individual wants or needs." The executive committee argued that its program "must become more sharply committed to create a black analysis of the condition of the black community, past and present." This analysis strove to clarify the political, economic, and social conditions facing the Black community and the current nature of White repression. The programs would be aimed at Black local leadership, who would use radical analysis as a "weapon of advocacy" in establishing Black self-determination. The committee called for individual meetings with the staff to discuss the future of the organization.[125]

The staff responded unfavorably to the essay and the meetings. Jualynne Dodson, for example, recalled objecting to the personal interviews. She based her objections on her 1968 experiences with the Black Student Union and Third World Liberation Front in the San Francisco State

University strike that led to the creation of the first Black Studies Department. For her, the "interrogation" process had not proved successful in the past; it was a "disastrous and unnecessary experience." Her response to the principles was "mixed." She was "happy" to see the IBW define itself on clearer terms, but believed that "no commitment or commitments are monolithic." She further believed that some personal responsibilities, such as raising her daughter, were more important than the IBW. Consequently, she knew that if conflicts arose, "there's no guarantee IBW will be first." Dodson also recalled that her response reflected latent gender tensions inside the institute. Although her time at the IBW was one of the most intellectually and politically stimulating experiences of her life, she remembered instances in which associates inflicted "intellectual and gender putdowns." Despite these frictions, she also recalled that members could disagree yet still work together, creating a dynamic and productive environment. Harding, Strickland, and other male associates' lack of gender analysis needs to be balanced against the space the organization provided for Black female intellectuals. This calculus does not absolve the IBW's male leadership, but rather recognizes that the failings of its male associates regarding gender were also the failings of society in general. Moreover, many of the female members had not fully theorized the latent sexism that existed inside the organization. Bourke remembered that the gender dynamics were "*unconsciously*, rather automatically, male chauvinist," however, when the issue arose, it was managed critically and in the end was not the "cause of any great dissension."[126] The IBW associates failed to theorize gender clearly, and this was one of the major weaknesses of the organization.[127]

Given the financial difficulties associated with the IBW's independence, the executive committee's primary concern was saving the IBW, not theorizing gender. The executive committee's actions forcefully streamlined the organization in order to keep its doors open.

Female staff members were not alone in their concerns with the IBW's direction. Cofounder Stephen Henderson also harshly criticized the executive committee for its authoritarian tone. Although he agreed with the principles, policies, and program presented during reorganization, he also believed the executive committee was "quite heavy-handed" in its approach to the staff, and demonstrated a "flexing of [its] collective muscles." He argued that the leadership used "veiled threats and quasi-religious, quasi-sexual language" to push people out of the organization.

Specifically, he felt the essay used the word "submit" like a "bludgeon." In Henderson's mind, when this word was not qualified, it was "not merely abusive, but dangerous." Not found in previous reorganization essays, this term was dangerous because the IBW's "small size . . . and intimate working arrangements make it virtually impossible to separate personalities from policies." Henderson's concerns were not purely rhetorical—he also took issue with the executive committee's apparent lack of "respect for personality." He suggested that respect, not submitting to a "higher cause," be the source of discipline and liberation. He further identified particular principles and policies with which he disagreed. For example, he found the idea of paying a mandatory tax to the IBW in an attempt to maintain the organization's financial solvency "arbitrary, rigid, and arrogant." He also agreed with Dodson that other commitments might come before the IBW, especially family ones. The essay and meeting caused Henderson to question his role in the IBW. He wanted to continue his relationship with the organization he had cofounded, but he was "not willing to be bullied or insulted . . . or accept 'dogma' without an explanation," nor would he defend the institute's press releases without seeing them first. The May 1971 meeting marked a decline in Henderson's full-time participation in the IBW. In the fall, he accepted a teaching position, with the IBW's support, at Howard University; he continued to support the institute, but was no longer a part of its day-to-day activities or at the core of future programs.[128]

After SRS '71, the staff continued to express concerns about the lack of clarity in the IBW's refined purpose. Consequently, staff members organized in opposition to the executive committee. During the meeting, staff members characterized the IBW as a "bourgeois organization" concerned primarily with Black Studies. According to the notes, they claimed the IBW "had no firm or conscious political goals, and therefore, no consistency." The personnel wanted the institute to become a "revolutionary organization geared to the masses of black people." In addition, they identified a split between a "bourgeois, class-oriented, educational institution," and an organization "dedicated to education and politicizing the masses to take power." After a contentious meeting in fall 1971, members officially organized a staff caucus. They believed there was an "atmosphere of oppression" and that there were conflicts between old and new staff members. The caucus explicitly "moved to break the mold of policy being handed down by leadership and as a part of our own commitment and education to come to grips with the real problems of analy[zing] . . . IBW."[129] The staff formed a "committee-of-the-whole" to run the IBW, applying collective scholarship to briefly reform the IBW's leadership.

The experiment in leadership was truncated because of financial constraints. Beginning in January 1972, Harding took various university teaching positions in order to offset the burden of his salary on the IBW's budget. Over the next three years, Hill and Strickland followed Harding's lead and surrendered the IBW's day-to-day operations to Howard Dodson and others. In May 1972, the executive committee informed Douglass that she would not be retained as a fund-raising coordinator. The executive committee cited the lack of money and her political style as justification for her removal. Harding felt that Douglass was not successful in her job, because with Harding, Strickland, and Hill often away from Atlanta, the office needed "as many calm, cool and collected folks as we can get, folks who see in this period that our politics is best expressed in our work and not in our political conversations." Harding believed that Strickland needed to be in Atlanta so Douglass could be "reigned in [sic]."[130] The committee also suggested that Douglass, as a leader of a small group of women that included Patricia Daly and Sharon Burke, had disrupted the reorganization meetings, fostered alienation within the staff, and stood in the way of the IBW's advancement. Bobby Hill also made it known to the leadership that he would not "associate with an organization that has Jan and Pat in leadership roles."[131]

Douglass responded to these charges, concluding that the derogatory words were aimed at her because she was a woman: "The implications of these charges are that I am a mad woman responding to some internal fantasy." Moreover, in the executive committee's accusations toward her, Douglass believed that the IBW had violated the very principles that it established during reorganization. Douglass felt she had no choice but to leave the IBW, because "anything less, amounts to submission and capitulation on my part. My integrity will not allow me to do that."[132] The IBW's failure to address latent internal gender issues, as well as its lack of gender analysis, represented a major gap in the organization. Harding would later remember, "gender exploitation and Black patriarchy was often hidden under the mountain of the struggle that we were carrying on for freedom in relationship to White America." He admitted that much of this burying was unintentional, though sometimes, "more than was healthy, this was an intentional burying."[133] Douglass left the IBW to form a collective of Black women intellectuals in Atlanta called Sojourner South. Her new organization included Toni Cade Bambara, Dodson, and Daly, and they began to fill the gap on gender analysis left by the IBW.[134]

At the end of the IBW's reorganization process, Harding and Strickland stressed the need for a collective IBW approach, as a means to accommodate staff demands. Strickland noted that, "People came to IBW for all sorts of reasons and out of all sorts of backgrounds. . . . So there were a variety of perspectives and different, sometimes contrasting, visions of the meaning of blackness and the meaning of struggle." He and other associates believed the process of collective scholarship would reconcile these perspectives and, in the end, would be more stimulating and productive.[135] Harding came to a similar conclusion, arguing that the IBW's analysis "must include a sense of one's history and identity, a clarification of the nature of the earlier oppressions and struggles against them and the successes and failures of the past. It must include an accurate analysis of the structures and mechanism of oppression, past and present and contemplated; it must include many-sided analysis of the present situation and what is necessary for successful organization and struggle."[136] As the IBW headed toward 1972, associates concluded, "IBW's analysis of the social structure could set the perspective for political action; IBW would not necessarily do the organizing itself but would contribute to it," and their goal was to become "the most profound theoretical and research organization in the country."[137] The institute emerged from internal reorganization with a clearer focus regarding finances, identity, and leadership.

The IBW's reorganization was rocky. Associates such as Harding and Strickland addressed the organization's finances, identity, and leadership, each of which had been muddled by the separation from the King Center. The IBW developed strategies that insured survival, but also revealed weaknesses. First, without stable and consistent funding sources, associates eventually accepted jobs at universities, weakening the IBW's collective scholarship and its distinctive voice. Second, the IBW's decision to become a think tank devoted to Black activist communities seemed to run counter to the protest movements of the era. Around the time the IBW began its reorganization, activists of all types were embroiled in violent, decade-defining events. In May 1970, student activists were murdered at Kent State University and at Jackson State University. Three months later, the FBI placed Angela Davis on its ten most-wanted list for her alleged role in Jonathan Jackson's one-man plot to free his brother,

George Jackson of the Soledad Brothers. Activists rallied in support of Davis, making the "Free Angela" movement one of the decade's defining moments. Considering these high-profile actions, the IBW's decision to focus on an intellectual path toward black equality seemed incongruent with common conceptions of Black radicalism. Finally, the IBW's leadership failed to fully theorize and analyze how gender functioned inside the organization. The staff, spurred by women often operating in bridge leadership capacity, briefly ran the organization. Associates accounted for staff concerns by emphasizing the organization's collective methodology. The IBW's decisions during reorganization allowed it to survive its independence.[138]

Conclusion

In the late 1960s, Harding and Henderson envisioned an independent organization devoted to supplying critical support to the burgeoning field of Black Studies and to the larger Black Freedom Struggle. By the beginning of the seventies, this dream had become a reality: the IBW had played an instrumental role in analyzing and developing Black Studies programs. Moreover, Harding's personal connections with the King family allowed him the opportunity to affiliate the institute with the King Memorial Center, giving the IBW an independent base outside of the university. For most of 1970, Harding wanted to remain linked with the King Center because it provided an opportunity for independent analysis, while simultaneously affording the IBW the ability to use the center's rhetoric and representation to raise money for its projects. However, the King Center believed the IBW's radicalism damaged its capacity to raise funds from corporations, who had the assets necessary to generate the nearly twenty million dollars needed to complete the memorial.[139] As this conflict developed, Harding and other IBW associates realized that the structural autonomy they imagined that the King Center provided was instead a mirage. The King family and its advisors demanded strict ideological and political adherence to nonviolence, integrationism, and racial liberalism. Although IBW associates did not oppose these ideas, they chose to be experimental in terms of ideology because they believed that, in order to tackle the problems of the 1970s, the Black Freedom Struggle needed new synthetic ideas developed dialectally from a variety of ideological perspectives. The IBW's lecture series, which included talks by people of differing perspectives, allowed for the discussion of various ideological and political alternatives. The opposing approaches taken by the IBW and the King Center led to a difficult, but mutually agreed upon, separation.

The separation from the King Center exposed internal weaknesses in the IBW's structure, forcing internal reorganization. Financially, the IBW relied heavily on White foundation grants for support. These grants were not guaranteed annually, forcing associates to develop alternative funding sources. Associates began to articulate a theory of small organization, one which encouraged associates to give lectures and even take faculty university positions to offset expenses. Taking such positions was not an ideal situation, but it was the surest way to lower operational costs. The IBW also developed an extensive network of supporters who regularly donated to it. In addition, associates agreed to not take on any new programs, because they realized the group could not financially support them. Organizational restructuring let people inside and outside the IBW know that it was not a school. It also reduced Harding's role by moving the decision-making process to a formal committee, only after the staff led by female members directed the organization. After reorganization, Harding, Strickland, and Hill defined the IBW as an independent center for research, analysis, and advocacy. A Black think tank "came closest to the task we saw for ourselves," suggested Harding.[140]

The IBW associates' decision to become an activist think tank provided an opportunity to produce analysis that could create a narrower, issue-based consensus than had previously existed. The IBW's experiences of separation and reorganization led to a more clearly developed pragmatic nationalist framework that was rooted in synthetic analysis, not a hopeful unity based on race. After its internal reorganization, the IBW was more fully prepared to meet the demands of its core audiences: Black elected officials, academics, and grassroots activists. The approaching 1972 election was an opportunity to produce a political synthetic analysis for Black elected officials and activists. This role made an independent IBW a key player in the 1972 Gary Convention.

3

"Toward a Black Agenda"

The IBW and a Black Political Agenda for the Seventies

In February 1972, members of the IBW highlighted some of the crises in Black communities and offered potential solutions. Vincent Harding, William Strickland, Lerone Bennett Jr., and other political analysts drafted the "Preamble" to the National Black Political Convention in Gary, Indiana.[1] In it, they asserted that "a Black political convention, indeed all truly Black politics must begin from this truth: The American system does not work for the masses of our people, and it cannot be made to work without radical fundamental change."[2] The Gary Convention, as it was informally known, constituted the height of Black Power–era politics, as Black elected officials and grassroots activists, including traditional civil rights and emerging Black Power organizations, forged a national Black political agenda in preparation for the 1972 presidential election. The "Preamble" identified crises facing Black communities nationwide and stressed how structural racism permeated Black life. "Our cities are crime-haunted dying grounds. Huge sectors of our youth—and countless others—face permanent unemployment." Furthermore, "neither the courts nor the prisons contribute to anything resembling justice or reformation. The schools are unable—or unwilling—to educate our children for the real world of our struggles. Meanwhile, the officially approved epidemic of drugs threatens to wipe out the minds and strength of our best young warriors." In addition, "economic, cultural, and spiritual depression stalk Black America, and the price for survival often appears to be more than we are able to pay. . . . The crises we face as a black people are the crises of the entire society." A Black political agenda that engaged structural racism would address these problems and possibly lead to "true self-determination."

The first step toward improving the situation of Black Americans suggested in the "Preamble" was an independent Black political movement, a "determined national Black power, which is necessary to insist upon such change, to create such change, to seize change." The Gary Convention was at "the edge of history," but it also came at the moment when the IBW began to fulfill its practical goals of research, analysis, and advocacy. The IBW associates helped to forge a hard-earned, albeit temporary, unity between themselves, grassroots activists, and Black elected officials by developing synthetic analyses of social, economic, and political problems. Through the organization's use of collective scholarship, the IBW developed and promoted a "Black perspective," a mode of analysis that built on their earlier work on the Black University and reflected the split from the King Center. Under Harding and Strickland's leadership, the IBW's Black perspective was one that emphasized structural racism as a methodology to examine the social, political, and economic problems facing Black communities. The Black perspective formed the basis of a national Black political agenda and marked the IBW's full transition to an activist think tank. It also solidified the organization's position as the radical intellectual wing of the Black Power era.[3]

Between 1971 and 1973, IBW associates developed a broader analytical perspective, moving beyond academic concerns about Black Studies. In doing so, associates firmly established the organization's identity as an activist think tank. After the IBW's separation from the King Center and its internal reorganization, associates recognized the need for a strong analytical framework that could facilitate issue-oriented consensus among the various ideological entities of the Black Freedom Struggle. Harding and Strickland produced synthetic political analyses that were not ideologically driven, but were instead based on issues affecting Black communities. This shift does not suggest that IBW associates were nonideological, as a pragmatic Black nationalism best describes their approach, but rather that they understood that ideologies functioned as paradigms that limited problem-solving capabilities. Consequently, associates employed social, political, cultural, and economic analyses dialectally as a means to confront complex racial problems, such as poverty, and to find radical yet attainable solutions.[4] To create the organization's Black perspective, associates relied on its collective network of colleagues and friends.

The process of collective scholarship produced the IBW's Black political agenda, which emphasized the need to address structural racism.

Institute of the Black World associates developed a synthetic "Black perspective" predicated on the complex realities, past and present, of Black life. This approach did not reflect racial essentialism or an assumption of homogenous Blackness, but it appreciated that in the post–civil rights era Black people still had to protest the continued manifestation of anti-Black racism in American institutions.[5] Moving beyond the singular nature of institutionalized racism, the IBW assessed structural racism. As Strickland put it, "we are calling attention to the fact that every institution in the land, north and south, east and west, has been structured with the clear purpose of keeping blacks on the bottom or on the outside." Strickland insisted that Black people needed to play a "key role" in changing these institutions, and that it was the IBW's job to promote a sense of "historical and political relevance" that would allow Black people to become the "makers of history." The process of advancing historical and political ideas embodied the institute's rationale of producing "scholarship in the context of struggle." In this case, Strickland thought the IBW needed to help produce ideas and concepts to foster continual struggle against "white power." These struggles would be based on analytical thinking, "evaluated in terms of their consequences (not just mindless ideology)," with the hope of taking power based on "new forms of social, economic, political and cultural organization." The IBW's Black perspective placed structural analyses before ideology.[6]

The IBW's Black analytical perspective expanded ideas about structural racism. Although similar to the concept of institutionalized racism introduced by Stokely Carmichael in *Black Power*, structural racism has a broader and more comprehensive analytical frame. According to scholars Andrew Grant-Thomas and john a. powell, structural racism "shifts attention from the single, intra-institutional setting to *inter-institutional* arrangements and interactions."[7] Structural racism provided broader analysis of the issue by interpreting racism as a "societal outcome," understanding it for its effects rather than its content, appreciating both "overt and covert" forms, and recognizing it as a historical phenomenon. "The structural perspective," according to the scholars, "understands contemporary disparities as partly derivative from norms and conditions established long ago, including some established without racial intent."[8] This structural framework was the basis upon which the IBW attempted to forge issue-specific agreement between activists and elected officials.

According to the IBW's 1969 "Statement of Purpose," it planned "a Black Policy Studies Center," but plans were delayed because of the organization's initial interest in Black Studies and the growing conflict with the King Center. The original 1969 statement of purpose included the goal of analyzing contemporary Black politics in the hopes of achieving Black self-determination. Harding noted that a Black political agenda "might well become the central *corporate* task of the Institute Staff for the next 2–3 years." Specifically, in the 1970s, the institute's associates formulated a political agenda, with the goal of generating broad consensus among Black elected officials and grassroots activists. This Black agenda represented an attempt to produce "a humane society in America." The IBW concluded that any political agenda must address the systemic problems of education, economic development, political organizing, police control, health and welfare, approaches to the Third World, research on Black historical experiences, and cultural development.[9]

On the heels of reorganization, IBW associates positioned the group as an activist think tank with three main constituencies—academics, Black elected officials, and grassroots activists. As the 1972 presidential election approached, the IBW provided these groups with its Black perspective, a structural analysis of racism. The IBW applied its Black perspective by creating, through its Black Agenda Network (BAN), a Black political agenda for the 1972 presidential election. The IBW's agenda-forming activities culminated in the key role it played during the March 1972 Gary Convention. The IBW's "Preamble" to the convention underscored the importance of analyzing structural racism. When the convention formulated its Black political agenda, the IBW used the policy initiatives developed in BAN as a model. Finally, after working on the national agenda with mixed success, IBW associates used their skills in support of Maynard Jackson's 1973 mayoral campaign in Atlanta. Jackson's decision to reach out to the IBW demonstrated that the organization had become a leading voice on radical structural analysis. As the IBW moved toward a Black political agenda, it also progressed toward more fully becoming an activist think tank.

From Protest to Politics

The IBW's shift away from Black Studies and toward its role as an activist think tank reflected the broader transition from protest to politics engulfing the Black Freedom Struggle at the end of the 1960s. Civil rights strategist Bayard Rustin anticipated this transition in his 1964 essay "From Protest to Politics." He noted that the 1963 Birmingham campaign marked the end of the "classical" phase of the civil rights movement, and the next step was political power. Rustin believed this change was necessitated by the "rise of *de facto* segregation in our most fundamental socio-economic institutions." He did not believe that liberalism, with its emphasis on individualism, or a "no-win" Black militancy were the answers in the next phase of the movement, because each approach failed to address the legacy of segregation embedded in institutions. "It is institutions—social, political, and economic—which are the ultimate molders of collective sentiments. Let these institutions be reconstructed *today*, and let the ineluctable gradualism of history govern the formation of a new psychology." Rustin argued that revolutionary change was the product of changing institutions, which could only be accomplished by a political coalition of progressive forces. The passage of the 1964 Civil Rights Act and the 1965 Voting Rights Act set the stage for a tremendous increase in the number of Black elected officials (BEOs) representing Black communities.

Black voters had record turnouts in 1964 and 1968, which led to an increase in the number of BEOs.[10] Between 1970—the first year statistics on BEOs were collected—and 1972, there was a nearly sixty-five percent increase in the number of local, state, and federal Black officials.[11] In Congress, thirteen Black congressmen and women led by Shirley Chisholm, William L. Clay, Louis Stokes, John Conyers, and others formed the Congressional Black Caucus (CBC) in 1969. The CBC's goal was "to promote the public welfare through legislation designed to meet the needs of millions of neglected citizens."[12] In addition to the formation of the CBC, the election of the first Black mayors occurred in the late sixties, beginning with Carl Stokes in Cleveland, Ohio, Richard Hatcher in Gary, Indiana, and Kenneth Gibson in Newark, New Jersey. These and other electoral victories made BEOs a growing force in the Black Freedom Struggle and gave credence to Bayard Rustin's suggestion to move from protest to politics.[13]

The growing number of BEOs validated Harding, Strickland, and other IBW associates' decision to become a think tank. Black elected officials were the second constituency (Black Studies programs were the first) of the IBW's research and analysis. In deciding to assist BEOs, the IBW competed with other think tanks in trying to shape Black political opinion. For example, integrated think tanks like the Joint Center for Economic and Political Studies analyzed political and economic data in a progressive manner, but refrained from activism. As a third-wave think tank that emphasized influence on both politicians and the activist communities, the IBW never focused exclusively on public policy. The IBW supplied sociopolitical analysis that stressed structural change to politicians, civil rights activists, community organizers, academics, and Black people. The decision to make the IBW into an activist think tank reflected associates' emphasis on synthetic analyses and pragmatic decisions that could immediately improve the lives of Black citizens, as well as provide the IBW with the financial backing to survive.

While the IBW and the Joint Center vied for influence among BEOs, most of whom were Democrats, another group of well-funded third-wave think tanks began to support conservative principles. Conservative think tanks wanted to overturn the liberal norms, ideas, and programs instituted during the New Deal and the Great Society. Despite Richard Nixon's election in 1968, many conservative bureaucrats felt that their ideas were marginalized, in part because the Democratic Party still controlled both houses of Congress. Nixon insiders and cabinet members opposed the policy positions advanced by liberal and moderate groups such as the Brookings Institute, the Ford Foundation, and the Institute for Policy Studies, wanting an alternative "repository of its political beliefs." A conservative institute materialized when Edwin Feulner and Paul Weyrich formed the Heritage Foundation in early 1972. With a $250,000 donation from Joseph Coors, owner of the Coors Brewing Company, the Heritage Foundation officially opened in 1973. By 1977, the foundation's annual budget exceeded $2 million. The Heritage Foundation relied on direct mailings that featured concise conservative recommendations.[14] The Institute of the Black World operated on the opposite end of the political spectrum from the Heritage Foundation, and in the early 1970s, it was unclear whose policy perspective would win out.

The 1972 presidential election was crucial in determining America's future political direction. Richard Nixon won the 1968 election in part due to the backlash against the excesses of Black Power and the student movement. Millions of Americans watched the violence and chaos surrounding the 1968 Democratic Convention in Chicago. Coming only four months after Martin Luther King Jr.'s assassination and amid the continuing fighting in Vietnam, ten thousand protesters descended on Chicago in an attempt to influence the Democratic Party to end the war. In a clash between protesters and the Chicago Police Department, more than 600 were arrested and over 150 officers were injured. Nixon's platform of peace in Vietnam and law and order at home resonated with voters, and he won easily over Democratic nominee Hubert Humphrey and Independent Party candidate (and former segregationist) George Wallace.[15] For the 1972 election, questions remained about whether Nixon's coalition could hold or if progressives would organize to defeat the incumbent. Progressives pointed to America's continued involvement in Vietnam as Nixon's weakness. South Dakota senator George McGovern honed in on this topic when he announced his plans to run for president. He described the Vietnam War as "a moral and political disaster—a terrible cancer eating away the soul of the nation."[16] The 1972 election was about ending the Vietnam War and how to achieve equality domestically. Progressives suggested stronger governmental action, while conservatives believed in the natural workings of the market.

In a context where conservative and progressive forces tried to shape the direction of American domestic policy, Black activist communities had to get their house in order. The successes of the 1960s also led to ideological confusion in the 1970s. Black Power inspired a variety of ideological perspectives and agendas. The wide-ranging discourses of Black Power found agreement in challenging liberal civil rights. However, as scholar Adolph Reed Jr. has pointed out, the discourses produced "a muddled intellectual world of vague ideas and conceptual confusion."[17] The IBW associates saw this confusion as well, asserting, "white America is in a state of profound crisis, black America is in a state of profound confusion."[18] The disarray that the IBW and others observed in the Black Freedom Struggle was, in part, a product of ideological disunity after Martin Luther King Jr.'s assassination.

Ideological, political, and analytical confusion over the future direction of the Black Freedom Struggle provided the IBW with a tremendous opportunity to develop synthetic analytical frames that would create issue-based consensus. The IBW associates saw the creation of specific recommendations developed through collective scholarship as a means to produce consensus between grassroots activists and BEOs. The associates' decision to develop a Black political agenda coincided with what historian Komozi Woodard calls the Modern Black Convention Movement, which included the 1967–69 Black Power Conferences, 1970 and 1972 Congress of African People Conventions (CAP), and the 1972 Gary Convention. These conferences and conventions, led by Black activists under the banner of Black unity, pushed the freedom struggle from questions of equal access to ideas of structural change and, ultimately, Black liberation. During the convention movement, Black Nationalists exposed racial liberalism's policy failures in its inability to rectify systemic problems facing Black communities, such as poverty, police brutality, and structural racism. Black Nationalists countered weak liberal policies by creating alternative social, cultural, and economic institutions to fill the voids. Traditional civil rights organizations and BEOs also tried to get the government to draft legislation that addressed structural inequalities by proposing plans for universal health care and a guaranteed income. The Modern Black Convention Movement was a moment when BEOs, Black Nationalists, and civil rights organizations came together in an attempt to pressure legislators for structural change. The IBW's participation in these conferences demonstrated its identity as a think tank.[19]

The Black Agenda Network

Amid its reorganization, the IBW began applying a preliminary structural analysis of contemporary issues in Black America with the goal of producing policy recommendations. In 1970, IBW associates mailed their governing council a series of essays, "Black Agenda Working Papers," on key issues facing Black communities. The papers served two functions. First, IBW associates began to think critically about areas for a Black political agenda to address. Second, the essays and critical responses laid the foundation for the IBW's Black Agenda Network (BAN).

The "Working Papers" presented preliminary arguments on politics, Black art and culture, education, economic development, and police brutality. The essay on politics, written by Strickland, argued that the 1970s was a new political era, because at no point in American history had more Blacks been registered voters, yet the Black vote "has never been so powerless." A solution to this crisis was to build a Black political movement based on political education and accountability. The IBW's role, naturally, was political education, or to "propagate the analysis of what is happening."[20] In his essay on Black art and culture, Henderson outlined "priorities for research, for criticism, and for creation," to achieve "black liberation and black celebration." Henderson called on Black scholars to research African cultural production and thereby eliminate distorted interpretations. He wanted scholars and students to view Black art and culture as "Black Humanism." Henderson recognized that Black problems were rooted in economics and politics, but he also believed that "behind any realistic drive to reach permanent solutions there must be a regeneration of the spirit." This was the role of Black art and culture.[21] Chet Davis's essay on education argued that Black education in the 1970s had declined on many levels, including the institutional repression and co-optation of Black Studies.[22] Davis wanted more research on Black education, the creation of a communication network to exchange ideas, the use of media to promote Black educational analysis, and community control over education.[23] Economist Robert S. Browne and Strickland wrote the essay on economic development, wherein they concluded that because Blacks had been traditionally excluded from the financial "levers of power," and faced systemic structural racism, the only solution was political mobilization. "What I am suggesting is," wrote Browne, "that any significant economic development which we achieve will come about largely through political maneuvering, and we must therefore be very together and know exactly what we are doing." Strickland added, "There can be no economic development apart from political power."[24] Finally, Strickland also wrote an essay on police brutality, calling for additional Black officers in supervisory positions.[25] Altogether, the essays called for research and analysis to advance Black political consciousness and culture.

The IBW held an October 1970 meeting of approximately fifty of its national associates in Idlewild, Michigan, to form the Black Agenda Network (BAN). In preparation for this meeting, IBW associates reviewed the critiques of their Black Agenda Working Papers from the governing council. Literary critic Addison Gayle responded that the essays were "adequate," and he was "in total agreement with each of them." Other reviewers criticized the analyses. Julius Lester found the essays by Browne, Strickland, and Davis "highly disappointing and inadequate," and wondered if he should even attend the October meeting. Atlanta University political scientist Mack Jones thought the essays were "too reformists—civil rightish [sic]." Jones did not see "bold new departures," but instead "an argument for more of the same old stuff." Despite his criticisms of the essays, Jones was excited over the meeting. The October meeting in the Black resort town, Idlewild, historically known as a retreat for the Black intelligentsia, promised to be a major event; work and leisure, all in the name of a Black political agenda.[26]

The purpose of the IBW's Black Agenda Network was to assess the problems facing Black communities and to identify resources that could address and perhaps solve these troubles. The BAN consisted of eight groups composed of ten to fifteen people each. The network was an "unprecedented attempt to create a sustained, precise, collective analysis of some of the major problems facing the [Black] community in America." The BAN planned to put forth "specific programmatic proposals" in critical areas of education, economic development, political organization, health and welfare, communications, cultural definition and survival, organized religious resources, and Pan-African history and relations.[27] The associates understood the need to identify urban problems and suggest potential solutions. The IBW constructed the objectives of the BAN based on questions examining the present and historical conditions of Black people, the systemic forces acting upon Black communities, and various attempts, past and present, to achieve self-determination. All the questions aimed to identify the "long-range plan of analysis" and programs in the eight task force areas. After analyzing the problems, the IBW wanted each committee to "disseminate the results of the work of the BAN task forces in as wide and as deep a milieu as possible, placing special focus on the black community." By entering the marketplace of ideas, the IBW exemplified a think tank, producing the kinds of perspectives and systemic analyses that would make it possible for the Black community "to move towards authentic self-determination." For the IBW's leadership, a Black political agenda was the embodiment of their responsibility as intellectuals and as an activist think tank.[28]

The BAN committees' members prepared policy assessments outlining future plans. The political organizing committee's report, for example, identified powerlessness as the basic political condition of Black people. The report located the source of this powerlessness in three areas: "the machinations of white power," "the absence of a political methodology for organizing blacks on behalf of their own self-interest," and "the absence of a political ideology which expressed self-interest." The committee members examined the need for developing Black methodology and ideology as a "precondition to any victorious struggle with white political power." The report concluded, "electoral politics can be a viable *tactic* for liberation if it is converted from transient political *campaigns* into a *permanent political movement*. All agreed that politics must be transformed from an end in itself (political participation) to a concrete means of liberation."[29]

Shortly after the retreat, Harding and Strickland published their ideas about a Black political agenda in the *New York Times*. The IBW associates assessed the 1970 midterm elections by demanding new political ideas. They concluded that, by not supporting Black communities, both political parties had misunderstood America's political reality. Democrats and Republicans continued to see Black problems as separate or divorced from national concerns. However, the institute's lead associates argued that these notions of Black particularity illuminated "America's profound decay" and "are thus the central issues of [American] life."[30] The authors expressed hope of an "eventual development of humane alternatives to all the basic political, economic, and cultural systems of America." They promoted progressive solutions that emerged from the BAN retreat, such as radical tax reform, withdrawal from Vietnam, overhaul of the prison system, community control of the police, endowment of Black education as a national resource, a Marshall Plan approach to the urban problems, and unconditional aid to Africa, among other things. To accomplish these goals, the authors suggested a "black reconstruction," which could be attained through "independent, insistent, black political power." Harding and Strickland argued that these issues were national concerns, because a Black agenda was the only "humane agenda" remaining.[31]

The *New York Times* column represented high hopes for developing a Black political agenda, but belied the BAN's organizational weaknesses. The logistical and financial problems of organizing numerous committee members nationwide crippled the network. The IBW lacked the financial resources to sustain the network's goals. Fortunately, the IBW incurred few expenses at the initial Idlewild meeting. A philanthropist paid the boarding expenses, and another participant covered travel expense for some attendees through his institution, although it was unclear whether this was a business, a foundation, or an academic institution.[32] Despite their inability to maintain the BAN's lofty goals for logistical and financial reasons, core members of the institute kept working on key policies they believed should be included in a Black agenda.

At the end of 1971, the IBW summarized the year's activities. Associates admitted that it was tempting not to look back, "as if the past were not connected to the path ahead," or to pass simple judgments couched in the rhetoric of Black Power slogans. Nevertheless, the associates believed it was "absolutely necessary to look as hard as we can at what black people have just been through." The year-end review essay reflected the IBW's Black agenda work as it assessed the effect of the government, Vietnam, and revelations that the FBI's Counterintelligence Program (COINTEL-PRO) was aimed at the nonviolent component of the civil rights movement. They concluded that more attention needed to be paid to the structural dimensions of Black economics and crime, asserting, "We cannot end our powerlessness by pretending that a black ideological movement is the same as a black liberation movement." The experience gained by IBW associates in the BAN proved useful during the organization and operation of the 1972 Gary Convention.[33]

The Gary Convention and the Black Agenda

In preparation for the first presidential election of the seventies, several Black leadership conferences convened in 1971 to develop a strategy that would maximize the Black vote in the coming election.[34] At a key September meeting in the Chicago suburb of Northlake, Illinois, BEOs and grassroots leaders debated the appropriate strategy for the election. Georgia state representative Julian Bond proposed that each state or city with a large Black population run a "favorite son or daughter" as its candidate, stating that such candidates would help increase the Black voter turnout. Others, such as John Cashin, chair of the Alabama National Democratic Party, wanted no Black presidential candidate. Percy Sutton, Manhattan Borough president, opposed Cashin, arguing, "Running a black Presidential candidate creates a strategy and a sense of internal unity which carries far beyond the convention floor and the election of 1972. It carries with it a political awareness that will flow into the local election of every city, town, and village in America where black people live."[35] Grassroots leadership wanted a more democratic process that provided activists such as Congress of African People's (CAP) Amiri Baraka and Congress of Racial

Equality's (CORE) Roy Innis political capital in a realm increasingly dominated by elected officials. Baraka proposed a national convention as a method of accommodating the various ideas and developing an electoral strategy. However, both nationalists and BEOs had misgivings about these suggestions. Nationalists believed that no work could be accomplished given the diverse ideologies. Elected officials were wary of accountability to their constituencies, fearing that some of the inflammatory rhetoric used by Black Power advocates would cost them votes.[36]

Black elected officials held a separate conference two months later in November 1971 that continued the progress toward the Gary Convention. More than three hundred officials attended the Washington, D.C., meeting. Fourteen workshops covered diverse topics including "Black Political Power in the Seventies," "Money Resources," and "Problems of Aging." Lerone Bennett Jr. utilized the keynote speech to promote the IBW's Black agenda work.[37]

Bennett's address echoed themes from the IBW's earlier BAN meetings. He stressed that it was imperative for the leadership community "to develop a series of comprehensive plans identifying the black interest and the black position in every field." In essence, he called for Black politicians to support and use the IBW's work. Bennett named five reasons that the IBW's work was vital. First, he stressed the need for the creation in the 1970s of a plan to tackle issues of employment, welfare, education, prison reform, and health. Second, he suggested that a Black agenda must demand, as the basis for cultural, political, and economic improvement, Black control of resources and bureaucracies. Next, he wanted an agenda that would renew the "structures, energies, and values of the black community." Fourth, he stressed the need for a massive mobilization of the community's resources, including labor, capital, intellect, and the ballot. This mobilization, declared Bennett, must "transform political structures so that people will not have to be aliens and adversaries for resources and services that governments should provide routinely." Finally, a Black agenda should transform "the institutions of America which threaten or prevent the fulfillment of items one, two, three, and four." Echoing the IBW's mantra, the *Ebony* editor concluded, "It is necessary for us to disengage ourselves from white people's arguments and *redefine* all concepts and associations in terms of the fundamental interest of black people." Bennett's association with the IBW influenced his suggestions for developing a Black agenda and assured the IBW's participation in any future discussions on the topic.[38]

After BEOs gave Bennett's speech a standing ovation, Michigan congressman Charles Diggs made the official call for the Gary Convention. The call for a national convention, however, did not resolve the concerns initially expressed at the Northlake conference by grassroots nationalists or BEOs. In fact, the naming of three co-chairs, Gary, Indiana, mayor Richard Hatcher, Congressman Diggs, and Baraka, exemplified the cleavages underlying the banner of unity. With three months remaining before the March summit, the co-chairs relied on established activist networks, such as the CAP, the CBC, and the IBW, to coordinate the massive undertaking.

The IBW's "Preamble" to the Gary Convention symbolized the organization's synthetic yet pragmatic outlook, one that moved beyond traditional politics and called for structural change. This perspective worried many BEOs and Black civil rights organizations, despite their harmonious rhetoric before the convention. The NAACP was the first to oppose the transformative perspective promoted by the IBW in the "Preamble." John A. Morsell, assistant executive director for the NAACP, called the introduction unacceptable because of its separatist rhetoric. Morsell said that the preamble withdrew "from the American political process on the thesis that this is 'white politics,'" and it proclaimed "a doctrine of black racial superiority in that it holds that only persons of African descent are capable of spearheading movement toward desirable change in the society."[39] The NAACP believed the document pursued revolution rather than reform. According to the NAACP's press release, "We are committed to a practical politics of accomplishment, utilizing the system as we find in the conviction that its own processes provide the mechanism for needed changes in it."[40] The NAACP's refusal to explore even the proposition of new political ideas, frameworks, and organizations ultimately relegated it to the margins of the convention. Moreover, the national office's failure to participate in the convention demonstrates how some civil rights organizations closed off the possibility of alternative strategies, echoing the IBW's separation from the King Center.[41]

In the March 1972 issue of the IBW's *Monthly Report*, associates responded to the NAACP's position by exposing the oldest civil rights organization's reliance on a liberal framework that emphasized individualism and a free market economy, ultimately maintaining the status quo. Institute of the Black World writers asserted that the current system had not and possibly could not work for the betterment of vast numbers of Blacks. Members of the IBW declared,

> the "system as we find it" is already in an advanced state of collapse, not even working for the oppressor, much less for the oppressed. ... Commitment to the system can only lead to more collapse, with high unemployment, large welfare rolls, overcrowded prisons, and a soaring crime rate; inflationary prices, inadequate housing, increasing pollution, and a drug problem of crisis proportions; plus a cynical foreign policy which coordinates warfare in Asia, with big-business protectionism in Europe, and C.I.A.—initiated coups in Latin America.[42]

The presumed failure of the American system identified here had a two-fold effect. First, it undermined the NAACP's status quo position in favor of the need for radical change. Second, the assumption of American collapse allowed the IBW associates to position themselves at the forefront in creating a new system. Although the IBW's claim of an American collapse seemed extreme, the impact of the Vietnam War as well as the revelations of domestic and international corruption had taken their toll on American society; the Gary "Preamble" captured this angst. The NAACP's opposition was an early warning of looming problems between moderates and radicals. Racially moderate organizations like the NAACP wanted reform. Moderates presumed that the end of legal segregation concluded the civil rights movement and felt that Blacks should rely on the normal avenues of change, like electoral politics. On the other hand, through their systemic analyses of Black America's social, economic, and political problems, the IBW associates urged the need for structural change. In their work, associates argued that many communities, Black and White, would continue to suffer under the aegis of normality unless there was structural change. Overt racism was no longer an accepted part of normal American affairs, but the IBW asserted that poverty, pollution, inadequate health care, and wealth inequality remained embedded in the American system. Structural change, they argued, was a solution, even though many moderates recoiled from it because of its radical implications. An early example of the fracturing of the Black Freedom Struggle's fragile unity at Gary, the NAACP controversy was a preview of the dissension to come.

In preparation for the Gary Convention, the IBW associates submitted to the planners an outline of a Black agenda based on the BAN's proposals. The purpose of the outline was "to suggest some of the major changes we need to begin to eliminate racism and exploitation from American life." The proposal assumed that institutional transformation was necessary for radical change, and that it would "move us forward in the struggle for a new humanity." Although the IBW had spent considerable amounts of energy and resources developing this outline over the previous two years, the institute's submission was not a finished program or solution, but a "starting point" to provide "a sense of direction."[43]

The IBW's proposed agenda addressed six key areas—politics, economics, human development, communication, Africa and the Third World, and environmental protection. Under political concerns, the outline suggested a national constitutional convention to change "the anti-Black racist control . . . built into the present Constitution." The IBW's agenda proposed proportional racial representation in Congress and full employment. In regards to voting, the agenda called for an end to all gerrymandering, because it was diluting Black political power. In addition, it called for the establishment of a permanent voting rights act, one that did not have sections requiring periodic renewals from Congress. The plan also addressed local concerns, such as home rule of Washington, D.C., and community control over police.[44] The institute's Black economic agenda proposed aggressive taxation, including abolition of income tax for families that made less than $20,000, a federal tax of fifty percent on all corporate profits, and the creation of a National Black Development Council to control a share of Black taxes. The National Black Development Council would be responsible for the "planning and execution of . . . new initiatives in housing, land, schooling, jobs and health for the black community." The outline recognized the centrality of urban problems by promoting an urban-based homestead act that addressed the need for "humane housing." The agenda also addressed rural concerns, calling for a reorganization of the Department of Agriculture away from agribusiness interests, and the incorporation of a "well-funded black agency" to promote Black rural development. In addition, the economic section tackled day-to-day difficulties such as increasing the minimum wage from $1.60

to $2.50 per hour, guaranteeing an income of $6000 for families, increasing Social Security by 100% and making the benefits available at 50, ending discrimination in employment and unions by making it a felony, and offering free public transportation.[45]

The IBW's outline presented ideas to improve the lives of Blacks beyond politics and economics in its discussion of social issues. The agenda promoted nationalized health insurance for all citizens and free medical care for families with incomes under $10,000. The proposal also demanded the elimination of capital punishment. Moreover, the IBW continued to support Black education by calling for a National Foundation for Black Education, an organization "funded from public sources, to develop and encourage national and local planning and experimentation in the creation of new models of black education at all levels." The IBW insisted on free public education for all Black people up to their "highest attainable level," believing that, "after centuries of exploitation, we are due at least this much." Finally, the document called for community control of some radio and television outlets in the communications section.[46]

Although the IBW's proposed agenda focused on the needs of American Blacks, it also contained suggestions on international matters. It called for increased economic aid to the Third World, a withdrawal of support from minority White rule in Southern Africa, and a removal of all troops from Vietnam. The IBW's concern with environmental protection appeared in its discussion of the need to prosecute "industrial polluters" in urban areas. It also stressed the need to limit the production of private automobiles and the building of highways. Finally, following the revelation of the COINTELPRO program in 1971, the document demanded J. Edgar Hoover's resignation from the FBI. The IBW's agenda suggested that the resources used to spy on civil rights activists could be spent instead on "eradicating the national traffic in narcotics." The IBW presented the outline of its Black agenda to the National Black Political Convention Committee, embodying its role as a think tank for Black progressive forces and promoting its politics of self-determination. The IBW knew its work was visionary, but associates declared, "at every critical moment of our struggle in America we have had to press relentlessly against the limits of the 'realistic' to create new realities for the life of our people." The Gary Convention was the next bend in the river of Black resistance.[47]

The IBW's proposed agenda was extremely ambitious. Although the agenda was couched in the language of Blackness and seemed too radical for racial moderates and the White mainstream, the IBW's plans were synthetic, pragmatic, and designed to gain the widest amount of support possible. The people who briefly served on BAN committees represented an array of political perspectives. For example, the political committee included long-time activist Ella Baker, IBW associates Strickland and Mitcham, academics Mack Jones and James Turner, representatives of politicians H. Carl McCall and Richard Hatcher, journalist Alex Poinsett, and religious leaders Leon Watts and Robert Chapman. This diverse committee used the collective scholarship process to produce synthetic proposals. Agenda items such as increasing the minimum wage, improving health care, strengthening education, and promoting public transportation could have received broad support in Black communities and across racial lines. The IBW's progressive program offered attainable items with appropriate support, political consciousness, and political willpower. Delegates discussed and revised these preliminary plans at the Gary Convention.

The convention opened on Friday, March 10, under the leadership of the three co-chairs: Baraka, Diggs, and Hatcher. More than 3,500 delegates from 44 states poured into Gary that evening. By Saturday there were nearly 10,000 participants, all of whom demonstrated unbridled enthusiasm and excitement. As delegate Ben Chavis remembered, "There was a lot of electricity in the air. I mean, it was truly a time in Gary, Indiana, when African Americans were self-determined. When there was no intimidation. In fact, there was affirmation all over the place. And I would say there was a sense of pride, just to be there. To know that we'd made it out of those local struggles around the country to come into this convention to express the aspirations of the people we left back home."[48] As the state delegates caucused at their hotels Friday evening, their interactions with each other transformed local problems of employment, health care, education, and social welfare into national concerns.[49]

Over the course of the weekend, grassroots activists and elected officials debated the merits of independent politics. However, the cleavage between grassroots activists, who comprised a significant portion of the state delegates, and the BEOs, who envisioned themselves as leading spokespersons, threatened to destroy the convention. Saturday evening, Baraka and CAP leaders worked with state caucuses to assuage fears that their agenda items would not be formally included. The delegates felt disrespected by Congressman Diggs' authoritative moderating earlier in the day, and believed he and his allies might block their agenda items. The delegates and Baraka realized that a Black agenda was the centerpiece of the convention.[50] After a long night of caucusing with state delegates and Black leaders, Baraka moderated the tumultuous Sunday session, where a Black agenda was completed. Baraka masterfully managed the session, in which state delegates demanded that their agenda items be included in the final draft. The delegates worried that elected officials' program would eclipse grassroots activists' concerns. Strickland noted, "Imamu [Baraka] emerged as the strongest black political force on the scene."[51]

Two additional contentious issues, busing and the Israeli-Palestinian conflict, put Baraka's skill as a grassroots organizer and moderator to the test. Each agenda item created rancorous debate on the assembly floor. There was a strong split between civil rights moderates and BEOs on the one hand, and grassroots activists on the other, regarding busing. Elected officials trumpeted the civil rights perspective that promoted integration, seeing busing as a simplistic yet effective strategy to achieve this goal. Grassroots activists' attitudes reflected growing opposition to busing in Black communities. Activists questioned the assumption embedded in the logic of integration that all segregated institutions are inferior. The activists and their supporters also noted that in many cases it was only Black students who rode buses, often for hours, to integrate schools. Consequently, Black students bore the burden of this policy. Parents and activists believed that it was time to question the assumption that integrated education was synonymous with quality education. Following intense deliberations, the anti-busing resolution overwhelmingly passed. This signaled a different direction for the Black Freedom Struggle. Grassroots activists' anti-busing position ostensibly aligned them with President Nixon's anti-busing platform. Many moderates argued that the convention's anti-busing resolution helped Nixon begin rescinding civil rights advances. As the NAACP's Roy Wilkins said, "black separatists such as Roy Innis [who introduced the anti-busing resolution at the convention] and his little band of bitter men had in effect supported Richard Nixon's position that blacks did not want busing."[52]

The convention also passed a pro-Palestinian resolution in response to the Israeli-Arab conflict in the Middle East. This position reflected the philosophy of Pan-Africanism and its call for people of color to unite against White oppression. The pro-Palestine resolution caused a similar backlash by the moderate Black establishment. In this case, the Michigan delegation, led by Coleman Young, walked out of the convention.

Young opposed "the dogmatic approach" of the Black agenda, believing that Baraka was forcing the document through the assembly, because, as Young recalled, "it was a blatantly separatist document."[53] Some of the Michigan delegates remained, denouncing Young as a pawn of the United Auto Workers (UAW), and accusing him of not allowing non-UAW Blacks to speak during the convention.[54] The media focused almost exclusively on these and other controversies during the convention. The attention given to these conflicts at some level reflected the contentiousness of the convention, but it also obscured some of the convention's positives, such as the Black agenda. Institute of the Black World's Strickland noted the media portrayal of "Gary as a mess, as a great black confusion," and he positioned the IBW to counter these images.[55]

Strickland noted several key problems that the National Black Assembly, the Gary Convention's official organization, needed to address before publishing the agenda in May. First, for Strickland, the Gary Convention signaled an overt challenge to BEOs, whose visibility and importance had grown since 1968. He believed activists and community members repudiated the power of the CBC and BEOs during the convention. He suggested in internal memos that many of these politicians used race and Black Power rhetoric to get elected, but once elected were not accountable to their Black communities. A new set of circumstances arose out of the Gary Convention: "the question [was] not simply black representation but black representation" bound to Black people and "accountable to them [rather than] to ambition or to white political parties." It was a shift from "symbolic black politics to politics of genuine struggle." In contradistinction to the media's view of the conflict as representing failure, Strickland saw it as the beginnings of renewal. The ability of local activists to promote an agenda over elected officials' objections was a part of "The Great Democratic Revolution."[56]

Although Strickland saw the convention as a direct challenge to BEOs, he did not believe the events in Gary absolved Black Nationalists from scrutiny. As he stressed, "there must be some new thinking on nationalists as nationalists," for that category "is mystical and vague and allows in too many kooks." Despite some Nationalists taking credit for the events in Gary, Strickland believed their position did not lead to "effective unity," in part because they had "no vision by and large." The split between nationalists and non-nationalists was "unhealthy and ignorant," and political positions needed to be taken on "issues not ideology." Ultimately, for

Strickland, there were serious and less serious "folks," and he wanted "to bind the serious forces together." He argued that political theorists, grass-roots activists, and BEOs needed to develop the independent Black political thrust of Gary in a truly democratic way, going beyond both BEOs and "some of the sectarian nationalists." According to Strickland, new Black politics must "come to transform the society not . . . nestle within it." The politics of transformation, he argued, should move from "elitism to mass movement," thus creating a new type of politics that would be accountable to Black communities.[57]

Strickland's analysis of BEOs and Black Nationalists exemplified the IBW's synthetic analysis, while his call for accountability to Black communities signaled a political pragmatism. Building on the IBW's Black Agenda Network, Strickland believed that transformation of Black politics was established through the creation of a political movement, rather than through the election of Black officials or through a political party. A movement would instill accountability in politicians of all races and would emphasize political consciousness. Political issues, not race, would be the basis of a political consensus. Such a transformation would alter the power dynamics between Black communities and their elected officials. He and other IBW associates urged the National Black Assembly to embody this goal with the Black agenda.[58]

The IBW believed the Gary Convention's Black agenda was an ideal location to initiate larger changes in the political culture. Associates argued that because some of the agenda items ratified in Gary were contradictory and controversial, they needed to be taken to Black communities for town hall-style debate and endorsement. Associates believed that the community ratification process would have highlighted the democratic themes of the convention, deepened political consciousness in the Black community, and held activists and BEOs accountable to the needs of the various constituents there. The democratic spirit, which Strickland believed had not been witnessed since the assassination of Martin Luther King Jr., indicated the need for new thinking, new political structures, and, eventually, a "new politics of liberation." Strickland thought the first step in this process was a response to the media's inaccurate portrayals of the event, and he believed the IBW was positioned to counter these depictions. The IBW associates told the National Black Assembly that "they did not see this role of mass black public education happening," and wanted to begin the process by producing a broadside and pamphlet for the Black press in an attempt to reach the masses. By emphasizing the democratic spirit of Gary, the IBW wanted to ensure that the structure of the National Assembly was representative of activists, elected officials, and community residents.[59]

The institute presented the idea for a broadside to the National Assembly steering committee, but it was not accepted. The National Assembly kept to its May 19, 1972, publication date of *The National Black Political Agenda*, without additional discussions in Black communities, because leaders believed there was not enough time to hold meetings and alter the agenda before the November elections. The IBW demonstrated its acceptance and embrace of its role as an activist think tank by suggesting that the agenda be approved through a democratic town hall-style meeting, so that the media's portrayal of the convention could be counteracted, and by providing critical support for the National Black Assembly. Although its idea for a broadside was ignored, the IBW made its presence felt at the Gary Convention and afterwards.[60]

The National Black Political Agenda was officially released on May 19, Malcolm X's birthday. It contained many of the recommendations in the IBW's original agenda outline, but was a flawed document because of unresolved contradictions. Composed of eight sections, *The Agenda* addressed key proposals on political empowerment, economic improvement, human development, international policy, communications, rural development, environmental protection, and District of Columbia politics. *The Agenda* began by calling for a National Black Assembly, because "the bondage of Black people in America has been sanctioned and perpetuated by the American political system—for the American political system is one of politics dedicated to the preservation of white power." The assembly was to function as a research organization, a provider of political education, and a mechanism for political mobilization, but not as an official third party. *The Agenda*, like the assembly itself, was contradictory. For example, the political agenda section supported the creation of a National Black Assembly, which many activists saw as the prelude to the creation of a third party. It also supported the Republic of New Africa, an organization that demanded the United States give Black America five Southern states as reparations for slavery. At the same time, the political agenda called for the registration of Black voters in the United States. How one organization could support the creation of a third political party, nationalist-based separatism, and traditional electoral politics that reinforced the status quo simultaneously was not reconciled or explained. The convention's discourse of unity permitted contradictions such as these to remain uncontested. Rather than debate these resolutions and identify specific areas of focus, all were included, forming a gumbo of political agenda items.[61]

Many of *The Agenda's* recommendations agreed with the Institute of the Black World's BAN agenda submitted before the Gary Convention. Topics such as political education, home rule for Washington, D.C., community control over police, schools, and media, the end to discrimination in labor unions, and economic support for Africa and the Third World appeared in both the IBW's platform and *The Agenda*. However, there were key differences that made the IBW's proposals more substantive than those offered in *The Black Agenda's* often-contradictory Black Nationalist rhetoric. For example, both documents located the source of Black economic disadvantage in the structural racism derived from the historical legacies of slavery and Jim Crow. The assembly's *Agenda* insisted, however, that there was a debt owed to Black America and that the assembly must "not rest until American society has recognized our valid, historic right to reparations, to a massive claim of the financial assets of the American economy." *The Agenda* employed nationalist rhetoric in calling for a committee to calculate reparations, pressure organizations and corporations for them, and create alternate economic structures. Although IBW associates understood that Black economic inequities were rooted in slavery and Jim Crow policies and that reparations were desirable, they knew that political realities made reparations quite improbable. Therefore, the IBW's initial demand for a guaranteed income, an increase in the minimum wage, and an end to income tax for families making less than $20,000 was more transformative and politically expedient than the calls for reparations in *The Agenda*. By not taking the agenda to communities for debate and discussion, the National Black Political Assembly (NBPA) settled for the radical, idealist economic platform of reparations over the IBW's more pragmatic program. Perhaps the IBW's transformative economic program rooted in pragmatism would have received tremendous support. After all, with nearly one-third of Black families below the poverty line, countless others just surviving, and a looming recession in the mid-1970s, the ideas offered in the IBW's agenda could have made a real difference for individuals and communities. The IBW's plan for national health insurance and free public education for Blacks "to their highest attainable level" was also more progressive than those plans offered in the National Black Assembly's final agenda. The IBW's program addressed structural inequalities that would have benefited Black communities and could have appealed to a larger constituency. These and other limitations of *The Black Agenda* encouraged IBW associates to analyze its weaknesses.[62]

In the months following the document's official release, Strickland published his concerns and represented the IBW's stance on the Gary Convention and *The Black Agenda*. He recognized that *The Black Agenda* was essential to understanding the meaning of the convention, despite the media's interpretation of events. He explained in *Negro Digest*,

> We came to Gary to adopt a National Black Agenda and to attempt to unite Black people around our common interests by adopting a program that could come before the election of candidates. We created a program that would break with the traditional history of American politics of personality; we came to Gary to break with this tradition of ignorance that sees the liberation of Black people being invested in the election of some white or Black Messiah. . . . That is what Gary stood for at its best, and that was the essential spirit of the Black Agenda which was adopted at Gary.[63]

Strickland stressed that in order to meet the potential of Gary, the National Black Assembly must take *The Black Agenda* to the masses of Black people to be ratified in some populist fashion. Allowing the people to approve the agenda would ensure the process was democratic and would allow Black communities to address the plan's contradictions and limitations.[64]

Strickland's suggestion of taking *The Black Agenda* to the masses never occurred because much of the document's dynamism was immediately undercut by what Harding termed "politics as usual." The fragile unity of the Gary Convention began to fall apart soon after the summit. Black Elected Officials immediately rescinded their support of *The Black Agenda*, fearing that alignment with the more controversial sections of the document would cost them votes in future elections as well as political capital among their White counterparts. In June 1972, the CBC issued a "Black Declaration of Independence" and a "Black Bill of Rights." The CBC undercut the Gary agenda by trying to get presidential nominees to support its documents. The assembly also had planned to present *The Black Agenda* at both conventions. Then, based on which party offered the strongest support, the National Black Assembly would endorse a particular candidate. By using the same tactic, the CBC let the presidential nominees avoid addressing more progressive agenda items. As such, the CBC's program was a comparatively weaker version of the Gary agenda. The "Black Declaration of Independence" and "Black Bill of Rights"— names clearly designed to invoke a Black connection to American ideals and not separatism—were not developed out of a mass political process, but rather represented a return to elite political forms that marginalized grassroots activists and everyday people. Moreover, the CBC's program did not include some of the IBW's transformative recommendations on guaranteed income, national health insurance, and free Black education. As political scientist Ron W. Walters concluded, "the politics of Gary and the strategy of Black elected officials were at irredeemable odds."[65]

Scholars have thoroughly explored the failure of the Gary Convention. Political scientist Robert C. Smith argued that the Gary Convention proved that the ideological diversity of the Black community does not allow a single organization, like the National Black Political Assembly (NBPA), to represent the race. He also suggested that the tendency of supporters of Black Nationalism toward utopianism often allows the extreme elements of the tradition to dominate. He even suggested that despite nationalism's importance in Black communities, its leaders "adopted an ideology and rhetoric that effectively separated them from the grassroots."[66] Smith further asserted that when BEOs and integrationists underestimated the importance of nationalist ideology, they weakened their connection to the Black mainstream.[67] Recently, Cedric Johnson described the Gary Convention as a "shotgun marriage of the radical aspirations of Black Power and conventional modes of politics."[68] The hastily formed unity failed, according to Johnson, because of incongruent purposes among elected officials, radicals, and nationalists. The multipurpose NBPA tried to meet everyone's needs, but in doing so actually met nobody's. Despite the various conclusions about the failure of Gary, most scholars agree that the IBW's plan for a more democratic approach toward ratifying *The Black Agenda* would have been a positive step in the right direction, one that would have allowed for political accountability. Although BEOs and nationalists claimed they spoke for their communities, their refusal to take *The Black Agenda* there for further dialogue and discussion demonstrated otherwise, rendering Black communities silent. The primary reason for failure at Gary was the organizers' failure to institutionalize further accountability. The explanations for the decision not to hold additional town hall meetings included a lack of time and money. However, regardless of the rationale, Black people who did not attend the Gary Convention were silenced when the assembly did not take *The Agenda* to communities for further discussion. The Gary Convention's weaknesses also exposed "the dirty little secret" of Black politics: the demobilization of the Black poor benefited many BEOs.[69] The IBW's demand for accountability would have provided a solid base for the NBPA to build its political hopes and dreams upon. As it turned out, *The Agenda* was used by nationalists to fuel their ambitions as community spokesmen and by BEOs to secure and strengthen their electoral base, while it promoted a centrist and often unaccountable agenda. Despite the failures at Gary, IBW associates hoped that insurgent Black mayors could play a vital role in transforming local communities, so Harding, Strickland, and other members turned their attention to Black politics in Atlanta.

Black Politics in Atlanta

The limited outcome of the Gary Convention irritated Strickland. In particular, he was frustrated that Julian Bond, Jesse Jackson, John Conyers, and others supported George McGovern's presidential candidacy in 1972 without demanding additional accountability. At the Black Political Science Association Conference in May, Strickland suggested that independent Black politics could not be based exclusively on BEOs, and that it needed a strong community base. However, he recognized that "never before has a significant sector of the petty bourgeoisie [BEOs] come together to take a position of opposition to the American system. This is new." He later added that political power was the only mechanism through which Black people could compete against "state-monopoly-capitalism." The rise of insurgent Black mayors who wanted to implement a progressive political and economic agenda was an opportunity for the IBW to continue its duties as a think tank. In essence, just as the IBW supplied theory to *The National Black Political Agenda*, it could try to influence the public policies of Black mayors. The logical starting point was Atlanta.[70]

The election of Black mayors in the 1960s and 1970s resulted from demographic shifts, as Blacks migrated from the rural South to southern, northern, and western urban industrial centers. The migration process reflected a continual pattern that had begun with the end of the Civil War and was fueled at this point by America's participation in World War II, which opened jobs in the defense industry. In addition, racialized housing policies, such as redlining, racial covenants, and unequal mortgage lending, sped White migration to the suburbs. The percentage of Blacks in the populations of cities like Detroit, Chicago, Gary, Atlanta, and Los Angeles grew exponentially. In addition, the Southern civil rights movement inspired Black northern and western populations to assert their political power. In 1967, Carl Stokes of Cleveland and Richard Hatcher of Gary were elected mayor of their respective cities. Two years later, aided by the popular support of Baraka's Committee For a United Newark (CFUN), Kenneth Gibson became mayor of Newark. Theoretically, the victories signaled a new type of Black leadership that represented both the successes of the civil rights movement and the insurgency of Black Power. Despite these hopes, Black mayors faced deindustrialization that gutted urban coffers. In addition, their narrow election victories meant centrist politics were required to effectively govern. Nonetheless, the electoral successes of these insurgent Black mayors set the background for the Gary Convention in 1972 and for the rise of Maynard Jackson.[71]

Jackson's electoral victory was the culmination of traditional, moderate Black politics in Atlanta and student civil rights activists demanding equality at all costs. Jackson's grandfather, John Wesley Dobbs, had been the principal Black politician in Atlanta in the mid-twentieth century. Dobbs cofounded the Atlanta Negro Voters League in 1949, which, with the lessening of the stranglehold that Jim Crow laws put on Black political life, made Black votes a force in Atlanta politics. Black Atlantans knew Dobbs as the "mayor of Auburn Avenue," the main street through the Black middle-class community in Atlanta. Jackson set out to create his own path and add to his family legacy. In 1956, he graduated from Morehouse College at eighteen years of age. He then earned a law degree from North Carolina Central College (now University) in 1964. Jackson returned to Atlanta as a lawyer and entrenched himself in the local Black middle-class community of which his grandfather had been "mayor." By the late 1960s, Jackson entered local politics, determined to become more than the symbolic mayor of the Black community.[72]

In the 1960s, student activists upended Atlanta's tradition of Black brokerage politics, which favored stability over radical change. The young activists thrust themselves on the political scene through protest that upset the carefully constructed biracial support of the White Atlanta business class. In 1960, Black students ushered in the sit-in phase of the civil rights struggle with a full-page advertisement, "An Appeal to Human Rights," denouncing Atlanta's image as the "City Too Busy To Hate." As home to SNCC headquarters, Atlanta received a steady stream of student activists demanding equality and urging others to do the same. Local students joined SNCC and followed up the "Appeal" with direct-action protests against Jim Crow discrimination in Atlanta-area stores and restaurants that eventually led to the arrest of Martin Luther King Jr. in October 1960. When presidential candidate John F. Kennedy called King's wife after her husband's arrest, he earned votes from Black communities nationwide. These votes provided Kennedy with a slim margin of victory in the November 1960 election.[73]

Some SNCC activists turned to electoral politics, directly challenging White moderate rule in the city. For example, in 1965, Julian Bond ran for and won a seat in the Georgia State Legislature in the predominately Black 136th District. Bond's election symbolized the rising tide of Black electoral politics, but the state legislature refused to let the freshman congressman take his seat. Georgia declared that Bond's ties to SNCC, which had recently opposed the Vietnam War, meant he was guilty of treason against the United States and the State of Georgia. Activists nationwide rallied to Bond's cause, and he was reelected in a controversial special election.[74]

Outside of electoral politics, activists created the Atlanta Project, which organized the impoverished Vine City neighborhood surrounding the Atlanta University Center. The Atlanta Project, led by SNCC activist Ivanhoe Donaldson and others, used Black Power rhetoric, which further undermined the city's biracial political coalition and heightened racial tensions. In 1966, a Black Atlanta neighborhood rioted after police wounded an unarmed suspected car thief. When Mayor Ivan Allen Jr. paternalistically tried to calm the growing east Atlanta community of Summerhill from atop a police car, protesters rocked the cruiser until he fell. The crowd yelled "Black Power" as it grew increasingly chaotic. The overt repudiation of Allen, the earlier election of Bond, and Atlanta's legacy of Black activism demonstrated that it was ripe for a dramatic change in leadership. The alliance between moderates, Black and White, would not survive. In this changing political landscape, Jackson set his sights on electoral success. In 1968, he ran an underfunded campaign for the United States Senate against segregationist Herman Talmadge and lost. Next he eyed city hall, using the growing Black population (51% by 1970), the tradition of Black middle-class politics, and student activism to achieve his first electoral success.[75]

By 1969, Atlanta's emerging Black leaders refused to act as silent partners of the moderate, White, business-dominated political coalition. Their tenuous partnership ended when the White business elite, including outgoing mayor Allen, refused to support vice mayor and fellow Democrat Sam Massell, a Jewish realtor, in his mayoral candidacy. The business elite and Allen instead threw their support behind Republican alderman Rodney Cook. On television, Allen suggested that Massell withdraw from the race because his brother, Howard, had solicited campaign contributions from nightclub owners while escorted by a police officer. Massell was confused by the mayor's actions and declared, also on television, that the timing of the accusations seemed suspicious. Massell suggested that the entire episode demonstrated prejudice rearing its ugly head to prevent the election of a Jewish mayor. Recognizing discrimination, Black leaders broke with their White business counterparts and strongly supported Massell. The decision to forge a separate political path marked the first time in decades that Atlanta's White elite and Black middle-class leadership did not support the same candidate.[76] During this situation, Jackson announced his candidacy for vice mayor. In the 1969 runoff for mayor, Massell received 95% of the Black vote and 25% of the White vote to capture city hall. Jackson easily won with similar levels of support, making him one of the first BEOs in the South since Reconstruction. According to Atlanta University political science professor and IBW associate Mack Jones, "the black vote settled what must be characterized as an intrafactional fight among the white business and commercial elite and sent to city hall an administration beholden to the black community." Despite the election of Jackson and other local officials, Jones suggested that Black politicians were ineffective because they had no agenda for the Black community.[77]

As vice mayor, Jackson looked to the IBW to help formulate a local Black agenda for Atlanta. During Jackson's 1969 campaign for vice mayor, he sought Strickland's advice on how to understand retiring Atlanta mayor Allen's "attack" on Massell. The IBW associate advised the candidate that he needed to find a way of "bringing together Black leadership in Atlanta," especially after he and another Black mayoral candidate, Horace Tate, ran for office without the support of established Black leadership. Strickland believed that the basis for unity would have to be "non-political . . . a kind of non-partisan freedom program for black Atlanta." As Strickland relayed the details of his meeting to Harding, he wondered what role, if any, the IBW could play. In 1973, when Jackson pondered a run for mayor, he realized that he needed to consult the IBW. Despite the fact that Jackson solicited support from over 150 community organizations to increase voter registration and turnout, the IBW's Black Agenda Network and its work on *The Black Agenda* made it a logical source for political analysis of the Black community.[78]

During Jackson's campaigns for vice mayor and mayor, the IBW crafted policy interpretations that reflected its pragmatic nationalism emphasizing structural racism. The institute drafted Jackson's press release on the 1971 Attica prison rebellion, which included his comments on Governor Jimmy Carter's redistricting plan to dilute the Black vote. The statement linked the "urban crisis" with Attica: "there is no more an urban crisis today than there was a prison crisis at Attica. They both are part of America's racial crisis[,] simply played out on different scenes." Both events, the press release continued, were racial crises that reflected "the immoral arrogance with which white men wield power over blacks." Jackson, under the IBW's guidance, made it clear that "open politics" was the only real option.[79] A year and a half later, Jackson announced his intention to run for mayor. His candidacy revealed the potential of progressive Black electoral politics. With crime a major campaign issue in the race, Jackson echoed the Gary Convention Preamble.[80] In his campaign announcement, he said that too many people turn to crime "because of the very hopelessness of their plight. So we must do more than throw people in jail to relieve our crime rate. We can start by recognizing the causes of street crime, among which are drug abuse and unemployment."[81] This subtle nod signaled, at least initially, that Jackson planned to forego the regressive law-and-order backlash agenda that had led to conservative political ascendancy since the late 1960s. Jackson's use of the IBW's analytical perspective signaled its importance as a think tank.

Jackson sought Strickland and Harding's services during his mayoral campaign, asking them to "write something . . . that needed to be said to the people of Atlanta." Strickland and Harding crafted a speech that introduced "present and future ideas." The speech used the growing Watergate scandal as a point of departure, because they hoped Jackson, and in turn the IBW, would receive national exposure from the address. They wrote two versions of the speech for Jackson. A longer, original version of the essay indicated "more fully our [the IBW's] thoughts on a number of matters." The shorter, speech version, "Atlanta in the Best and Worst of Times," called for a "search for new directions" and viewed Atlanta, and the possible election of Jackson, as "the way to a new kind of life." The speech again put crime in a broader context, planning "to prevent [crime] with honest compassion and intelligent planning." It also recognized the slim majority Blacks held in the city and reached out to all communities by placing "human values foremost" and emphasizing Atlanta as "a pluralistic city which will rejoice in our special gifts and histories." In the end, Strickland and Harding tried to "write a statement of significance and integrity that does not retreat from projecting the kind of vision we feel the city and the society needs, but that also fits comfortably and logically within your own campaign strategy and winsome personality."[82]

Racial antagonism quickly became the focal point of the 1973 mayoral contest that pitted Jackson against incumbent Massell. Heading into the October 1973 runoff election against Jackson with his political future hanging in the balance, Massell openly raised the specter of a Black mayor running Atlanta. Despite the racial animosity Massell experienced as a Jewish mayoral candidate in a Southern city in 1969, he campaigned as the last White hope for the city, the only candidate who could stop the implicit Black menace. His appeal to racial fears was apparent in his campaign slogan, "Atlanta is too young to die." Other Massell supporters followed his lead. The Atlanta Real Estate Board took out a full-page advertisement in the *Atlanta Constitution* in support of Massell. The ad, aimed at White voters and their economic fears, declared, "It's Cheaper to Vote Than to Move." The police department also got in on the act. In an organizational newsletter, Fraternal Order of Police (FOP) second vice president R. T. Roland argued that the election of Jackson "could very well be the downfall of the department." Roland portrayed Jackson as an outspoken opponent of the department because as vice mayor Jackson had demanded an end to police brutality and an increase in the number of Black officers. Roland continued, "he is clearly a black racist" who "would be happy to see every white officer fired and the entire department composed entirely of blacks." Roland wanted fellow officers to strengthen the FOP in order to stop the "Mad Man."[83] The antiblack language used by Massell and his supporters backfired. On election day, Black voter turnout was nearly 70%. Jackson received nearly 95% of the Black vote and 18% of the White vote to become the first Black mayor of a Southern city.[84]

Black Atlantans saw Jackson's election as a mandate for local government to improve their lives. Jackson tried to fulfill these hopes. First, the newly elected mayor worked to transform the police department by hiring more Black officers and appointing some to positions of power. This effort was best exemplified in Jackson's attempt to fire Police Chief John Inman and replace him with Reginald Eaves. The newly elected mayor believed that an increase in the number of Black police officers would reduce police brutality in Black neighborhoods. Second, Jackson implemented an affirmative action plan to incorporate Blacks into the city's financial structure. Much to the consternation of White businesses that previously had a monopoly on city contracts, Jackson awarded city contracts to Black companies. Within two years of his election, Jackson had awarded approximately 25% of all city contracts to minority businesses. Finally, Jackson proposed that the construction of the new airport occur in the southern part of Atlanta, which would benefit the Black communities in the southwestern part of the city. Each of these decisions faced stern White opposition, especially from the business community that had historically dominated the city's economy. These plans, in a reduced form, were ideas promoted by the Institute of the Black World's BAN and during the Gary Convention. Although the IBW's role in the Jackson administration was purely advisory and mostly limited to his campaign, during his first term in office Jackson tried to enact several of the ideas promoted in the IBW's Black political agenda, particularly those regarding police brutality, affirmative action, and Black economic development.[85]

Jackson's position as a progressive and insurgent mayor did not last. The White business community reacted to Jackson's agenda by threatening disinvestment from downtown. The *Atlanta Constitution* ran a series called "A City in Crisis," which perpetuated the antiblack rhetoric used in the mayoral campaign by Massell. The threat of an empty downtown pulled Jackson away from his early progressive policies. Black and White business leaders, according to political scientist Clarence N. Stone, "had a strong incentive to overcome differences and reestablish biracial cooperation in governing the city."[86] In 1975, Jackson yielded to White community demands that the Black public safety director, Reginald Eaves, resign. Eaves had been plagued by media exposés on his secretary's criminal record and his special treatment of one of his relatives. In another case, Jackson relinquished some of his progressive credentials by supporting business interests over labor. In 1977, with support from business leaders and Black middle-class leadership including Martin Luther King Sr., Jackson broke an American Federation of State County and Municipal Employees (AFSCME) sanitation workers strike. The workers, who demanded a fifty cents per hour pay increase to their below-poverty wages, led the strike. Jackson expressed sympathy for their demands, but argued that the city did not have the money for such raises. When negotiations abruptly ended, Jackson issued an ultimatum—return to work or be fired. One day before the ninth anniversary of Martin Luther King Jr.'s assassination while demonstrating support for striking sanitation workers in Memphis, Jackson fired 1,024 Atlanta sanitation workers, a majority of whom were Black.[87]

By this time, the IBW's financial difficulties prevented them from providing a penetrating analysis of the situation. Jackson's retreat from the insurgent politics that helped him win office exemplifies how many BEOs failed to be accountable to the Black working-class constituents that elected them. Jackson's subsequent electoral victories relied less on a politically mobilized Black working class and more on the traditional Black middle-class leadership that cooperated with business. Although this strategy may have been politically expedient, and perhaps even necessary, it contradicts the insurgent politics that led to the election of Jackson and other Black mayors, giving credence to Harding's complaint of "politics as usual." Associates' frustration at both national and local electoral politics meant their work as a think tank for politicians had to be connected with analysis aimed at Black activist communities. By raising community awareness, IBW associates hoped to hold politicians of all colors accountable to their constituents.

Conclusion

Between 1971 and 1973, the IBW shifted away from its focus on Black Studies programs and moved toward developing a Black political agenda, in the process becoming an activist think tank. The IBW associates relied on collective scholarship to develop a synthetic, pragmatic, yet radical agenda based on an analysis of structural racism. Beginning with the BAN and continuing at the Gary Convention, the IBW created a Black political agenda that called for creating national health insurance, supporting Black education, increasing the minimum wage, and promoting other progressive ideas. The IBW associates designed an agenda that would garner the broadest amount of support. Therefore, the IBW's agenda did not include controversial Black Nationalist items, such as reparations or the Republic of New Africa's call for five Southern states as repayment for slavery and segregation. Although these ideas were important, they would not generate a broad base of support in Black communities and would also instigate intense opposition. When some of these extreme positions appeared in the Gary Convention *Agenda*, the IBW stressed the need to take the agenda to Black communities for town hall-style ratification. The National Black Assembly decided against the IBW's suggestions, considering it too logistically difficult.

The IBW associates used the experience they gained with the BAN and the Gary Convention to advise Maynard Jackson in his run for Atlanta mayor in 1973. Harding and Strickland wrote speeches that connected local concerns, such as crime, to structural racism. Moreover, Jackson's early agenda as mayor, which transformed the racial composition of the police department, implemented affirmative action, and located the new airport in south Atlanta to benefit Black communities, reflected the IBW's pragmatic agenda. Stiff opposition from Atlanta's business district, however, kept Jackson from implementing a more radical agenda. Nonetheless, the Atlanta mayor remained a supporter of the IBW's work. In the late seventies he awarded the IBW city grants to publish its newsletter and to keep its doors open. On both the national and local scenes, the IBW associates, led by Harding and Strickland, demonstrated the organization's value as a think tank. At the same time that they created a Black political agenda, the associates produced various publications that allowed scholars, politicians, and the Black community to witness and benefit from their analytical and interpretive skills. In essence, the IBW associates published their developing synthetic analyses for various Black activist communities.

4

"Collective Scholarship"

Developing and Promoting Synthetic Analyses

In 1974, the IBW published a collection of essays, *Education and Black Struggle*, based on lectures from the 1971 Summer Research Symposium. In the lead essay, "The Vocation of the Black Scholar and the Struggles of the Black Community," Vincent Harding challenges intellectuals to reassess their purpose and questions whether intellectuals' roles are "out-of-style." In the context of deprived Black communities, his answer to this rhetorical question is that intellectuals need "to speak truth." Harding's version of truth-telling requires studying Black experiences, defining a "hard black analysis," identifying the systems and individuals (Black and White) that opposed Black liberation, and acting upon these analyses. As he defines it, "becoming personally involved in the concrete, active struggle for liberation, entering deeply into its life, and opening our own lives to its risks, is, of course, the most unrespectable aspect of the vocation of the black scholar." Harding and his IBW associates tried "to speak truth" by shaping popular consciousness with their publications.[1]

Although the Gary Convention and Maynard Jackson's mayoral campaign exemplified the institute's active role in shaping a political agenda, after its separation from the King Center, the organization also sought to shape popular Black political consciousness by marketing its ideas to Black activist communities. The IBW, through its publications and its expanded network of associates and friends, promoted and developed increasingly radical social, cultural, political, and economic analyses. During the 1974 Summer Research Symposium (SRS '74), the IBW used Walter Rodney's expertise to strengthen class and economic variables in the institute's analytical perspectives. The institute followed SRS '74 with personal and political conversations with Rodney and Detroit radicals James and Grace Lee Boggs about ideology, sociopolitical analysis, and activism. The IBW designed these "roundtable discussions" to address the increasingly contentious race-versus-class debate that fueled dissension in the 1970s Black Freedom Struggle. Through its publications, SRS '74, and interviews with leading Black radical intellectuals, the IBW promoted a synthetic brand of Black radicalism that went beyond the growingly doctrinaire platitudes of the post-Gary 1970s.

"The Great Debate" and Dissension in the Black Freedom Struggle

In the aftermath of the Gary Convention, many organizations and activists switched their ideological perspective from Black Nationalism to Marxism. For example, Owusu Sadaukai, born Howard Fuller, organized African Liberation Day (ALD) based on and influenced by the unity of the Gary Convention. The Pan-African event continued the unity experienced at Gary and was designed to make the African diaspora "aware of the political conditions in Southern Africa and the armed struggle being carried out by the brothers and sisters there," to educate people on the relationship between African and the New World diaspora, and to organize a "national protest demonstration against the United States foreign policy which supports European colonialist rule in Southern Africa."[2] Coordinated by activists nationwide, including Harding on behalf of the IBW, tens of thousands of people protested against colonial rule at various sites nationally and internationally on May 27, 1972. In Washington, D.C., more than ten thousand people marched past the Portuguese embassy, the Rhodesian Information Center, the South African embassy, and the U.S. State Department. According to political scientist Cedric Johnson, ALD "was the largest, post–World War II demonstration concerning Africa affairs held in North America."[3] Following the success of ALD, organizers formed a permanent organization, the African Liberation Support Committee (ALSC), which ultimately raised over forty thousand dollars for African revolutionaries fighting colonialism. This was done initially in the name of Pan-Africanism.

By 1974, this display of unity fractured over ideological debates on the correct political line—race or class. Sadaukai, ALSC's main organizer, along with IBW's cofounder Abdul Alkalimat, shifted the organization to Marxist-Leninism. This shift in ideological perspective raised the ire of nationalists in ALSC. In the summer, Howard University held a conference about the future of the Black Power movement. Its theme was "Which Road to Black Liberation?" During the conference, arguments erupted between Pan-Africanists and Marxists. Activists continued this debate in preparation for the June 1974 Sixth Pan-African Conference (6-PAC) held in Dar es Salaam, Tanzania. During 6-PAC, revolutionary African leaders such as host Julius Neyere urged American Black Nationalists to "oppose racial thinking." In the months after returning to the United States from 6-PAC, Amiri Baraka publicly made the switch from Black Nationalism to Marxism, transforming the Congress of African People into a Marxist organization.[4]

Dissension also beset the National Black Political Assembly, as BEOs continued to separate themselves from grassroots organizations. At the National Black Political Assembly's second convention in Little Rock, Arkansas, in 1974, dissonance emerged between integrationists, Black Nationalists, and Marxists. Based on the limited number of BEOs who attended, it was clear that many were trying to separate themselves from nationalist grassroots organizations. Assembly president and congressman Diggs did not attend, and Los Angeles mayor Thomas Bradley and Detroit mayor Coleman Young also avoided the meeting. Some BEOs still attended, including Atlanta mayor Maynard Jackson, Gary, Indiana, mayor Richard Hatcher, and congressman John Conyers. The central issue at the Little Rock convention was the creation of a third political party, which was ultimately rejected. During the conference, debates erupted over ideology—Black Nationalism, Marxism, or integration. By the end of 1974, it was clear that the mirage of Black unity could not be sustained given the diversity of thought. Amid the growing ideological and strategic dissension among Black activists after 1972, the IBW sought to develop and promote synthetic analyses about discrete issues that could generate consensus through considerable debate. The IBW's publications reveal the organization's evolving analytical perspective, which was designed to navigate the growing dissension in the movement.

The IBW's Publishing

Like the decision to develop a Black policy center, extensive publishing was one of the IBW's original goals. The IBW associates viewed publishing as an important means to reach activist communities, the organization's third constituency. Moreover, the institute's shift away from creating Black Studies programs to an activist think tank also meant that publishing and media access became crucial to its work. As part of the "third wave" of think tanks that focused on advocacy, the IBW and similar groups placed more emphasis on short policy briefs than on book-length manuscripts. They hoped that these shorter documents would immediately transform political consciousness through media access. In this context, the IBW was not different from better-funded think tanks that sprung up nationally. The IBW associates, often through collective authorship, gave their ideas general visibility by using several formats to publicize their various forms of scholarship. In the "Black Papers" series, the *Monthly Report*, a newspaper column titled "Black World View," and a journal with the same name as the newspaper column, the IBW hoped to reach and influence a variety of activist communities.[5]

The IBW's "Black Papers" were a series of scholarly pamphlets that were "presented not as an alternative to white scholarship on . . . selective subjects, but as its replacement." These pamphlets included Lerone Bennett's *The Challenge of Blackness*, which was the keynote address from the Black Studies Directors' Conference, Harding's *Beyond Chaos: Black History and the Search for New Land*, Margaret Walker Alexander's *How I Wrote Jubilee*, and St. Clair Drake's *The Redemption of Black Africa and Black Religion*. The institute published most of these essays in a joint venture with Third World Press. The IBW intended these essays for, and sold them to, educational institutions, thus providing the scholarly foundation for Black Studies. The "Black Papers" constituted the IBW's primary publications from 1969 to 1972, but expanding costs and the IBW's shift away from Black Studies reduced the significance of the "Black Papers" in the institute's publishing plans after 1972.[6]

The IBW designed the "Black Papers" to transform the scholarship of the Black experience, but its *Monthly Report* had a different audience. The *Monthly Report* targeted institute associates, contributors, friends, and Black communities nationwide as its readership. The idea for the newsletter came from Robert Hill during the reorganization meetings in 1970 and 1971, and it became the most consistent form of communication provided by the institute. It began in 1971 with a circulation of fifteen hundred. By 1973 the number of copies printed had tripled, and by 1979 more than eight thousand people and institutions received the monthly updates. The *Monthly Report* had a variety of uses. According to the IBW, "It has been used in many kinds of teaching situations in colleges, high schools, prisons, and community groups to give people a politically informed, historically accurate, black interpretation of current events." The newsletter was also important in soliciting donations for the financially strapped organization. Counting on the success of the newsletter, the institute included its newspaper column in the bulletin beginning in September 1971.[7]

The IBW's syndicated newspaper column, "Black World View," appeared in more than twenty Black newspapers, including the *Atlanta Voice*, *Chicago Defender*, *New York Amsterdam News*, and *Oakland Post*. Black newspapers' circulation numbers were dramatically declining in the 1970s, but the "Black World View" column also ran in the Nation of Islam's *Muhammad Speaks*, which reportedly had a circulation of six hundred thousand. The columns addressed topics ranging from Malcolm X and Louis Armstrong to the 1971 Attica prison rebellion. Besides its inclusion in newspapers, some Black radio stations read the columns as political commentary over the air. The "Black World View" put the IBW's analysis directly in the hands of Black communities. By the mid-1970s, "Black World View" evolved into a journal publication that included the newspaper column and added more substantial analysis.[8]

The first newspaper column, which appeared in June 1971, interpreted the meaning and significance of Malcolm X for the seventies. The column argued that Malcolm X was a model of the "New Black Man," one who anticipated the Black Power era's promotion of self-transformation. The editorial moved beyond "specific political viewpoints" and examined Malcolm as a model of "an overriding, powerful, personal and political methodology for change." The IBW's decision to emphasize the Muslim's "self-criticism and self-education" was no surprise, especially considering its identity as a think tank designed to provide education and critical support to organizations during the Black Power era. The column also reflected the Black Power era's optimistic hope that Black self-understanding, unity, and liberation were within reach.[9]

Other early columns primarily addressed Black culture and politics. A July 1971 piece described the importance and legacy of jazz musician Louis Armstrong in a political context. The media coverage following Armstrong's death lauded his musical contributions but attributed them to his individual genius, divorcing him from the Black community from whence he came. During Armstrong's quiet and simple funeral, which bore no resemblance to the New Orleans funerals he played while honing his craft, poet Robert Frost received a larger ovation than did Dizzy Gillespie.[10] The IBW challenged the public interpretation of Armstrong's life, reminding its audience that, "musicians and other black artists now know that *whatever* they do as Blacks in a racist society has political overtones." The IBW's column continued, "whatever the level of his political consciousness, Armstrong's life and art must be seen as a national Black Treasure as well as an objective lesson in America's exploitation of black citizens. For those who sought to exploit Armstrong have consistently tried to deny the validity of the Black Culture which he helped to create." The IBW associates urged their audience to acknowledge how Armstrong's life in the Black community shaped him and his art.[11]

In an August 1971 column, the IBW commented on Vice President Spiro Agnew's African trip, which signaled increased American economic and military aid, as well as control, on the continent. Using the diplomatic visit as a point of departure, the column called for broader politics that included a more substantive analysis of foreign policy. "The vision of black people must be enormously expanded: beyond the narrow pursuits of black capitalism and black careerism . . . beyond 'civil rights.'" The IBW urged its readers to take action and to pay attention to the world and events around them. Despite their timeliness and appropriateness, these editorials lacked the urgency present in the IBW's analysis of the Attica prison rebellion.[12]

The Attica rebellion epitomized the radical prison movement of the late 1960s and 1970s, and the IBW's analysis probed its racial and social implications. The rebellion began in August 1971, as prisoners at the upstate New York penitentiary staged a one-day fast to protest the murder of George Jackson, a prisoner on the West Coast. In the prisoners' minds, Jackson epitomized the injustice faced by Black men who were unfairly punished by the judicial system, and he demonstrated the radicalism growing behind bars. Jackson, who was seventeen at the time of his arrest for a series of petty crimes, trusted the poor guidance of his public defender, and plea-bargained to second-degree armed robbery for stealing seventy dollars from a gas station. In 1961, the judge sentenced nineteen-year-old Jackson as an adult under California Indeterminate Sentence Law to "one year to life." Although Jackson's accomplice, who confessed to instigating and leading the robbery, was released from prison after two and a half years, Jackson remained incarcerated. By 1970, he had become a legend inside the prison system for his physical and mental regimen, which included thousands of push-ups each day as well as extensive reading and writing. Jackson's intellectual development and activities in prison corresponded with those of leftist activists in the San Francisco Bay area who were influenced by a crude Marxist analysis of prisons; these activists based their analysis on Ho Chi Minh's idea, "When the prison gates fly open, the real dragons will emerge." While in prison, Jackson joined the Black Panther Party. Other Panther leaders who had served time in prison, such as Huey Newton and Eldridge Clever, also promoted the belief that prisoners were the vanguard of revolutionary leadership.[13]

The convergence of Black Panther prison ideology and Jackson's personal and extensive prison education resulted in tragedy. In January 1970, after Jackson and two other prisoners were charged with killing a prison guard in retaliation for the murder of three Black prison activists by a tower guard, the three men endured solitary confinement twenty-three hours each day. The "Soledad Brothers," as they were known, drew worldwide attention and support from congressmen, celebrities, and UCLA professor and Marxist theorist Angela Davis in particular. Jackson became the revolutionary prison spokesman with *Soledad Brother*, a collection of his prison writings smuggled out by his lawyer and published. The letters argued that street crime was a form of political protest, among other things. As Jackson wrote, "*Pure* nonviolence as a political ideal, then, is absurd: Politics is violence."[14] A failed August 1970 jailbreak, organized by his brother, increased Jackson's profile among Black Power activists. Davis subsequently went to trial for her alleged role as the mastermind behind the failed escape attempt. Her arrest and trial further galvanized Black Power activists. These events placed Jackson in the pantheon of Black Freedom Struggle activists and made him a threat even behind bars. On August 21, 1971, guards at San Quentin killed Jackson. The authorities released an "official" story reporting that an eight-inch gun was smuggled to Jackson by his lawyer and hidden in the prisoner's afro. This fabrication was used to justify Jackson's murder by prison guards. In the wake of the murder, protests erupted worldwide. French philosopher Michel Foucault described Jackson's death as an "assassination," musician Bob Dylan penned a song to the slain Jackson, and the prisoners at Attica in upstate New York staged a one-day fast.[15]

The Attica prisoners' one-day fast evolved over two weeks into a takeover of the prison by its thirteen hundred inmates, who demanded better-quality food, water, and shelter. In addition, they wanted "complete amnesty from physical, mental, and legal reprisals," improvement of the educational system, freedom of religion behind bars, and drug treatment for those inmates who desired it. Historian Manning Marable concluded, "Attica prisoners wanted to be treated like human beings." The prisoners requested honest negotiations and asked that leading Black Power activists observe the process. Despite positive inroads during the negotiations, New York governor Nelson Rockefeller ordered a forceful retaking of the prison, which resulted in the killing of twenty-nine prisoners and ten guards.[16]

The Attica rebellion and its demise captured the attention of Black activists, who organized protests and interpreted the significance of the events. In Atlanta, on September 27, 1971, approximately five hundred students held a "Remember Attica Rally" that culminated in a two-mile march from the Flipper Temple AME Church (near AUC) to the Georgia State Capitol. Rick Reed, southeastern coordinator of the Black Workers' Congress, led and organized the rally, which included speakers Julian Bond, Mack Jones of Atlanta University, IBW's William Strickland, and Dorothy Bolden of the Domestic Workers Union. According to FBI agents at the event, "the general theme expressed by the majority of these speakers referred to Attica, minority oppression, the Vietnam war, Nixon's wage freeze, and advised the audience that the solution to these problems was unification of the blacks and other minorities." When the marchers arrived at the capitol, they met with Black legislators, Ben Brown, Bobby Hill (not of IBW), and Julian Bond in the House Appropriations Committee room, where they discussed the "genocidal policies of the prison system" and the "People's Indictment" of Governor Rockefeller. Those meeting with Black legislators blocked Georgia state legislator James H. Floyd, Appropriations Committee chair, from entering the room. In response, Floyd ordered the contingent arrested, but Governor Jimmy Carter intervened, preventing the meeting from escalating out of control. The rally leaders inquired whether or not Black legislators supported the "People's Indictment" of Governor Rockefeller for ordering the violent retaking of the prison.[17]

The "People's Indictment" charged Governor Rockefeller with "MURDER IN THE FIRST DEGREE, of MASS MURDER, and other crimes," including excessive force, failure to achieve a peaceful resolution, physical abuse, withholding medical aid, depriving human rights, and fraud in the cover-up. Before the rally, the IBW distributed the "Indictment" to activists, students, and community members. Supporters signed copies and returned them to the IBW offices. In one month, more than two thousand names graced the bottom of petitions. The IBW drummed up support for the "Indictment" and the rally around the AUC by making round yellow stickers to place on dormitory doors that read "Institute of the Black World, Remember Attica" across the center and had the office address at the bottom. The top of the sticker urged students to "Mobilize." In addition to collecting signatures, the IBW analyzed the rebellion in its newspaper column, stating the belief that the rebellion was a case where "history takes a revolutionary turn." The IBW wrote, "Attica is a new event in history. Nothing like it has ever happened before. It is a symbol that black men whom white society has consigned to its deepest dungeons have, instead of succumbing, rediscovered themselves and reeducated themselves to rise up and strike back at the system which intended that they should never survive at all—and certainly not as men." Attica was a radical event, according to the IBW, because the prisoners seized the prison and "ran it autonomously and humanely." It was a place where the "power of freedom had triumphed over the power of repression" and created "new men." The IBW associates challenged Black leadership to provide "radical alternatives to the existing practices of American society."[18]

In the months between the fall 1971 Attica protests and the spring 1972 Gary Convention, IBW associates explored the implications of the prison rebellion. They also examined events in the Black Freedom Struggle since the assassination of Martin Luther King Jr. In the October 1971 column, "The American State vs. Black People," the IBW declared that "the Black struggle in America is at an historical crossroads." The source of Black problems mirrored that of America's problems, but it also reflected the movement's reluctance "to forge an independent vision for itself." Protests did not continue after the Attica rebellion. Instead, the event faded into the background as all Americans struggled against rising inflation and unemployment. To associates, the lack of anger signaled "the inadequacy of the Black vision of social change in America." Attica, in the institute's eyes, represented the complex phenomenon of "the State as murderer," which needed further analysis. The IBW described the prison rebellion as only the latest example of lethal force being used against protesting Blacks—others included the murder of three Black students on the South Carolina State University in Orangeburg campus (February 1968), the murders of Chicago Black Panthers Fred Hampton and Mark Clark (December

1969), and the killing of unarmed George Jackson by prison guards (August 1971). Associates determined that, "Blacks must rethink their relation to the existing system of American justice and the State responsible for it." The IBW associates further saw a problem in the fact that these state murders were treated as local "incidents," obscuring Americans' inability to accept "the inviolability of Black life." The IBW believed that for Black leadership to confront this axiom in the 1970s, the institute needed to provide, and the leadership needed to offer, "radical alternatives to the existing practices of American society."[19] This perspective formed the IBW's point of departure in working with Amiri Baraka, Congressman Charles Diggs, and Gary mayor Richard Hatcher at the Gary Convention. In the end, "real power" for the institute was to "redefine America anew."[20] The "Black World View" columns served a key cog in this redefinition.

The IBW published the Gary Convention "Preamble" in its "Black World View" column and in its *Monthly Report*, which trumpeted the convention's significance across the diaspora. The "Preamble" redefined America and the future of the Black struggle. Marcus Garvey's widow, Amy Jacques Garvey, who received the "Preamble" in the *Monthly Report* at her home in Jamaica, described the document as "a manhood expression of self-reliance and self-determination." She also told Harding, after the NAACP's opposition to the Gary Preamble, not to worry about the "Old Guard," as they "mostly got a hand-out from the White System."[21]

The failure of the Gary Convention to live up to its attendees' expectations resulted, in part, in an expansion of the IBW's class analysis. The associates needed to understand why the ideals of the "Preamble" were not fulfilled. Furthermore, BEOs who betrayed the tentative unity of the Gary Convention and later supported George McGovern's Democratic Party nomination for the 1972 presidential election without consideration for *The Black Agenda* became a target for the IBW's political analysis. The institute chastised Black politicians for not seeing McGovern as a political opportunist who used protesters from the 1968 Democratic Convention as a base. Despite an increased presence by Blacks and liberals, the IBW observed that, "Gary and the Black Agenda were bartered away for a mess of porridge." Associates added, "some of our elected representatives were sincerely mistaken, others were hopelessly corrupt, but all, the best and the worst, including Shirley [Chisholm], delivered up our real and potential black political power. They delivered it up willingly, graciously, cleverly, in the belief, one supposes, that by advancing white politics they were somehow advancing our own."[22] A year after the Gary Convention, the IBW lamented, "It is fair . . . to suggest that the vaunted black political strategy of 1972 by and large reflected the vested interests of black politicians as a class and only peripherally those of black people."[23]

The institute's solution to expanding and continuing the Black struggle was developing political consciousness and a movement "rooted in the people." Ideally, this would lead to a Black politics of self-reliance that engaged "black people at every juncture and every point to participate in the search for new direction." This answer to improving the lives of Black people replicated IBW associates' reasons for taking the *National Black Agenda* into Black communities for debate and ratification and their support of Maynard Jackson. A year later, the IBW was still promoting associates' political dreams that had been introduced in their publications at Gary.[24]

The centerpiece of the IBW's publications was *Education and Struggle.* The edited collection was a collaborative effort between the IBW and the *Harvard Educational Review* (*HER*) that grew from the 1971 Summer Research Symposium. The collection included essays from Harding, C.L.R. James, St. Clair Drake, Grace Lee Boggs, Walter Rodney, Tanzanian president Julius Nyerere, and Vietnamese activist Nhan Dan, as well as letters from Black prisoners. The IBW used the volume of essays to "affirm an essential unity of identity between black America and the Third World" based on a "common history of bondage to the white West." The goal was to find "an alternative path," and to demonstrate that new forms of education were essential. "Our commitment is to our people, to the pursuit of truth, to new answers, to the development of new black men and women—and to struggle." Harding's opening essay, "The Vocation of the Black Scholar," demanded that intellectuals speak truth. Despite this goal, he recognized that "there will be no uniformity in the ground we find." Echoing Frantz Fanon's *The Wretched of the Earth*, Harding believed that any transformation of Black communities required new concepts.[25] The edited collection became the IBW's most widely distributed and best-selling publication, with more than twenty-five hundred copies sold in one year.[26]

The IBW's various publications were important for three reasons. First, associates' production of scholarly essays, newspaper columns, and a newsletter demonstrated the IBW's position as an activist think tank. Associates used their analyses to influence perceptions and interpretations of the Attica rebellion and the Gary Convention. Second, the publications provided a tangible connection to Black communities. Individuals from all walks of life sent money in response to requests in the *Monthly Report*, allowing the IBW to keep its doors open. Black organizations and people used the IBW's analyses to clarify their own thinking. Correspondence between prisoners and the IBW discussing essays and newspaper articles shows that the associates' analyses were reaching all corners of Black communities.[27] Finally, the IBW's evolving ideas criticized the dominant ideologies of Black Nationalism, Marxism, and Liberalism. The IBW's concerns did not mean that the institute withheld support from a variety of organizations, but rather that associates placed a premium on synthetic analyses. Institute of the Black World associates published analyses of social, cultural, political, and economic activities aimed at improving Black communities. The goal of these assessments of the leading ideologies was to identify political issues that would generate widespread support. Through its collective scholarship, the IBW worked to forge a pragmatic unity. This legacy of collective scholarship was continued and enhanced during the summer of 1974, when Walter Rodney arrived in Atlanta. By the time of his arrival, Black activists were sharply divided on the question of whether race or class should be the salient feature of Black ideology, analysis, organizations, and activism.

The 1974 Summer Research Symposium

After the Gary Convention, the IBW associates determined that race or "Blackness" as an analytical and organizational tool had inherent limits. Across the movement landscape, many activists began to expand their economic analysis. Harding and Strickland had applied a nuanced racial analysis that focused on structural racism. However, many activists used a simple racial discourse that assumed that unity would result from explicit recognition and acceptance of Blackness. The IBW associates identified self-interested Blacks who used the rhetoric of unity and community as a cover for their "collective hustle"—in terms of personal acquisition of finances, employment, and political office—as the most obvious example of this simplistic racial discourse.[28]

"Individualism is undermining the race," wrote the IBW in "Racism and the Black Depression," which appeared in the September 1972 *Monthly Report*. Furthermore, the column continued, "instead of trying to get free, we have been too busy trying 'to get over.'" By 1974, the associates were working to enhance the organization's Black analytical perspective by moving beyond simple Blackness and expanding their analysis of structural racism. To do so, they focused more on American political economy, using an analytical frame applied by Adam Smith and Karl Marx that suggested that labor, rather than land, was the source of economic value. The associates' decision to further their analysis of the political economy reflected their frustration with Black activism during the mid-1970s.[29]

Associates theorized that the existence of a racialized political economy synthetically explained both race- and class-based exploitation. The theory provided meaningful insight into emerging self-interested, middle-class Blacks who, as the IBW saw it, undermined the struggle for Black liberation with their embrace of rugged individualism. Associates bemoaned the fact that those who focused on individualism often took for granted the sacrifices of all citizens during the civil rights era, attributing the unequal effects of the movement to personal genius or hard work. In addition, the IBW associates held that this point of view was devoid of any structural analysis; it did not take into account the effect of a racialized economy or the longitudinal results of unequal education. Acknowledging that the civil rights movement created opportunities for BEOs and a growing Black middle class, associates posited that racial discourse without economic analysis often resulted in a celebration of "Black firsts." Furthermore, it provided little accountability to a working-class Black majority who continually struggled against racialized social, political, and economic inequalities. The IBW associates, recognizing the conceptual weakness of simple racial discourse, augmented their analysis in order to study the effects of a racialized political economy. Associates pursued this analytical change through collective scholarship with Walter Rodney at the 1974 Summer Research Symposium (SRS '74).

The SRS '74 introduced participants to "the theory and methodology of political economy as a frame of reference for analyzing Black American social, economic, and political development," and used the theory to study the "contemporary situation of black people" in the United States and the diaspora. The 1974 symposium was comprised of three distinct, but interrelated, programs. First, there was a public lecture series on the theme "Black Struggle and the International Crisis: Towards the Next Stage," which featured lectures by Rodney, Harding, Strickland, and Hill. The second component of the summer program was a six-week research project on "Social Structure and the Black Struggle." Rodney and Strick-land served as codirectors for the research project, which investigated the political economy of Black and White America, the social structure and Black struggle, and the history of race relations between Black and White Americans. Participants tested the applicability of development theory as employed in Rodney's *How Europe Underdeveloped Africa* and Amilcar Cabral's *Return to the Source*. Finally, the summer ended with a three-day symposium, "Where do we go from here?" The panel discussions were designed to develop future directions for a declining Black Freedom Struggle.[30]

The institute organized the SRS '74 differently than it had the 1971 symposium. The different strategies reflected the dramatic changes that had occurred in the intervening years, including the decline of the Black Studies movement, the rise of BEOs, and the growth of the Black middle class. The 1971 symposium, as Strickland wrote to Rodney, rode "the crest of the black studies movement," and thus "tried to alert a class of black educators to the relationship between scholarship and struggle." The difficulties facing the SRS '74 differed because, the institute believed, "the struggle for black education, along with the larger black movement itself, [had] dissipated." As a result, associates used collective scholarship to expand the institute's analytical frame. As Strickland asserted, "a new perspective must be poised against this vacuum and we want to try, with the help of some of our friends, to develop it." The institute conceived of the SRS '74 as an "in-house seminar," through which associates hoped to answer five key questions: "What are the requirements of the present and future struggle and how is our understanding of these requirements to be best communicated to black people? What has been the historical development of Black America? What is the relationship between the social structure and black struggle? What has been the developing political and economic relation between black and white America?"[31]

The institute invited Rodney to lead several sessions devoted to analyzing the political economy. Rodney's experiences before 1974 paralleled much of the IBW's history. As had the IBW, he had questioned the role of the university and the Black middle class in the social order, and fostered Pan-African projects and radical analysis as alternatives. As mentioned earlier, Rodney arrived on the Pan-African intellectual scene during the 1968 Black Writers Conference in Montreal. Before the conference, Rodney's reputation had grown in progressive Caribbean circles. As a student at London University's School of Oriental and African Studies, he had studied under C.L.R. James. Working with James provided the young scholar with valuable lessons in the application of Marxist theory to experiences of the African diaspora. Rodney recalled James's scholarship as "a model of the possibilities of retaining one's intellectual and ideological integrity over a protracted period of time."[32]

As a professor at the University of the West Indies—Mona, Rodney "grounded," or talked and bonded with, Rastafarians in Kingston, Jamaica. By interacting with Rastas, Rodney stepped outside the bounds of traditional middle-class behavior and signaled his unity with the working class of Jamaica. After a violent confrontation between the State and the Rastas in 1963, officials stringently enforced antidrug statutes, prohibiting the smoking of ganja that the Rastas infused with spiritual meaning. As a result, the newly independent Jamaican government labeled the Rastas criminals for their nonconformist lifestyle. When Rodney began teaching at the University of the West Indies, many government and university officials believed that a responsible professor would not affiliate himself with such a group. Rodney believed, however, that "the black intellectual . . . must attach himself to the activity of the black masses."[33] It was this perspective and experience that Rodney brought to Montreal for the writers' conference.[34]

As a scholar, Rodney connected his research on African history to the Black Power movement of the late 1960s, asserting that Blacks "must define the world from our own position." For him, African history was not separate from "the contemporary struggle of black people." Furthermore, he argued, intellectuals "must not set up false distinctions between reflection and action." The Montreal conference signaled the passing of the torch from an older generation of Caribbean intellectuals, such as James and Richard B. Moore. The IBW emulated this generational shift in both of its Summer Research Symposiums.[35]

After the "Rodney affair," the Guyanese historian taught and lectured in Tanzania and other parts of Africa. Moreover, Rodney's reputation as a scholar-activist opened lecturing opportunities for him in the United States. Although Hill knew Rodney from Jamaica and Montreal, Harding and Strickland first met him at the 1970 African Heritage Studies Association's annual meeting at Howard University.[36] The IBW subsequently invited Rodney to participate in the SRS '71, but he declined because he was completing research in East Africa. It worked out for the best, however.

Rodney's focus on neocolonialism's impact on the Caribbean made him the perfect keynote speaker and panelist for the SRS '74. His analysis illuminated similarities between the situation in the Caribbean and the incorporation of the Black middle class in the United States. According to one biographer, "what emerges from Rodney's work is not only a critique of empire and capitalism in general but a dissection of the domestic political elite that assumed political authority from the colonizers in Africa and the Caribbean as well as an analysis of the process of recolonization. Rodney tried to understand why the movement of independence was also the moment of recolonization."[37] As Rodney interpreted it, neocolonialism in the Caribbean and Africa allowed for the apparent transfer of power to the "natives" while maintaining imperial power relations. This analysis appealed to the IBW, because it sought to understand the failures and weaknesses in America's Black communities that had been exhibited since the Gary Convention, and it offered steps to continue the Black struggle during the second Summer Research Symposium.

In spring 1974, Howard University Press published an American edition of Rodney's *How Europe Underdeveloped Africa*. With Rodney's help, IBW associates subsequently applied development theory to the American situation. Both Rodney's neocolonial analysis and his development theory relied on a Marxist theory of political economy. Systemic inequality, for Rodney, was derived from Western capitalistic exploitation and petit-bourgeoisie manipulation. His use of Marxism appealed to the IBW associates because of its nondogmatic quality and strong reliance on empirical evidence to produce theory. *How Europe* used development theory in its examination of the economics and social facts of African life. Rodney believed a society develops economically "as its members increase jointly their capacity for dealing with the environment" in terms of "understanding the laws of nature (science)" and "devising tools (technology)" to organize society. Development theory identified exploitation by European capitalists as central to understanding the underdevelopment of Africa, Latin America, and Asia. This mode of analysis appealed to the institute as a methodology for comprehending the state of American ghettos.[38]

Rodney's *How Europe* continued his critical focus on Black neocolonialists. Clearly the imperialist system bore a major responsibility for the underdevelopment of Africa, but Rodney also identified as culpable "those who manipulate the system and those who are either agents or unwitting accomplices of the said system." He did not reduce Africans' responsibility for their own underdevelopment, but argued that "not only are there African accomplices inside the imperialist system, but every African has a responsibility to understand the system and work for its overthrow."[39] This perspective aligned with the institute's, and the IBW saw Rodney's presence at the SRS '74 as a necessary first step in the development of a post-Gary conceptual framework that emphasized class as well as race.

Rodney also relied on a nondogmatic Marxism in his analysis of neo-colonialism. The Guyanese scholar based his deft application of Marx on historical evidence, encouraging the institute's associates to enhance their class analysis of the United States. In Rodney's "'Labour' as a Conceptual Framework for Pan-African Studies," which was delivered at the 1970 African Heritage Studies Association, he argued that the category of labor could "provide an entrée to the study of all history," and that "man's work is the basis for other global approaches to human history which present their analysis in terms of class and other social formations." This approach was not an attempt to establish class as the universal radical category of societal reorganization, but rather a method that grew out of his analysis of the empirical evidence. Rodney did not want scholars and activists to view these classes or any other divisions as static, but instead as categories that needed to be understood in "broad historical dimensions." Rodney's flexibility in approaching class analysis stood out against the backdrop of the increasingly doctrinaire Marxism emerging in the 1970s.[40]

Rodney continued this analytical trajectory at the SRS '74. In a lecture titled "Politics of the African Ruling Class," he examined the "present state of affairs on the African continent." He concentrated on the ruling class, which he defined as "not really an African ruling class," but rather as "capitalists who live in London, in Paris, in New York, or in Washington." Africans in this arrangement were the "governing class" who took their orders and cues from abroad. This link was important because, as Rodney pointed out, "the present African ruling class fulfills essentially the same kinds of functions as the old colonial regimes used to fulfill." Moreover, the African ruling class in newly independent nations spent a disproportionate amount of state money on reproducing itself through its bureaucracy. Rodney posited, "as important as the state was in the colonial period as a means by which a certain class expressed itself, it is even more important in the post-colonial period." He observed that the

African ruling elites were the nationalists of the 1950s and 1960s, but that their nationalism was limited to attaining "constitutional independence." The ruling elites often failed to capture control of the national economy or the productive forces in African states, opening them to critiques from the left. Unable to control the economy, but still wanting to retain power, the ruling class would "resort to oppression, to wiping out the left, where the left exists, and to wiping out a large number of people not necessarily because of any ideological difference." Rodney noted that the results of this oppression were one-party states, often based on regionalism and "so-called tribalism." Despite the cataloguing of the "weaknesses and ills" of Africa, Rodney believed the positives "portray[ed] the African people as once more fully engaged in making their own history," and showed that "an indigenous process of contradiction, evolution, revolution and struggle is going on."[41]

In a joint seminar with Strickland at the SRS '74, Rodney further elaborated his class analysis by emphasizing that it was one of many historically generated categories of inclusion and exclusion—a division based on definitions. "In effect, Europe came to define what was developed and what was not, with their own technology and way of life as the standard of excellence, for 'those who can define are the masters' and vice versa." He insisted, later, that scholars could err in their analysis if they fail to "understand that all these categories are historically interchangeable. What is a white man today may not be a white man tomorrow." Rodney's flexible use of class analysis recognized that understanding the values of a given society might require an examination of other categories as well. However, it was the dominance of capitalism that led to his use of class. He acknowledged, "society creates certain values. And I mean, those of us who have had experience as black people shaped by this same society, black men given power in a capitalist society are not less bestial and brutal than white men given power in capitalist society." A given society's values functioned to structure its organization, and these values were historical rather than racial. Rodney concluded,

I'm saying each [race and class category] [has] a validity of its own. In other words, one is not just purely derivative of the other. There may be at one particular point in history the racial contradiction may have derived from the basic class contradiction. At another point the class contradictions reinforce or react upon the race contradictions and so that what I'm getting away from is a sort of simplistic analysis which takes one of these factors, either one, and ascribes to them the sole or preponderating determining historical influence in a society like this [America].

Rodney's insights helped associates who were struggling to make sense of the significance and contradiction of a growing number of BEOs who campaigned on platforms of racial unity, but had limited ability and desire to transform lives and create opportunities within the Black community. Moreover, he led the IBW associates to further explore race and class implications in the United States.[42]

Rodney's presence at the SRS '74 was important for the IBW associates because it enhanced their analysis of political economy and provided another example of a committed Black intellectual. Rodney displayed "tremendous intellectual discipline" during the SRS '74, and his analysis of political economy depended on "a mastery of—but not slavery to—dialectical materialism." Moreover, Rodney's attendance at the symposium helped the senior associates "to crystallize much of our thinking about the role of black intellectuals in our own society, and the role that IBW might play in that development." The IBW associates further developed their class analysis, but they still believed that any investigation of the American situation must include a strong racial analysis. In the joint SRS session with Rodney, Strickland argued that class cleavages in America were resolved because of racism. He and Rodney constantly debated race and class theories of the American social system, but their conversations were based on mutual respect.[43]

The SRS '74 serves as another example of the IBW's collective scholarship. Associates used Rodney's class analysis to further their understanding of a racialized political economy. This flexible perspective explained continued racial subjugation and a rising Black middle class that reinforced the American dream. Despite some minor differences on race and class analysis, the various positions presented during the six-week symposium did not contain the hostility that had begun to creep into the movement. The IBW concluded that the SRS '74 was a success. The IBW associates' summer experience with Rodney led them to establish a program through which they held conversations with leading Black intellectuals to expand their understanding of a racialized political economy.

The Roundtable Discussions

Following the SRS '74, the IBW again reassessed its "mission and objectives in light of the work that had been done during the Symposium."[44] During a staff retreat in Pennsylvania, the executive board, which now included Patricia Daly and Howard Dodson as well as Harding, Hill, and Strickland, decided to conduct "roundtable" discussions centered around the debate over "race vs. class" analysis and "nationalism vs. socialism." This "Great Debate" dominated the Black activist and intellectual landscape from 1973 to 1976.[45] It was in this context that the IBW associates, as leaders of intellectual work during Black Power, planned interviews with "black students, black politicians, black ex-prisoners etc. in order to get an all-sided view of black America." Through these interviews, the IBW tried to carve out a synthetic path in the highly contested and combustible ideological debate.[46] The IBW's goal for the roundtables was "to clarify for ourselves and for the Black struggle the relationships between these diverse tendencies and the role that they will play in shaping the next stage of struggle."[47]

Beginning in the fall of 1975, the IBW transformed its free *Monthly Report* into a subscription-based journal, the *Black World View*.[48] Because of the financial difficulties plaguing it, the institute mailed only a few issues of the monthly newsletter after the symposium. The shift from a newsletter to a journal allowed the IBW to build on the SRS '74 and to highlight a growing number of progressive Black intellectuals' ideas. Although it included essays from feminist scholar Toni Cade Bambara, historians Robert Harris Jr. and Manning Marable, economist Robert S. Browne, and educational theorist Barbara Sizemore, the cornerstones of the *Black World View* were its interviews with James Boggs and Rodney. These "roundtables," according to executive board member Howard Dodson, helped the IBW "to sharpen our own analysis of this problem [the race versus class debate]."[49]

On April 30 and May 1, 1975, IBW senior associates Harding, Hill, Strickland, and Dodson held in-depth conversations with Rodney. In the eight months since the SRS '74 concluded, Rodney's professional life had fallen into turmoil. In early 1974, Rodney had received a position as professor and chair of history at the University of Guyana. Although excited by the prospect of returning to his home country, Rodney recognized that he would face difficulties as a result of his analysis of neocolonialism, which accurately described the Forbes Burnham regime and his People's National Congress (PNC). Burnham, a former Marxist, defeated former colleague Cheddi Jagan of the People's Progressive Party (PPP) in the 1960s by manipulating racial fears in the diverse nation—approximately forty percent of the population was of East Indian descent, thirty percent African, fifteen percent mixed, and the remaining fifteen percent divided between Amerindians, Chinese, and Europeans. Burnham broke from the PPP, which he had helped to found with fellow Marxist Jagan in 1950, and mobilized African support to win a majority of the newly elected government. Burnham recognized the Cold War political landscape, and declared he was not a leftist radical like Jagan. In Cold War politics, Burnham's anticommunism and racially polarizing position guaranteed American support for his party. Once elected, Burnham passed the repressive "National Security Act," giving the police the ability to search and arrest anyone at will.[50]

Observers viewed Rodney's appointment to the University of Guyana as a sign that Burnham was open to progressive change. The IBW associates described it as a "clear victory for Walter and his supporters, a vindication of his vision." Rodney planned to continue his activism, organizing the working classes in Guyana when he returned home. However, just before the fall 1974 academic semester began, the university, caving to pressure from the Burnham-led government, canceled Rodney's appointment. Despite losing his faculty position, Rodney decided to stay in Guyana so that he could continue organizing the Marxist Working People's Alliance (WPA) to challenge the autocratic rule of Burnham's PNC. Rodney often returned to the United States as a lecturer and teacher to financially support his family. In the spring of 1975, Rodney met with IBW associates at the University of Massachusetts—Amherst, where Strickland had recently accepted a faculty position. The conversation consisted of three topics: Rodney's personal educational development, the race versus class debate, and intellectual responsibility.[51]

During this roundtable discussion, Rodney recounted his educational and intellectual experiences for IBW associates. Growing up during the organizational height of the PPP—the first mass and multiracial party in the West Indies and an openly Marxist political party—influenced Rodney. According to him, Guyana during the 1950s "was very significant in my life, because what it did for me was to raise in my own mind a conviction about the seriousness and potentiality of our own people." Observing the PPP's mass organizing introduced Rodney to the class question. During his time at the University of the West Indies in Jamaica (which coincided with the country's quest for independence), Rodney witnessed the nationalism inside and outside the classroom that spurred the movement. These events motivated him to explore African history more thoroughly. As a result, Rodney enrolled in graduate school in London, where he extensively studied Marxism under the tutelage of C.L.R. James and his wife Selma. These two intellectuals exemplified "the power of Marxist thought." Finally, Rodney's time teaching in Tanzania and the Caribbean, along with "grounding" with locals, solidified his commitment to Marxist and neocolonial analysis.[52]

The ideological debate between Black Nationalists and Marxists that had begun to rip the Black Power movement apart in the 1970s discouraged Rodney. He attempted to rationalize both sides of the argument. In his mind, the Sixth Pan-African Conference was the key moment in heightening the contentious debate between advocates of race and class analysis, for African revolutionaries had dismissed racial consciousness and ideology as irrelevant to Pan-African liberation. Rodney reminded the IBW associates that the "historical conditions" differed across the diaspora: "I think we must beware of being trapped into generalizations that are supposed to be valid for the whole of the Pan-African world . . . it does not help to generalize." The African revolutionaries used their experiences to trump the Black American delegation's desire to incorporate race as a category of analysis. As the debate raged in the United States, many former Black Nationalists became "instant Marxists," a derogatory term denoting the sudden shift in ideological perspective. Rodney encouraged "more and more study," discipline, and humility from all activists. Moreover, he assessed the dogmatic style used by both sides in the debate, which resulted in a failure to find common ground. "The style of the debate" had such intensity that it was "near violence almost, where some people seem to line up on one side or another, I feel that the form has sometimes assumed more importance than the substance." The two positions, he continued, are "unnecessarily antagonistic." Although the Guyanese scholar believed "it was within the context of capitalism that racism developed," he reminded the IBW that "race and class are not absolutes," but instead concepts that arose historically. Rodney asserted that both nationalists and Marxists needed to do "much more work to examine what may be the uniqueness of the American situation." This analysis was the responsibility of intellectuals, and Black communities would re-inforce it with their support.[53] In addition, Rodney wanted scholars, like IBW associates, to become "guerrilla intellectuals." The major responsi-bility of intellectuals, according to Rodney, was to "struggle over ideas." He opposed the "artificial distinction between mental and menial labor." Rodney reaffirmed the IBW's purpose: "I still feel that the people that one is attempting firstly to influence are black people, young black minds above all else."[54]

The roundtable discussion with Rodney, as well as his participation during the SRS '74, demonstrated the IBW's collective approach to analy-sis. This approach privileged analyses of social, economic, cultural, and political structures over a predisposed radical ideology. As a result of their emphasis on a pragmatic and empirically based analysis, the IBW associ-ates continued to posit that race in the United States formed the essential category of analysis. However, their interactions with Rodney provided direction through the quagmire that was the race versus class debate. In their next roundtable discussion, the IBW planned to meet with James and Grace Lee Boggs, veteran activist-intellectuals who had employed the lenses of race and class in their analytical work on America.

Amid the explosive mid-1970s debates over race versus class, the IBW's choice to talk to James and Grace Lee Boggs was a logical one, especially considering the Boggses' influence on associates' analysis. The Boggses' paths toward radicalism began before they met. Grace Lee, a Chinese-American, became involved in radical organizing after she completed her dissertation at Bryn Mawr College in 1940 and moved to Chicago. There she joined the Workers Party (WP), a Trotskyite group, which or-ganized Black tenants on the city's south side. Later, she joined a smaller group of Marxist intellectuals led by Raya Dunayevskaya, a Russian-born, self-taught Marxist, and C.L.R. James. The group took its name from the pseudonyms used by Dunayevskaya and James—F. Forest and J. R. Johnson. The Johnson-Forest Tendency broke with the WP because the James-led group theorized that Stalin's Soviet Union was state capitalism instead of a bureaucratic collective or a workers' state.[55] James and Du-nayevskaya's "humanist approach," as opposed to rigid economic deter-minism, attracted Lee to the group. The Johnsonites moved to Detroit, renaming themselves the Committees of Correspondence (later just Correspondence), and arguing that marginalized groups such as Blacks, youth, women, and workers comprised the new revolutionary forces.

Once in Detroit, James Boggs joined James and Lee in the small radical organization.[56]

James Boggs was an organic intellectual in the truest sense of the term. He was born in Black Belt Alabama in the aftermath of World War I and was one of the millions of Blacks who left the South in search of new opportunities on the eve of the Second World War. Riding the rails north and then across the Midwest, Boggs performed odd jobs before he arrived in Detroit. In 1940, with increased job opportunities for Blacks as a result of World War II, he found work at the Chrysler plant. Steady employment sharpened Boggs's understanding of racial and labor politics. He became an activist in a nearly all-White United Auto Workers (UAW) local union. In the union, he organized on two fronts: against discrimination inside the union, and on behalf of labor against management. As Cold War politics cracked down on the radicalism inside industrial unionism, Boggs heard James's speech, "The Revolutionary Answer to the Negro Problem." The Trinidadian-born James had spent much of his time in the United States from 1938 to 1953 traveling to Black communities across the Midwest and Upper South, observing Black communities and organizing workers. In this speech, James underscored Black people's agency in transforming their lives, and he broke with Marxist orthodoxy by arguing that an independent Black political movement could be the catalyst for revitalizing an activist proletariat. Boggs admired the argument, and after learning that James was creating an organization in Detroit, he joined Correspondence. Boggs and Lee married in 1953, forming a personal and political partnership that lasted until his death in 1993.[57]

By 1963, the Boggses were leading organizers in Detroit, heading up economic boycotts and protesting police brutality. They also helped organize the Northern Grassroots Leadership Conference, where Malcolm X delivered his "Message to the Grassroots" speech, arguably his most influential. The same year, James Boggs wrote a series of essays that called for a new set of ideas. He believed that both the racial and class characteristics of America's social structure must be understood. Boggs argued that liberals failed by not seeing Blacks' "social, economic, and world role in relation to the accumulation of capital." Furthermore, Marxists failed to comprehend or recognize the racism of the White working class. In 1963, three years before Stokely Carmichael's proclamation of the slogan in Greenwood, Mississippi, Boggs offered Black political power as a solution to the problems faced by Black communities.[58]

Boggs's theories appeared in *American Revolution: Pages From a Negro Worker's Notebook* (1963) and *Racism and Class Struggle: Further Pages From a Black Worker's Notebook* (1970). During the reorganization of the IBW in 1970–71, Strickland based his analysis on Boggs's books, leading a seminar on the topic during the SRS '71 called "The Evolution of Revolution: James Boggs and American Social Analysis."[59] Strickland recalled, "I am also convinced that racism is much more than ideology, prejudice, and discrimination. The only person I had met at the time who was dealing with the concept of racism and was dealing with it at a much profound level than anyone else was Boggs."[60] Furthermore, Strickland continued, "it was Jimmy who did the most important work on racism. . . . Boggs's essay 'Uprooting Racism and Racists,' . . . is still the best-condensed critique and explanation of racism that has ever been written in my judgment." The Boggses' theoretical framework was consistently employed during the IBW's early years, and associates used the roundtable discussions with them to strengthen the organization's analysis.[61]

Grace Lee Boggs's analysis of education was also key to the IBW's educational emphasis in the mid-1970s. Her essay, "Education: The Great Obsession," in the IBW's *Education and Black Struggle* argued for a redefinition of the purpose of education based on a philosophy of history, clearly defined goals, and community responsiveness.[62] In addition, Lee Boggs participated in the IBW's 1976 conference "Quality Education and the Black Community."[63] At the conference she argued, "education in the United States can no longer be for the purpose of earning or for achieving the 'good life' or for fitting people into—our present industrial society. Education must now be for the purpose of governing, that is, for the purpose of changing society and for changing ourselves simultaneously."[64] Harding fondly remembered the effect of the Boggses' "disciplined grounding in Marxist thought." Harding noted that the couple insisted "that we must develop an American revolutionary ideology that will be based far more on our unique national experience of struggle than on anything that has come before us."[65] The approaching bicentennial of the American Revolution set the stage for the IBW's roundtable discussions with the Boggses.

Conversations with the radical couple occurred in June 1975 and included associates Bennett, Harding, Hill, and Strickland. The institute followed Lee Boggs's advice—"it is impossible for the intellectual to develop except in a continuing dialogue with the community"—by making the roundtable a public forum. Lee Boggs suggested new approaches to the race and class question based on temporal relationships rather than on "relationships between those who are on top and those who are on bottom." She recalled how scholars had valorized Blackness, but "didn't look at the traps" that separated many inside the Black communities. The Boggses continued to emphasize the duality of race and class. Although the roundtable discussion was too long and therefore too expensive for publication, the IBW published *Questions of the American Revolution: Conversation with James Boggs*, which summarized Boggs's life and revolutionary theories.[66]

The IBW described the interview with the Boggses as "must reading for anyone who is seriously attempting to learn from what has happened in America over the past forty years in order to prepare for the next stage of struggle."[67] James Boggs argued that poverty relief and welfare functioned as pacification programs. Instead, he insisted that "in order to make a revolution in the United States, we have to transform people's bourgeois thoughts. . . . What most blacks really mean when they talk about revolution is that they want what 'the Man' has; but the irony of it all is that 'the Man' has all these material goods due to the fact that blacks are in their current predicament." Boggs maintained that any successful revolution must attack culture and the state simultaneously. He continued by talking about the weaknesses of Pan-Africanism and Black Nationalism. In his view, Pan-Africanism functioned to oppose capitalist exploitation outside the United States, whereas the Black Freedom Struggle in America needed to "fight capitalism itself." He suggested that Pan-Africanism was for Africans. Boggs also believed there was a need "to go beyond black nationalism, for we could have black nationalism and still not make a revolution—that is the reorganization of the whole society." Boggs insisted that "a revolutionary vanguard party" and its vision of the future would prove the key to any societal transformation.[68]

Although Boggs criticized Marxists for failing to update Marx's analysis, he firmly believed that racism was an effect of capitalism. Boggs wanted people to understand the interconnectedness of race and class.

Racism and capitalism complement each other—just as imperialism and capitalism complement each other. In other words, racism is a tentacle of capitalism for exploiting people inside the United States—just as imperialism is a tentacle of capitalism for exploiting people outside the United States. And blacks (although they don't want to hear this) benefit from imperialism—just as whites benefit from imperialism. The difference, though, is that whites benefit from imperialism and racism.

The key for Boggs, as for Rodney, was to break with dogmatic Marxism. He asserted that Marxism was "a method of thought," not "truth for all time." Boggs's analysis looked to forge a path in the sectarian race versus class debate of the 1970s. Moreover, Boggs extended the radical tradition in his statements on sexism.[69]

The IBW's incomplete analysis of gender and its role in the Black struggle constituted a profound weakness that was never completely addressed. Boggs challenged the IBW and its readers to consider the role of gender and how this weakness undermines the freedom struggle. Boggs maintained that "long before there were classes there was the woman's question." Furthermore, he articulated a path along which to push feminists, nationalists, and Marxists toward a more progressive social analysis. Women needed to challenge male chauvinism and "carry the struggle against the system itself." Many women, according to Boggs, had narrowly focused on "being against men," instead of aligning against the system. Boggs also observed that sexism was a "tentacle of capitalism." He argued that this premise should be the basis of unity between Black and White women, because "*all* women are oppressed in this society—no matter what color they are." Boggs maintained that Black Nationalism, and all nationalisms, were "reactionary on the woman's question." They did not necessarily grapple with the issues, instead resorting to gut reactions in a way that hindered them. "Black nationalists contend that the white man castrated them, so black women have to take a back seat in order to compensate for the degradation to which black men have been subjected—as if *two* wrongs could ever make a right." Boggs wondered how a revolution is to be made if half the population is "un-political."[70] Due to Boggs's analysis on sexism and an increasing number of female associates, including Toni Cade Bambara, Barbara Sizemore, Pat Daly, and Sylvia Wynter, the IBW took the issue to heart. The institute hosted a conference, "Role Alternatives for Black Women: Where to from Here in the Black Freedom Struggle," in 1977. This conference did not completely rectify the marginalization of gender in the IBW's analysis, but it started to address a profound weakness.[71]

Boggs concluded his interview by outlining future directions for the movement, especially the need for intense study of racial and economic issues and possible solutions. He called for "disciplined scientific thinking and disciplined political organization." This meant, for the political theorist, the need to move beyond Black electoral politics. Black organizations needed to address not only what they opposed, but also what they supported. In essence, Boggs suggested that those Black organizations consumed by the race versus class debate needed to go through the process of reorganization, because they had retreated to sectarianism. Political scientist Cedric Johnson described this process: "the mid-seventies turn to ideological education favored a mode of politics that inhibited principled political debate and issue-driven, temporal collaboration. Instead of galvanizing public sentiment around discrete policy matters or programmatic efforts capable of generating identifiable gains, Marxists and cultural nationalist activist intellectuals became mired in esoteric debates that rarely had anything to do with the issues of immediate concern to the broader black citizenry."[72] The IBW's publication of the Boggses' interview exemplified how it avoided the land mine that was the race-class debate. Moreover, the roundtables reaffirmed the IBW's commitment to synthetic analyses that could generate issue-oriented consensus.[73]

The product of the IBW's interactions with Rodney and the Boggses was the further development of the organization's analytical perspectives. Building on the insights gained at the SRS '74 and the roundtable discussions, the IBW began in the mid-seventies to promote a racialized political economy as a synthetic perspective amid the race versus class debate. The IBW's analysis of a racialized political economy critiqued capitalism. However, it also recognized that economic production was not the only organizing principle of society, and that race and racial ideology were modes of inclusion and exclusion that attached themselves to the economic structure. American history is replete with examples of White workers choosing their racial identity over class identity, and in the seventies, associates witnessed members of the Black middle class choosing their class identity over racial identity.[74] In both cases, understanding how the racialized political economy operated proved essential. Rodney and the Boggses offered a nuanced analysis in their ways of dealing with and examining the variables of race and class. The IBW's decision to publish these interviews and essays signaled its adoption of a nuanced Black radicalism that stood in contrast to the increasingly sectarian debates plaguing other Black activist organizations in the mid-seventies.

For example, the IBW published a "Special Report" in July 1975 that demonstrated its evolving analytical perspective. The lead essay, "America in Crisis," emphasized economic conditions, describing the decline in production, unemployment, national debt, and bankruptcies. Despite the economic emphasis, the IBW noted, "The effects of this general crisis, of course, bear down with special intensity on the backs of Black people. We have been made to absorb more of the devastation around us than any other sector of the American population. . . . We will continue to be among its chief victims." Given the economic crises, the IBW concluded that the "fundamental task of all politics in this country is the reconstruction of American political economy through the role of the State." The IBW's publications after 1975 employed an analysis of a racialized political economy. In many ways, the institute's analytical development logically follows from its attention to structural racism during the Gary Convention. In the context of the Great Debate between Black Nationalists and Marxists, the IBW's analysis functioned to mediate the split in the movement.[75]

Conclusion

As an activist think tank, the IBW promoted its ideas to Black activists, scholars, and communities. The institute used a variety of publication outlets aimed at a broad audience: academics read and used the "Black Papers" in their classes and research, and Black people and communities found that the newspaper column "Black World View" and the *Monthly Report* provided instant analysis of issues relevant to them. These publications allowed the IBW's analyses of Black political, social, artistic, and economic conditions to reach different levels of the Black community. Moreover, the colonized world was a subject of the IBW's columns, and its commentaries on Africa, Vietnam, and the Caribbean regularly appeared in Black newspapers nationwide. The IBW's analyses strengthened relationships between intellectuals and organizations across the diaspora. Finally, the SRS '74 and the roundtable discussions with Rodney and the Boggses helped the IBW carve a path through the minefield that was the race versus class debate of the mid-1970s.

The publications, the SRS '74, and the roundtable discussions symbolized the IBW's commitment to collective scholarship. The publications were products of the entire IBW staff; all members had the opportunity to comment on them, and the essays often bore the organization's imprint. According to Harding, the "varieties of opinion" meant that the IBW shied "away from ready made labels."[76] Moreover, collective scholarship allowed the IBW to avoid the destabilization caused by ideological tensions in the movement. The IBW, unlike the African Liberation Day protests, survived the "Great Debate." As Harding recalled,

> One thing that was important to us was to encourage the concept of collective scholarship and work—a collectivity of scholarship that was not simply in the hands of traditional scholars, even Black ones. We felt that we should take the intellectual tasks we had to work on into the midst of the people who were not only scholars, but also artists, organizers, and activists. The Black experience was so broad and so varied and so moving that only such a wide gathering of experience could help clarify it.[77]

The use of and emphasis on collective scholarship prevented the IBW from becoming a dogmatic organization that dictated ideology.

The IBW's belief in collective scholarship also demonstrated its commitment to synthetic, yet radical analysis over dogmatic or doctrinaire ideology. Diverse ideologies were adopted and adapted by IBW associates. The institute's association with and study of Black intellectuals recognized the limits of Marxism. Consequently, the organization's pragmatic nationalism allowed it to shift its analytical perspective toward a racialized political economy, a position that served as a middle ground in the increasingly hostile race versus class debate. Although the IBW survived the Great Debate of the mid-seventies, the institute's embrace of a racialized political economy along with its earlier activities made it increasingly difficult for the organization to survive. The institute's radical synthetic analysis attracted local and national police forces determined to "investigate" the organization, and it also made already limited funding scarce. In fact, the IBW's increasing radicalism marked the beginning of the end for the organization.

5

"The Tapes Were the Heart of the Matter"

The IBW's Infiltration and Decline

On the evening of March 11, 1975, there was a break-in at the IBW office. The intruder(s) came in through the back door of the white frame house at 87 Chestnut Street, using bolt cutters to make a hole in the heavy-gauge wire mesh that served as the IBW's mediocre security. The unknown subject(s) prowled through the offices, searching through administrative files, breaking into desks, and stealing "highly sensitive" audiotapes of meetings. The break-in resulted in the loss of seven thousand dollars worth of office equipment—mostly typewriters and tape recorders—as well as over one hundred copies of the March 1975 *Monthly Report*. Even though the offices were located on the edge of Vine City, a high-crime area, the robbery seemed strange. The typewriters and tape recorders could be resold through the underground market of stolen goods, but the files and audiotapes had no intrinsic monetary value. The IBW associates conducted their own investigation, recognizing the improbability of a thriving underground market for office equipment and the impossibility of a market for organizational files and tapes. Associates asserted that "the fact that certain tapes and *Monthly Report*[s] were taken suggests that the burglary was more than theft for financial gain. . . . There are suggestions of 'dirty' tricks similar to Watergate." The robbery crippled an already financially strapped IBW. Most associates believed that the theft of typewriters and tape recorders was a cover-up for a political break-in or "black bag job." Vincent Harding recalled that despite the stolen office equipment, "the [stolen] tapes were the heart of the matter," because they held discussions of future IBW activities and important staff meetings.

This break-in was the first of several over the next three months. The IBW associates and friends wanted to find out who was burglarizing their offices and why it was happening. The break-ins and the harassment of staff members in 1974 and 1975 represented the apex of domestic surveillance on the IBW. Moreover, the crimes suggest that the IBW's synthetic analyses and discussions with leading radical Black intellectuals had raised the ire of conservative forces as well as local, state, and federal police agencies.[1]

The IBW's radical intellectual work throughout its history—Black Studies, a Black political agenda, and analysis of the racialized political economy—signaled an evolving progressive analysis, but these activities resulted in increased scrutiny by police forces inside and outside Atlanta. This radicalism, existing amid an increasingly conservative political culture and a disastrous economy, caused the IBW's fragile financial situation to deteriorate. Harassment and dwindling funds reduced the institute's influence on the Black intellectual, political, and social landscape. Survival for the IBW meant withstanding a financial crisis and domestic surveillance.

Stagflation, Domestic Surveillance, and Declining Support for Black Activism

For nearly five years, the IBW stood on the verge of closing its doors, as the organization's budgets never matched its aspirations. The stagflation of the seventies along with the revelations of governmental malfeasance pushed the IBW closer to its end. At the beginning of Nixon's administration in 1968, inflation was at six percent, nearly five percentage points higher than in 1960. The sources of inflation were long-term structural issues in the American economy, including the rise of multinational corporations and their use of capital mobility, government spending in Vietnam, and the lack of corporate reinvestment in American factories. By 1971, America had its first trade deficit since 1893. In 1972, America witnessed soaring food prices. Following Nixon's reelection that year, twenty-five percent of consumers participated in a boycott of meat because of rising prices. Oil was the final piece of the inflation puzzle. Arab nations forming the Organization of Petroleum Exporting Countries (OPEC) raised the cost of crude oil three hundred percent between the fall of 1974 and January 1975. Inflation crippled citizens' purchasing power, making a 1967 dollar worth only 68 cents in 1974.[2]

Unemployment further increased economic anxieties. Corporations' rising fuel costs and reliance on capital mobility led to increased layoffs for blue-collar workers. In addition, unemployment for college graduates reached an all-time high in the early seventies. By 1974, the national unemployment rate had reached 7.2 percent, the highest since the Great Depression. For the Black community, the economic situation was more severe, as nearly forty-two percent were classified as poor or near poor. The American public grew increasingly disenchanted with its economic future. The revelations of governmental crimes and cover-ups only added to the pessimism.[3]

Given the economic recession and a growing political conservatism fueled in part by law-and-order campaigns that targeted Black and radical activists, Black activist organizations of all ideological perspectives suffered declining financial support. Sociologists J. Craig Jenkins and Craig M. Eckert noted that foundation support for Black activism peaked in 1972–73, and when foundations continued their support in the mid-1970s, most went to moderate organizations like the NAACP. Still, by 1980, foundation grants had declined by sixty-two percent.[4] The conservative political environment also meant that governmental support for Black activism waned. For example, financial and political support slowly diminished for former CORE leader Floyd McKissic's Soul City, a plan for a Black-owned town in North Carolina that was initially backed by President Nixon. By the 1976 Republican presidential primary that pitted Ronald Reagan against Gerald Ford, who took office after Nixon's resignation, Soul City was toxic. According to Reagan, the town, which had received millions of dollars in federal grants, signified a "federal giveaway." The inability of even moderate organizations like the NAACP as well as Republican-backed Black capitalist plans to maintain funding levels indicates just how scarce financial support for the IBW's pragmatic nationalism was in the mid-1970s.[5]

When the IBW associates connected the burglary of their offices with the "dirty tricks" of the Watergate scandal, such an assertion was not merely hyperbole. The IBW associates had consistently described American corruption, observed with their keen political and analytical insight. Their talk of corruption and dirty tricks also reflected the realization by a growing number of Black activists that they were under regular surveillance. The events of the 1970s exposed to the nation for the first time the scope and magnitude of the United States government's efforts to spy on its citizens.

In March 1971, details of the FBI's Counterintelligence Program (COINTELPRO) came to the public's attention. The "Citizens Committee to Investigate the FBI" stole files from an FBI office in Media, Pennsylvania. These files revealed the extensive surveillance program aimed at Black and radical activists as well as at White hate organizations like the United Klan of America. In terms of scope and focus, more than ninety-nine percent of the surveillance files dealt with radical or leftist organizations.[6] Originally, FBI director J. Edgar Hoover initiated COINTELPRO in the 1950s to undermine the Communist Party—USA (CPUSA). Using Cold War logic, government officials accepted this program.

The growth of the Black Freedom Struggle in the 1950s provided additional targets of scrutiny for Hoover's pet project. In the early 1960s, the FBI wiretapped Martin Luther King Jr.'s phones, ostensibly to explore his connections to communists. Furthermore, the FBI targeted King for surveillance in the hope of acquiring damaging information that would sully his public reputation or could be used to blackmail him. Hoover feared King's potential as a "messiah" who could unify the Black movement.[7] The progression of the Black Power movement also meant that activists like Stokely Carmichael and organizations such as the Black Panther Party came under extensive FBI investigation and surveillance. The FBI often used extralegal means in its investigations of Black organizations and individuals, including infiltration, psychological warfare, harassment through the legal system, and violence. The Federal Bureau of Investigation's COINTELPRO destabilized Black organizations and led to the death and incarceration of numerous Black activists. Historian Manning Marable notes that by July 1969, the Black Panthers had been targeted 233 times under COINTELPRO, and in that year alone 27 Panthers were killed and over 70 were arrested. Still, the final tabulation of radical activists of all races illegally imprisoned or killed may never be fully known.[8]

The revelations about COINTELPRO primarily concerned activists, but those concerning the Pentagon Papers and Watergate engulfed the entire nation. In June 1971, the *New York Times* began to publish a Department of Defense classified report on Vietnam, known informally as the Pentagon Papers. Daniel Ellsberg, a military analyst, leaked the report to the *Times*, and it showed that the government, including the president, misled the public about activities in Vietnam. The Nixon administration established a White House Investigations Unit, informally known as "the plumbers" because it was designed to stop leaks. The unit, led by G. Gordon Liddy and E. Howard Hunt, coordinated a break-in of Ellsberg's psychiatrist, Lewis Fielding's, office seeking information to damage the whistle-blower's reputation. It was not until Ellsberg's trial in 1973 that the public learned of this break-in. The charges of treason were dismissed because of governmental misconduct. The Pentagon Papers and the burglary of the psychiatrist's office set the stage for Watergate.[9]

Nine months after the break-in at Fielding's office, President Richard Nixon used the "plumbers" to spy on the Democratic National Committee headquarters at the Watergate Hotel. Nixon's use of illegal surveillance signaled his uncontrolled personal desire for reelection, but it also revealed the extensive nature of domestic spying on Americans of all walks of life. The Senate's investigation following Watergate revealed damning evidence of espionage to a stunned nation. When Nixon finally resigned ahead of the impending impeachment, America had a full view of the depths of illegal government surveillance. These revelations simply confirmed the suspicions of many Black activists.[10]

Although COINTELPRO officially ended in 1971, the FBI continued to monitor Black and radical organizations, including the IBW, throughout the decade. The FBI justified the continuing surveillance by asserting that the organization or person in question could become a potential danger to the United States. Through its informants, the FBI became aware of the IBW's conflict with the King Center. In addition, it kept tabs on the IBW as they organized lectures for "radicals" such as Stokely Carmichael, Shirley Graham Du Bois, and Robert Hill. Federal use of domestic surveillance encouraged local police agencies to develop similar investigative units, which were often federally funded. By 1973, the Atlanta Police Department had received at least $4 million in federal anticrime funds that were used against radical organizations.[11] In the mid-1970s, intelligence organizations had shifted from passive investigative techniques, such as the use of informants' reports, to aggressive techniques that included "black bag" jobs, or illegal break-ins. Negative public opinions about governmental counterintelligence activities made the shift in policy possible only if the FBI or another government agency could connect the IBW to potentially more dangerous radical organizations. Consequently, the FBI highlighted the IBW's weak and unverified connections to the Symbionese Liberation

Army (SLA) and the Venceremos Brigade to justify increased intelligence actions that further undermined the IBW's effectiveness and threatened its already limited financial backing.[12]

Spy at the *Atlanta Voice*

Nine months before the 1975 IBW break-ins, a web of police controversy snared the organization. The institute's attention to neocolonialism as well as its search for new meaning and direction in the Black Freedom Struggle put it in the crosshairs for external co-optation by the FBI and the Atlanta Police Department, straining the organization's limited finances. The sensational Symbionese Liberation Army (SLA) saga proved to be the catalyst for harassment of the IBW and became the justification for additional surveillance.

On February 4, 1974, the SLA kidnapped Patricia Hearst, the granddaughter of newspaper mogul William Randolph Hearst. The SLA, a splinter group of California New Left student politics, was part of growing prison radicalism. It was founded in a Berkeley commune by escaped convict Donald DeFreeze and White Bay area radicals who thought revolutionary leadership would emerge from prisoners. In response to the economic stagflation gripping the nation, the SLA kidnapped Patty Hearst, demanding a food distribution program for the Bay Area poor that would be financed by her wealthy grandfather in exchange for her release. By April 1974, Hearst and DeFreeze, who called himself Cinque M'tume, had become lovers. On May 17, 1974, the Los Angeles Police Department surrounded DeFreeze's east Los Angeles hideout and attacked. The police shot tear gas and more than five thousand rounds of ammunition into the house, killing DeFreeze and five other SLA members. After DeFreeze's death, there was a nationwide search for Hearst. She was eventually arrested in September 1975 in San Francisco. Hearst's defense counsel claimed that Stockholm syndrome was the reason she joined the SLA. Hearst served twenty-two months in prison for armed robbery, receiving a commuted sentence from President Carter in 1976 and a full pardon from President Clinton in 2001.[13]

The SLA and other extremist groups like the Weathermen fed a growing conservative backlash against all types of protest activities by Black and White activists. Politicians such as Richard Nixon and Ronald Reagan capitalized on this fermenting discontent to win electoral offices, using law-and-order rhetoric as a central campaign platform. This backlash also legitimized tremendous expansion of police forces and law enforcement funding. It also often gave officers free reign to eliminate radical people and organizations, despite the official end to COINTELPRO campaigns. Beginning in 1971, the Atlanta Police Department capitalized on the law-and-order rhetoric by using federal money to establish the Inspectional Services Bureau, which included a vice squad and an intelligence division under Police Chief John Inman's leadership. As vice mayor and as mayor, Jackson tried to control the renegade police culture. However, Inman was emboldened by a national mandate for "law and order," and attacked radical elements in Atlanta like the IBW and a local Black Panther Party chapter.[14]

Inman secretly began to investigate the progressive Black newspaper, the *Atlanta Voice*, in early 1974, believing it was involved in nefarious radical activities. In May 1974, the *Voice* uncovered the police operative in their offices and made it the newspaper's top story. Mayor Jackson requested the Fulton County attorney general investigate the legality of the operation, asking if the "extraordinary action" of using undercover Black policewoman Marion Lee was necessary or legal. The *Voice* reported that the police, under Inman's orders, planted Lee to locate the source for several stories the newspaper ran about the illegal surveillance of Black politicians over the previous two years. Inman approved Lee's assignment and defended the surveillance, but he did not explain why the espionage was necessary. Nevertheless, Jackson vowed, "Some heads are going to roll."[15]

On May 18, 1974, the *Atlanta Constitution* added to the controversy with a sensational front-page article that supplied the rationale behind the spying. The story reported that the Atlanta Police Department's Intelligence Division had placed Officer Lee at the *Voice* apparently as a follow-up to an earlier FBI investigation into "hard-core terrorists" in Atlanta. The FBI believed there was an SLA chapter thriving in the city. The article described the FBI's intelligence-gathering technique, through which agents attempted to lure into the open suspected Southern members of the SLA thought to be hiding in Atlanta and New Orleans. To carry out this goal, shortly after Hearst's kidnapping, the FBI placed false advertisements in the *Voice* and the *New Orleans Picayune* reading, "PAT IS OKAY." The FBI ploy got no response. However, when an article analyzing the SLA's tactics appeared weeks later in the *Voice*, it attracted the FBI and the Atlanta Police Department's attention. The Atlanta Police Department's Intelligence

Division planted Lee at the *Voice* hoping to gain information about the authors of the article and to sniff out extremist organizations.[16]

Melanie Finney and Adolph Reed Jr. wrote the front-page article on the SLA for the *Voice*. In the article, they sought to "deal with the basis, the conditions which gave rise to the ideas and the actions and the extent to which these actions can alter the conditions." The commentary called the SLA murder of Marcus Foster, the Black superintendent of Oakland, California, schools, "a serious tactical error," because it confused the Black community, on whose behalf the SLA acted. However, Finney and Reed suggested that the kidnapping of Hearst and the resulting media response lent "credibility to terrorism as a tactic." The column further argued that poverty and a desperate desire for equality created the context for organizations like the SLA. "The longer poverty and exploitation exists," the authors wrote, radicalism "will be the response of the victims as they rise up to demand the redistribution of wealth in America." Finney and Reed concluded that if the SLA were successful, several thousand Californians would be less hungry. The article did not endorse or condemn the SLA, but rather tried to understand its existence by relating it to the systemic poverty Black communities faced historically and during the recession. However, in the eyes of the FBI, the Atlanta Police Department, and the *Atlanta Constitution*, the authors' failure to condemn the SLA's actions was tantamount to support of the organization. The FBI subsequently conducted background searches on Finney and Reed. Through these checks, they discovered Finney was married to Michael Robert Finney, a well-known member of a Black Nationalist group called the Republic of New Africa. Reed belonged to Students for a Democratic Society (SDS), and he was supposedly "the main force behind a little known but devout terrorist organization."[17]

The *Constitution* article also indicated that the FBI believed Atlanta was ripe for terrorist activity. The FBI pointed to earlier articles in the *Voice*, especially Harding's "Watergate and the Restoration of Black Struggle," which supposedly argued that New Orleans rooftop sniper Mark Essex was an example of Black pride. Although the *Constitution* attributed "Watergate and the Restoration of Black Struggle" to Harding, Strickland wrote the controversial essay. Furthermore, the *Constitution's* reference to Essex was taken out of context. Strickland's essay addressed several problems, including the rise of a police state, the decline of the Black social movement, and a prescription for continuing the movement. The essay began with a commentary on political surveillance, using the Watergate scandal as a point of departure. It acknowledged that after years of the FBI "watergating" Black people, Whites had become the subjects of surveillance. Watergate shocked the nation, but Strickland explained how the Black Freedom Movement had faced the most intense surveillance. Strickland wrote,

> Political surveillance was not restricted to black leaders like Dr. King. It was aimed at the whole black movement because the American government felt that the black movement was a potential threat to the "American way of life." Fearful of the capacity of our struggle to turn America around, America's white ruling class responded to our peaceful picketing, our non-violent protest, and our legal petitions for our civil rights by establishing a national system of political intelligence to monitor the movement and contain it.

This surveillance had shifted from monitoring to sabotaging the movement. Strickland believed that Watergate and the use of similar tactics functioned to "preserve the façade of democracy."[18]

In response to the rise of the American police state, Strickland urged continual struggle. He saw Black America in the early 1970s as "accepting America as it is," with "the attitude of cynicism replac[ing] the habit of struggle." He asserted that Black America had lost its desire to struggle, and instead delved into sex and drugs as a treatment for continued marginalization. These problems stemmed from the failure of the civil rights movement to develop a theory of analysis. "The movement could not sustain itself on tactics alone, on confrontations and protest marches. The lack of theory and analysis, the evidence of the question of how in the world black people were ever to win their freedom within the existing American political and economic system, the failure to move as a national force with nationally defined goals and objectives to which all black people had been educated, all caused the movement to collapse from within." The IBW provided the systemic analysis needed, but Strickland recognized that the institute's material was not distributed as widely or deeply as possible. He saw this failure of distribution, a product of the IBW's limited finances, as damaging to the movement as a whole. Nonetheless, the IBW distributed its analysis to the extent possible amid a slowing protest movement and tremendous financial constraints.[19]

In the context of a faltering movement, Strickland's essay invoked the urgency and frustration of Essex. A recently court-martialed Navy sailor, Mark Essex had been fueled by the racism he faced in the armed forces and seduced by the violent fringes of the Black Power era when he conducted sniper attacks against New Orleans's Whites. Essex's attacks began with the murder of a New Orleans police officer on New Year's Eve, 1972, and ended in a deadly shoot-out with authorities at the downtown Howard Johnson Hotel. His reign of terror claimed nine lives, including those of five police officers (one Black), and injured over twenty people. The sensational affair and manhunt captured the nation's attention and, for a moment, many believed that the Black Revolution had arrived. In this vein, Strickland posited, Essex "took us back to what it was all about, grappling with our oppressor. . . . In doing so he breathed a little manhood, a little identity, a little purpose back into our souls, even if for a little while." As he tacitly supported the urban guerrilla warfare conducted by Essex, Strickland reiterated the IBW's focus on developing new ideas: "we must develop a new and conscious politics armed with the knowledge that white America will not reform itself and that all its systems dim, flicker and threaten to go out."[20]

Although Strickland contextualized his comments about Essex's violence, his seeming support of guerrilla warfare proved to be a poor editorial decision. Essex's actions were damaging for at least two reasons. First, they resulted in increased repression of all forms of radicalism. Any organization working to transform America into a more just and equitable system already had a difficult time with police intervention. However, Essex and the SLA's actions provided justification for police agencies to shift from investigating radical organizations to actively repressing them, ostensibly to prevent violent outbreaks. This repression breathed new life into COINTELPRO-type activities by providing a plausible justification for surveillance that both conservative and liberal politicians could agree on. There would not be a national counterintelligence program, but the FBI field offices and the local police could defend their aggressive actions against activists as long as they could connect them to violent extremism. Second, Essex's violence, although couched in the militant rhetoric of the era, had no connection to any organizations. Strickland's decision to connect Essex to a larger, but declining, Black movement fed into police and conservatives' misconceptions of a vast Black Power conspiracy. For these reasons, Strickland's essay presented an opportunity for the police and the White press to link the IBW's intellectual work with the violent radicalism of the SLA, Essex, and others, thereby forcing the institute to spend precious time and resources defending itself.

The Atlanta Black community challenged the justification for spying used by police and the *Constitution*, and the IBW defended itself against the false charges of affiliating with the SLA. Mack Jones, chair of the Atlanta University Political Science Department and IBW associate, defended the SLA article's coauthor, Adolph Reed Jr. Jones asserted that the *Constitution's* front-page article continued the newspaper's "practice of covering the black community from the police blotter and unverifiable tips." He further noted the newspaper's shoddy police work in identifying Reed, who was a doctoral candidate at Atlanta University "with an almost perfect record," whose telephone number was listed in the phone book, and who could be "found almost any day in the departmental Reading Room." Jones explained how the *Voice* initially asked him to write the article, and that when they found he was unable to do so, the newspaper turned to Reed. The political scientist concluded that the article was another case of "intimidation" against those who spoke out against "white oppression," and that Inman "concocted post hoc the SLA scare" to justify the spying only after being caught.[21]

Harding also sent a letter to the *Constitution* editor, decrying the "local manifestation of the Watergate mentality." His letter, too, saw Inman's story as a "smokescreen" for an "illegal and unconstitutional act." Inman's actions reflected, in his view, "a narrow-minded, racist and discredited public official [who] used the public trust and the tax-supported public personnel to fight his enemies, including the crusading *Atlanta Voice*, which constantly exposed him, and the Black mayor who fired him." Finally, he mentioned the *Constitution's* error-laden reporting, explaining that Strickland was the author. He ridiculed the poor journalism, noting that the magazine *Black World* published the essay in December 1973 and the IBW mailed it to the *Voice* as copyrighted by Strickland. Harding noted that the IBW was not a part of the Atlanta University, the Republic of New Africa, or the SLA. Harding wondered if he was one of the *Constitution's* "hard core terrorists on the run," despite the fact that he had lived in Atlanta for thirteen years and had had the *Constitution* print an IBW editorial the previous year. Harding wanted the newspaper to retract its story and "admit to itself . . . that it has cooperated with Inman and his supporters to justify his illegal, vengeful and repressive acts, taken under the cover of so-called threats to the city's security."[22]

In an attempt to counter the negative press coverage, and fearing that the *Constitution* would not print Harding's rebuttal, the IBW staff sent a similar letter to its associates and friends. The letter referred to "flimsy, unattributed proofs" that Atlanta was a hotbed of terrorist activities. "Apparently the police were not troubled by the main thrust of the 2500 word essay, but [focused on] a brief 70 word reference to Mark Essex." Furthermore, the letter linked the attack against Harding's credibility to the general conflict between Jackson and Inman. The police department's actions were representative of constant surveillance against Black radicals over the last two decades.

> We are convinced that this spying incident is part of a larger pattern. We see Inman and his supporters (on and off the police force) as representative of those forces who are ever ready to use the shield of "national security"—in this case "municipal security"—to hide or justify blatantly political acts of repression, revenge, and self-defense. Like Nixon, Inman went on the offensive and used tax-supported mechanisms of governmental law enforcement to attack a courageous, truth-speaking Black newspaper [the *Atlanta Voice*] which had given his corrupt regime no peace.

The IBW asserted that the *Constitution* article used the institute as a vehicle through which it could discredit Jackson, and it served as an "attack on Black leadership." On May 27, one thousand protesters marched through downtown Atlanta calling for Inman's departure and implicitly supporting the IBW's analysis. Led by civil rights veteran Hosea Williams, marchers denounced "police terror" and held signs that read "Remember Mark Essex." However, the media's false connection between the IBW and the SLA proved to be only the beginning of the harassment; within nine months the IBW offices would be robbed.[23]

The Break-Ins

On the night of March 11, 1975, the IBW's discussions of infiltration became reality—criminals broke into the institute's office. The burglars stole seven thousand dollars in office equipment. However, the theft of other, monetarily worthless items caught the attention of the associates. The intruders also took a series of audiotapes which contained the roundtable discussions led by Harding, Strickland, Hill, and Dodson. These round-tables with leading Black intellectuals, including Walter Rodney, focused on the state of the Black movement during the 1970s. The disappearance of these tapes signaled to the IBW associates that financial gain was not the sole purpose of the break-in and that political motives were involved. Harding's press release acknowledged, "we were simply carrying out the work which we believe to be our responsibility . . . but we are well aware of the ways in which government and other forces could try to use the materials against us." The burglary had all of the signs of a "black bag job." The IBW associates' suspicions were not far from the mark. In the 1980s and 90s, former FBI agents reported that, beginning in the 1950s, hundreds of illegal break-ins occurred. In addition, in the 1980s, agents W. Mark Felt and Edward Miller were prosecuted (though later pardoned by President Ronald Reagan) for their roles in coordinating 1970s black bag operations against the Weather Underground. Many of these illegal operations occurred after the official end of the Federal Bureau of In-vestigation's COINTELPRO. The suspicious circumstances surrounding the IBW break-ins signaled that shadowy conservative and police forces linked the IBW's radical analysis with national and international radicals and extremist organizations.[24]

The first break-in marked the culmination of harassment against IBW staff member Don Edwards, and reflected the tendency of outside forces to see radicalism as homogenous. Edwards started an Atlanta chapter of the Venceremos Brigade (VB), an organization that supported the Cuban Revolution. The VB members were American leftists who began travel-ing to Cuba in 1969 to cut sugarcane, to "educate people about imperial-ism and the international revolution against imperialism," and to apply Communist principles.[25] As a result of this radicalism, VB members were continually under surveillance by the FBI, the CIA, and local police. In November 1974, Edwards began receiving harassing phone calls. The ha-rassment escalated in early 1975. Self-identified "anti-Castro forces" cov-ered Edwards's car with red paint and filled his gas tank with sugar in Feb-ruary. In March, after changing his telephone number, Edwards received his first threatening note.[26]

> You up'd the anty [sic], now so will wee [sic] Phone calls and paint on car were nothing by now car should be inoperable/ you like sugar

right? / ha-ha We can get new phone number through our phone company contacts home will be next. Don't let us have to get fiscial [*sic*] You, your wife, children, or friends could be the targets We also know some of the other people working with you in your Cuban support organization All activities must stop! the decision is up to you
—Cuba Si Fidel Hell No

The anti-Castro faction sent another letter to Edwards's wife on the morning after the IBW break-in, encouraging her to "talk sense into the heads of your husband and his friends before somebody gets hurt!" Edwards's previous harassment supported associates' belief that the burglary of their office was politically motivated. However, the institute was unsure of whose politics were being attacked—the IBW's, or Edwards's and that of the Venceremos Brigade. The IBW made it clear in its press release that it had "no structural ties to the Brigade," but realized that "such distinctions are irrelevant to the reactionary forces in America."[27]

The IBW's offices were burglarized again a few days later, confirming associates' assumptions that the attack was politically motivated and that "reactionary forces" did not make distinctions between the institute and the brigade. During the March 14 infiltration, the unknown criminal(s) only removed and searched files. The harassment continued ten days later, when more than twenty phone calls bombarded the IBW's offices. A cryptic note, the IBW's first, accompanied these phone calls.

> Institute of niggers
> Don and his friends must go You know now what we can do
> Our friends will use information if necessary
> We will blow mother fucking buildings up we mean business
> You have until mid April
> Niggers will not rule America
>   G.

The IBW assumed that the mysterious "G" stood for *Gusano*, Spanish for "worm," a term that had previously been used by anti-Castro exile groups in an earlier letter to Edwards. Another letter, signed by the same "G," threatened sexual assault on Edwards's wife and continued, "House will go very soon Office too as long as you are there Institute of Niggers knows now what we and our friends can do." The IBW responded to these attacks by creating a "vigilance committee," which would publicize the attacks and try to raise money to replace the stolen equipment. Harding encouraged friends of the organization to send letters to the Congressional Black Caucus and to the Atlanta Public Safety commissioner, Reginald Eaves. The Black Panther Party's letter to Eaves typified the support. "These attacks are clearly the work of organized elements determined to undermine and ultimately prevent the very valuable work done by the Institute of the Black World in the collection and dissemination of otherwise unavailable information on the Black Freedom Movement in this country and the world—work aimed at forwarding the freedom of all oppressed humankind." As a sign of their respect for the IBW's intellectual work, activists and intellectuals contributed more than seven thousand dollars to replace the stolen office equipment.[28]

Despite increased security measures—which included heavy-duty burglary bars, new dead bolts, and floodlights—a third theft occurred a month later, just as the letter had threatened. In mid-April, burglars stole five electric typewriters and again went through the IBW's files.[29] Another letter appeared several weeks later, taking responsibility for the break-in.

> Institute of Niggers
> Howard [Dodson]
> Don still there! You have had one week past warning
> deadline No more grace No more Bullshit
> Your buildings are still targets Don his cohorts
> and family are still key targets too We know that
> people who went with VB group will be back soon
> Look out Light stuff has been cut down Will soon
> stop—period. Will begin to fire heavy guns soon!
> Police work, lights will not stop us
> Last letter to you now Only actions that's all you
> Niggers understand.
> G.[30]

The IBW again declared to the media that the attacks were politically motivated. Captain Howard Baugh, head of the Atlanta Police Department's Intelligence Division, said that they would continue to investigate with the aid of the FBI. The harassment of the IBW waned, but Edwards faced constant threats against himself, his family, and his babysitter. Even with the IBW's harassment declining, ultraconservative Georgia congressman

Larry McDonald received an anonymous letter in July urging him to "make a few hits" against the IBW. "We are requesting that you assign several of your most trustworthy, dependable and efficient operatives to make a few hits," the letter stated. "They will be rewarded handsomely and your campaign fund will be enriched immensely." The letter from Atlanta suggested that "knives, guns, explosives, whatever is needed should be used," and that the institute's offices should be burned. McDonald turned over the threats to the FBI for inspection. Julian Bond called for a federal investigation into the terrorist threats leveled at Edwards, his family, and the IBW. However, for the IBW, the threats and harassment ended just as abruptly as they had started, only days before the press conference.[31]

The letters and the IBW breaks-in had all the signs of organized counterintelligence. Historian David Cunningham's examination of COINTELPRO identifies a typology of eight actions used in the campaign against the New Left: 1) create an unfavorable public image; 2) disrupt internal organization; 3) sow dissension between protest groups; 4) restrict access to group-level resources; 5) restrict the ability of target groups to protest; 6) hinder individual targets' participation in group activities; 7) displace conflict; and 8) gather information or intelligence. The break-ins and harassment of Edwards and the IBW fit seven of the eight categories, with the lone exception of creating dissension between protest groups (although one can imagine that difficulties emerged between the IBW, Edwards, and the VB). The letters, threats, harassing phone calls, and break-ins against the IBW fit the profile of counterintelligence activities and lent credence to the IBW associates' suspicions that these were "dirty tricks." An escalation in events rallied the IBW's supporters, and Bond called a press conference to illuminate the illegal activities. Edwards faced additional terror tactics when a brick was thrown through his apartment door on July 3 and another threatening letter was received on July 8. The last letter included a "contract" for the murder of Edwards's wife.[32]

Before Bond's July 16 press conference in front of city hall, the police notified the IBW that they had arrested the suspect believed responsible for the break-ins. Joseph Lewis, a Black man, confessed to burglarizing the IBW's offices. In an elaborate confession, Lewis explained to officers that he sold the office equipment, valued at more than $2000, to Joe, a White man, for $125. He also admitted to breaking in a month later and taking more office equipment. Lewis did not admit to the theft of the IBW's tapes and files—the phrase "20 used cassette tapes" was redacted from the police report, and there were no additional references to stealing the tapes therein. Lewis acknowledged, "I have since burglarized places, houses and businesses and took small appliances and other items, which I cannot remember just what they were," and he claimed to have sold them to the mysterious Joe. The officers recovered two typewriters with the arrest, but to the IBW associates, the missing tapes were more important. No tapes were recovered; the police assumed Lewis threw them away. Lewis's confession did not address the threatening letters that the IBW and Edwards had received, and the IBW was not convinced the police had the correct suspect. The IBW's staff doubted the robber could have pulled off all of the jobs single-handedly; it seemed to them a "physical impossibility" for a man who was only five foot seven and one hundred thirty-five pounds. Considering that the average 1970s typewriter weighed 20–30 pounds and the area surrounding the IBW's offices was densely populated with citizens and students, a crime of this nature, if committed by one person, would require criminal genius, superior strength, and considerable luck. These factors raised associates' suspicions. Moreover, "other aspects of the burglaries remain unresolved." However, with Lewis's arrest, the harassment of Edwards and his family abruptly stopped, marking Lewis as either the perpetrator of the crimes or the fall guy.[33]

The break-ins and harassment reflected a growing conservative backlash, anchored by a law-and-order campaign, against the radicalism of the 1960s and 1970s. Despite Lewis's arrest and confession, the IBW and others believed that the perpetrators of these crimes remained a mystery. Anti-Castro forces in America were at times strong, and were often supported by government agencies.[34] Consequently, associates believed that the FBI was behind the burglaries. Strickland asserted, "It was COIN-TELPRO." The IBW posited that the FBI's purpose in the robberies was to damage the increasingly radical yet fragile organization. There is some credence to Strickland's claim, despite the official end to the program in 1971. The IBW had been under surveillance by the FBI since 1969, so its apparent connection to the SLA and praise for Essex could have put it back on the FBI's radar. The stolen items, especially the audiotapes, had little value on the underground black market. Although the FBI's legacy of COINTELPRO makes it a likely suspect for the break-ins, the CIA also conducted domestic espionage. Beginning under President Lyndon B. Johnson, Operation CHAOS generated massive intelligence files known as the "family jewels" in agency circles. Furthermore, the CIA compiled a list of more than 300,000 American names and organizations and conducted extensive investigations into 7,200 citizens. Two factors give credence to the possibility of CIA involvement. First, the stolen tapes contained interviews with Rodney, so U.S. support for Burnham's anticommunist regime opens the possibility that the CIA could have been involved in the break-ins.[35] Second, Edwards's participation in the VB would have fallen under CIA jurisdiction. Regardless, the burglaries at the IBW's offices appear to be black bag operations, so labeling them COINTELPRO serves as a metaphor for all types of illegal surveillance. For the IBW, the results were crushing because, as Strickland remembered, the "word went out not to fund us." The break-ins and increasing financial difficulties made the IBW's future bleak. If the goal of the break-ins was to destabilize the IBW further, the operations were successful.[36]

The IBW's Financial Troubles

Although the break-ins took place during an intense period of surveillance that had a dramatic and highly publicized effect on the organization, the lingering problem, which the burglaries only exacerbated, was the IBW's financial situation. The institute strained to stay financially solvent during the recession. In this tight financial climate, it was difficult for the IBW to maintain a steady stream of money to support its extensive programs and publications.[37] The IBW used three financial strategies to survive the recession: it relied on foundations, donations, and associates' sacrifices. Each of these approaches allowed the institute to keep its doors open. However, they all limited the IBW's long-term effectiveness by narrowing or weakening its programmatic elements and preventing its associates from conducting the collective scholarship that made its early years so productive. In essence, the IBW's financial strategies allowed for its survival but caused its disintegration.

Foundations

From its beginning, the IBW's financial situation was a constant topic of discussion and source of concern. After it separated from the King Center, the institute estimated its budget to be between $200,000 and $300,000 per year. The institute remained solvent the first year thanks to several grants to support students studying there: $65,000 from the Ford Foundation, $30,000 from the Southern Education Foundation, $45,000 from the Cummins Engine Foundation, $96,000 from Wesleyan University, and $10,000 from Dartmouth College. Bennett's internal memo justified the IBW's acceptance of White foundation money but stressed "relative autonomy" through multisource funding. However, Sterling Stuckey resigned based on the IBW's acceptance of White foundation money and financial mismanagement. In addition, staff members complained of the institute's fragile financial status during the reorganization in 1971 and 1972. Despite a general desire to rely on Black funding sources, the IBW recognized that its yearly existence depended on support from White foundations and that this reliance was precarious.[38]

Robert S. Browne, an economist and founder of the Black Economic Research Center (BERC), became a chief link to foundational support for the IBW. Browne's extensive connections, research, and activism made him a natural supporter of the IBW's plans. A Chicago native, Browne earned an MBA from the University of Chicago after graduating with honors from the University of Illinois. He continued his graduate studies in economics at the University of Chicago and the London School of Economics in the early 1950s. He would eventually earn his doctorate in economics from the City University of New York in 1981. During the 1950s, Browne traveled extensively across the globe, mostly through his job with the International Cooperation Administration (the predecessor to USAID), where he was a trade advisor to Cambodia and to the United States' economic aid mission in that country. During his stay in Southeast Asia, he witnessed the effect of U.S. economic policies in the region.[39]

After returning to the United States in 1961, Browne engaged in the activism sweeping the country on the twin fronts of civil rights and the antiwar movement. He protested the growing Vietnam War, leading college teach-ins in the New York area and, at the request of New York congressman Benjamin Rosenthal, serving as a consultant to the Ad Hoc Congressional Committee on Vietnam. In addition to opposing the Vietnam War, Browne recognized the need to foster economic change in Black communities. He took part in the 1967 National Black Power Conference, serving as coordinator of the Economic Development Task Force. Two years later, he gave the keynote address at the National Black Economic Development Conference (NBEDC) in Detroit. At the conference, former SNCC director James Forman delivered his "Black Manifesto," which demanded $500 million in reparations to Black people, to be paid by White churches and synagogues. As a result of Browne's speech and the media attention surrounding the "Black Manifesto," Browne received grants from the National Council of Churches and the Ford Foundation to start the BERC.[40]

From its founding in 1969, the BERC became the leading authority on Black economic development, publishing the *Review of Black Political Economy*. Its goals were "to create a think tank where black economists could study topics of significance to the black community" and to become "the principle center for economic expertise on black America." The BERC, like the IBW, maintained its independence in the face of funding pressures. The Ford Foundation wanted the center to affiliate with a university, but Browne refused. He realized that such an association would result in a loss of autonomy and feared that the image of the center as a "black institution would be lost." The objectives expressed by Browne and the BERC echoed those promoted by Harding, Strickland, and other IBW associates.[41]

The relationship between Browne and the IBW was a longstanding one. Browne served as a member of the institute's advisory board for the life of the organization. He attended the 1969 Black Studies Directors Conference. Then, in July 1971, the IBW, the BERC, and the University of the West Indies-based Institute of Social and Economic Research (ISER), which was directed by economist George Beckford, held preliminary discussions about interinstitutional collaborations and conferences. A formal association never materialized, but the two American think tanks supported each other. The IBW named Browne co-chair of the Economic Development Committee of its BAN, and Browne advertised the IBW's "Black Papers" in the first issue of *Review of Black Political Economy*. More importantly, Browne's connections to foundations proved invaluable to the survival of the IBW.[42]

Browne was associated with the Association of Black Foundation Executives (ABFE), an organization under the leadership of James A. Joseph, then president of the Cummins Engine Foundation. Founded in 1971, the ABFE protested the lack of minority representation on the managing boards of philanthropic foundations. The ABFE took its lead from Browne, who suggested that "institution building" took priority in funding. As Browne wrote, "basically, one would attempt to favor projects which offer a strong potential for developing skills or for organizing and elevating Black awareness, or for building viable, strong, self-sustaining

Black economic and political institutions." The IBW fit this description and received funding from Black executives associated with the Cummins Engine Foundation and the Schumann Foundation.[43]

Browne was also on the board of directors of the DJB Foundation, a philanthropic organization founded in 1948 by Daniel J. Bernstein with the millions he inherited from his father. By the time the younger Bernstein died in 1970, he had concluded that "the chief enemy of mankind was not famine, flood, or disease, but quite directly the injustice of governments in general and that of the United States government in particular." After 1970, the DJB Foundation directors used more than $6 million to fund a variety of "controversial" projects. The DJB Board planned to liquidate the foundation over ten years, but used all its funds up by 1974. The foundation focused on smaller organizations and gave money "without imposing our ideas." The IBW associates' relationship with Browne facilitated the institute's receipt of more than $140,000 from the DJB in four years, making the IBW one of its leading beneficiaries.[44]

The IBW did not rely solely on Browne and the network of Black foundation executives to secure funding, and it wanted to establish a development office based in New York to enhance its fundraising. After separating from the King Center, Harding and Strickland met in January 1971 with consultants to discuss strategies that would help stabilize the institute's finances. Several realizations came out of the meeting, including the realities that the IBW would have to rely on White funding sources for at least the next two or three years, that serious fund-raising needed to be done by professionals, and that fund-raising would require money over what the institute had budgeted for programming. In an internal document that analyzed the role of Blacks at White foundations, Harding argued that Black executives needed to "be responsible to a concrete analysis of the needs of black America and to develop rational and prioritized plans for meeting those needs within the limit[s] of their resources."[45]

The IBW's plans for a development office merged with ABFE's goals of institution-building, and the IBW relied on two of the highest-ranking Black foundation executives to get it started. Joseph of the Cummings Engine Foundation and Harriet Michel of the Schumann Foundation were among the eight cofounders of the ABFE, and they used their organizations to support the IBW. Cost forced the IBW to scale back its original plans for a New York-based office and instead settle on one in Atlanta. The IBW received 60% of its $50,000 budget for a development office from the

Cummins Foundation and the Schumann Foundation provided an additional 20%. Despite these grants, the IBW discontinued its development office and depended on senior associates Harding and Strickland to solicit funds for the institute's survival.[46]

Donations

The second step that the IBW took to remain financially solvent was to solicit donations. Harding and Strickland made sure that the IBW used direct mailings and made calls for funds in the *Monthly Report*. Immediately after separating from the King Center, the IBW issued a direct mailing that netted approximately $10,800 in contributions and kept the office open in the financially vulnerable first months of its independence. Although the *Monthly Report* published the IBW's newspaper column and analysis of the social, political, and economic problems facing Black America, by May 1974, the headline was an appeal for funds instead of analysis. The pleas for support were answered by a variety of constituents. University professors such as Atlanta University's Mack Jones, Hofstra University's director of Africana Studies Canute Parris, Harvard University's Alvin Poussaint, and Cornell University's J. Saunders Redding were among the many scholars who donated to the IBW. In addition, senior associates and the advisory board often donated their honorarium from lectures given nationwide. University departments, such as Cornell University's Africana Studies Program, under the chairmanship of James Turner, helped by purchasing the IBW's audiotape series, inviting scholars for lectures, and donating money. Famed Black artist Elizabeth Catlett donated lithographs to the IBW to sell in a fund-raising effort. In addition, organizations like the Kuumba Workshop in Chicago as well as many unnamed people in Black communities donated money to the institute. These donations were just as important as the foundation money to the IBW's survival. In addition to providing monetary support, individual donations let the IBW associates know that they were reaching Black activist communities. More importantly, these donations represented steps toward building a Black fund-raising base.[47]

Associates' Sacrifices

The IBW's third and most important method of coping with its shrinking finances was allowing senior associates to take jobs at universities. Strickland recalled this decision as a choice for associates that was encouraged from the beginning of the organization, "We had developed this theory, which allowed those of us with degrees, to go out and teach." By mid-1971, senior associates Joyce Ladner and Stephen Henderson had taken jobs at Howard University. These positions not only improved the institute's financial situation, but they also offered the associates an opportunity for professional advancement. As the economic crisis took its toll on the IBW, more senior associates moved to universities, lightening the payroll. As of January 1974, Harding went to the University of Pennsylvania, Strickland to the University of Massachusetts—Amherst, and Hill to Northwestern University. Howard Dodson ran the institute's day-to-day operations while the senior associates were teaching at universities around the country.[48]

The IBW's three financial survival strategies—foundations, donations, and off-site teaching—allowed it to keep its doors open. However, in the end, the strategies reduced the IBW's effectiveness. Its increasingly radical analysis justified the reduction of support from many foundations. In addition, when the IBW solicited donations through its publications and direct mailings, it created extra costs that were not completely offset by donations. Finally, by allowing associates to accept teaching positions outside of Atlanta, the IBW drastically reduced the effectiveness of its experiment in collective scholarship. The vibrant intellectual space that had once been filled with the sounds of debates and collaboration had been reduced to the offices of an organization that was barely surviving. In 1974, DJB's vice president W. H. Ferry expressed concerns about the IBW's survival strategies to Browne; news of Harding teaching in Philadelphia raised "troubling questions." Ferry's letter peppered Browne with detailed questions. "Apparently other senior staff members are also absent from Atlanta for long periods. Who are they? Do they remain on salary? What are they doing? What is the day-to-day activity of the Institute that is left in the hands of three people whose names I never heard before?" Ferry believed that Harding's "rhetoric" did not completely explain the IBW's situation. Considering himself a friend of the IBW, he noted that, "to less friendly eyes this would all look like an elaborate rip-off." Mere survival strained the IBW's meager finances and weakened its prospects of future financial support. Despite continued public analysis in its *Monthly Report* and the *Black World View*, the IBW struggled to survive. In the mid-1970s, the IBW's financial situation forced another round of reorganization.

Reorganization in 1975

On the heels of the SRS '74 and the break-ins, Dodson led the 1975 re-organization of the institute. After Dodson arrived in Atlanta with his wife, Jualynne, in 1970, he constantly supported the IBW. When the senior associates accepted academic positions outside of Atlanta, Dodson stepped in to run the organization. During his time at the IBW, Dodson was involved in the 1971 reorganization meetings and served as the SRS '71 coordinator. Dodson's tenure in Atlanta made him the logical choice to direct the Atlanta offices after the SRS '74 and to lead the staff in re-organization in 1975. In preparation for another reorganization, Dodson solicited Harding's advice.[49]

In a letter to Dodson, Harding outlined potential changes to the IBW's program and structure. He wanted to distribute the IBW's analysis and intellectual materials, including taped lectures, films, and other items. However, he recognized that there were risks involved, because the associates, who also produced the majority of the analytical material, were not in Atlanta. Harding feared, "the work produced by those who are formally connected with IBW will increasingly fail to represent a synthetic 'IBW perspective,' as the separation from each other and the organizational base continues." Harding found no simple solutions to these problems. In regards to organizational structure, he promoted the creation of a new board of advisors that would eventually include Browne, Rodney, and Caribbean intellectual and scholar Sylvia Wynter. Harding also noted the need for a staff director and a staff council to lead the daily activities in the Atlanta office. In addition, Harding wanted to remove the "essential dishonesty" of his title of IBW "Director." He understood that such a decision would influence funding, but his infrequent visits to Atlanta justified the change. Harding felt a new title, chair of the board of advisors, was better suited to his position. Finally, the cofounder wanted Dodson to find "selective ways of relating to the local Atlanta scene," such as creating a bookstore, starting a reading program, and engaging in cooperative work in the community. These changes reflected the IBW's survival strategies and signaled the end of its experiment in collective scholarship that had defined the first five years of its existence.[50]

Dodson took Harding's suggestions to the staff in the November 1975 reorganization meetings. In a memo to the staff, Dodson noted that the

IBW's identity as a research center had ended primarily because of financial problems. He urged the staff to see the organization as an "Educational Resource Center." The educational resources that the IBW had published over the previous five years served as the basis for its new identity. The proposed bookstore intended to introduce, or reintroduce, the IBW's publications to the Atlanta area. In addition, the IBW would "supplement its own publications with print and audio material that deal with the same basic themes reflected in IBW's work."[51] This shift meant that the IBW would survive in name only. Over the next several years, the IBW continued to cosponsor conferences with its limited funds. For example, the "Quality Education in the Black Community Conference" in 1976 included Harding, Barbara Sizemore, Toni Cade Bambara, and Grace Lee Boggs. The conference analyzed past, present, and future educational philosophies, ideologies, and tactics, and reflected the IBW's renewed focus on the local scene. More than two hundred local parents, teachers, and administrators participated in the conference.[52] Despite this and other successful conferences, the dialectical methodology of collective scholarship that produced the IBW's synthetic analysis was clearly missing. Harding recalled that, as the seventies inched toward the eighties, the IBW "became less and less a center for people, who were in residence there and working and struggling with concepts, and became more of a resource center."[53] By May 1976, all full-time staff members were asked to volunteer at least twenty hours per week. Although most of the staff agreed to the terms, by the end of the year "several key staff persons had been forced to take full-time jobs elsewhere in order to make ends meet."[54] These decisions resulted in less analytical work, as the organization struggled to survive.

Conclusion

During the mid-1970s, the IBW fought to survive break-ins and constant financial crises amid the increasingly conservative political environment and stifling economy of the mid-seventies. The IBW's focus on synthetic analyses, rather than activism, did not put the organization beyond the scope of external subterfuge by local and national police forces. Beginning with the false connection to the SLA by the Atlanta Police Department's Intelligence Division and continuing through the harassment of IBW staff member Don Edwards and his family as well as repeated office break-ins, reactionary forces saw the institute as a threat. Moreover, the "black bag" burglaries exacerbated the IBW's precarious financial situation. Consequently, it employed survival strategies to stay afloat as an organization. The break-ins and constant financial pressure led to a crucial 1975 organizational restructuring that changed the institute's identity from an activist think tank to an educational resource center. These crises destroyed the IBW's experiment in collective scholarship and reduced the influence of the organization's analysis. The IBW's decline was similar to that of other Black Power era organizations in the 1970s; internal and external forces worked synergistically to cause the breakdowns.[55]

The change in the IBW's identity was costly in the intellectual environs of the 1970s and 1980s. As the seventies wore on, new ideas and analyses were needed to understand phenomena that included a growing Black middle class that was increasingly incorporated into the American structure, as well as the new popularity of ethnic pluralism and its effect on Black advances. The IBW had turned too much of its attention to survival, to the detriment of its intellectual work. The institute's physical space remained, but its intellectual space had disappeared.[56]

Epilogue

The IBW's Closing and Legacy

In the IBW's final *Monthly Report*, William Strickland commented on the weakened state of the Black Freedom Movement in mid-1979. In his essay, "The Rise and Fall of the Black Political Culture: Or How Blacks Became a Minority," Strickland makes two interrelated arguments. First, he laments the generational shift between the Black youth of the sixties, who fought to change America's racial orthodoxy, and the youth of the seventies, who reaped the rewards of those challenges but failed to continue the struggle. "In the sixties, black people were a people of vision and purpose: A people on the move, firm in the conviction that we were a part of history which we could make if only we acted upon our own best beliefs. Now that has all changed. . . . Somehow the link between what we were and what we have become has been broken: leaving us strangers to ourselves and our history." Strickland's second argument suggests that there was a "devolution from 'people' to 'minority.'" He notes how mainstream intellectuals had begun to equate the Black movement with the progeny movements of women, Chicanos, Native Americans, Puerto Ricans, and others. For Strickland, this subtle shift "submerged the troublesome questions of racism, revolution, social change, black power, and the like and moved the questions back to the less troublesome ground of civil rights." The IBW's senior associate writes that both the demise of the Black Freedom Struggle and the articulation of Blacks as just one of many minority groups occurred because Blacks "lost hegemony over the interpretations of our conditions and America's." Although Strickland is referring to the national movement, his analysis and conclusions also speak to the reality of the IBW's declining influence as an organization.[1]

The IBW celebrated its tenth anniversary in June 1980 with a symposium, "The State of the Race," that featured Strickland, Vincent Harding, Robert Hill, and others. The event represented one of the few times after 1975 that the key founding members of the institute were together. Pat Daly, the new director of the institute, recognized that the IBW had outlasted other organizations from its era.[2] However, it was a bittersweet moment that commemorated a decade of intellectual work while signaling the decline of the institute as an activist think tank. The very notion of a reunion indicated that institute associates were not together in Atlanta on a regular basis, and thus that the IBW's collective scholarship was a thing of the past. Within three years of the reunion, the IBW closed its doors for good.

The IBW's legacy and contributions should be evaluated in three areas—Black Studies, a Black political agenda, and its organizational methodology of collective scholarship. These areas show why the IBW was one of the most respected organizations during the long seventies, and demonstrate why new organizations in the 1990s and early twenty-first century have re-created many of the IBW's goals and themes.

Black Studies

Black Studies was a constant in the IBW's history (along with financial instability). Not only was the field the first topic of study, with the Black Studies Directors Conference in 1969, but college programs and departments were constant supporters of the IBW's work, buying the audiotape lecture series, donating money, and providing jobs to associates. Therefore, it was no surprise that near the end of the IBW's existence—when money rarely was available and Harding, Strickland, and Hill all taught in Black Studies departments at various universities—the institute reevaluated the state of the field. After the initial insurgency that led to the founding of Black Studies programs and departments, many such programs struggled and some even closed in the late seventies, most notably the one at the University of Chicago.[3] Harding noted that Black Studies in the 1980s lacked the insurgency of its origins because it "failed to carry to [its] logical, radical ends many of the challenges to the assumptions, ideology and structure of American higher education, [and it] failed to continue to press the critical issues of the relationship between Black people inside the university and those who will never make it."[4]

In the early eighties, the IBW used its remaining resources and connections to strengthen Black Studies programs, organizing the Black Studies Curriculum Development Project. The Curriculum Development Project was a series of three conferences held in 1981 and 1982, and it turned out to be the IBW's last major event. By the mid-to-late seventies, the IBW had become a resource center for distribution of the radical materials that the IBW had produced and supported. Consequently, the offices near the AUC became a bookstore that sold the IBW's publications, audiotapes, and other materials. The IBW changed its physical space to deal with financial constraints and to keep its doors open. Senior associates Harding, Hill, and Strickland had all accepted positions at various universities to relieve the IBW of the burden of their salaries. When Strickland and Hill moved to academic positions in Black Studies departments, the IBW naturally returned to its focus to this field.

In some ways, the eighties conferences were similar to the 1969 Black Studies Directors Conference, the IBW's first program. In both cases, the IBW examined syllabi and curricular concerns. However, the growth of Black Studies programs and departments in the period between the two conferences meant more attendees at the latter conferences. The IBW designed the Black Studies Curriculum Development conferences to examine and exchange new materials and approaches to Black Studies, to provide a critical self-evaluation of the field, and "to refine the issues, problems, and possibilities" of it.[5] For example, historian Manning Marable reviewed Black history syllabi, and Strickland reviewed curricula on the political economy. Marable concluded that the fifty-five course syllabi revealed "an appalling inability to think about education as a force in the liberation of Black people."[6] He referred to Grace Lee Boggs's redefinition of Black education, which had been published in IBW's *Education and Black Struggle*, as a model.[7] He added, "Black history is not the study of 'race relations.' It is first and foremost the analysis of our unique ideological and material conditions, written from the insights of the Black masses and their leaders."[8] In another evaluation of course material, Strickland noted that less than twenty-five percent of the submitted political economy course syllabi actually addressed the political economy, for most of the syllabi were "groping after a more adequate interpretation of the Black experience."[9] The supposed political economy courses differed only because they had a more conscious analytical framework than the other courses. The IBW's curricular analysis demonstrated that even after a decade of examining Black thought, associates still tried to advance the analytical framework for Black Studies and ultimately for Black communities.

During the conferences, however, Black women scholars "forcibly injected gender issues" into the discussions of Black Studies. Female scholars demanded that Black Studies take Black Women's Studies seriously. They noted that many model syllabi made Black women's cultural, intellectual, and scholarly contributions invisible.[10] The IBW's response to earlier charges of sexism set the stage for female scholars' demand for more attention, and for how Black Studies scholars reacted to these demands. Female scholars asserted that the IBW had marginalized Black women's contributions, both intellectually and personnel-wise, during its reorganization. Furthermore, the absence of Black Women's Studies highlighted the ways in which the IBW had consistently obscured women's perspectives in their intellectual work. As they noted, in the IBW's early years, the organization had marginalized gender analysis. The fact that female scholars had to stage a protest to have their voices heard further accentuated an analytical weakness within the IBW, Black Studies, and the Black Freedom Struggle in general. The freedom movement identified how race operated in the American social structure, but Black activists often willingly accepted cultural norms of gender, sexuality, and, to a lesser extent, class. Rather than exposing how cultural narratives of normality operated to form modes of inclusion and exclusion, activists simply viewed race or class as what Caribbean theorist Sylvia Wynter has termed "brute facts," not cultural facts.[11] The defining moment when female scholars demanded that Black women's experiences and perspectives be considered and incorporated into the Black Studies curriculum led to the creation of Black Women's Studies. In fact, no field within Black Studies has grown as quickly as the study of Black women.[12]

As a result of the staff's earlier accusation that the IBW was inattentive to gender, associates led by Harding targeted these issues for correction. First, the IBW included more women in its ranks. Led by Lee Boggs from Detroit and Pat Daly in Atlanta, the IBW explored gender-related topics and incorporated a systematic analysis of gender into its radical analysis. Not only did women play increasingly important roles behind the scenes, but the IBW's publications printed scholarship from more women. *The Black World View* included lead essays from Lee Boggs, Toni Cade

(Bambara), and Barbara Sizemore. These experiences allowed the IBW associates to recognize the seriousness of female intellectuals' demands. At a later conference, after the female scholars' intervention, the IBW's analysis of the syllabi pointed out that courses on Black women were among the best-developed and most strenuous courses, and should serve as models for Black Studies.[13] The IBW had used the challenge from female staff members to broaden its revolutionary intellectualism. Associates tried to transfer this perspective to the larger discipline of Black Studies.

The Black Studies Curriculum Project was the IBW's last gasp, not the organization's savior. Still, many Black Studies programs benefitted from the IBW experiment. Several associates became faculty members in Black Studies departments and programs nationwide. As professors, associates taught students about the history of Black scholarship, analyzing structural racism and Black political economy. A brief listing of associates in Black Studies programs provides a glimpse of their longer-term influence on the field. Strickland joined former SNCC member Michael Thelwell at the University of Massachusetts, where they eventually established a doctoral program in 1996. Robert Hill taught in the Black Studies and history departments at UCLA. Abdul Alkalimat developed Black Studies programs at Fisk University, University of Toledo, and the University of Illinois, and he has spent the last two decades promoting technology in the field. Finally, Sylvia Wynter, who was a board member of the IBW in the late 1970s, served as director of the Black Studies program at Stanford University. Other IBW associates continued their work in traditional departments. Harding taught in the department of history at University of Pennsylvania and at Swathmore College, as well as in the department of religion at Illif School of Theology at the University of Denver. Joyce Ladner and Stephen Henderson taught in sociology and English departments, respectively, at Howard University. Long-time supporter and associate Mack Jones headed the political science department at Atlanta University.

The former IBW associates not only influenced Black Studies with their presence, but they have also supplied theoretical concepts that have moved the field forward. Harding accurately captured the twists and turns of Black history with his river metaphor in *There is a River*. He stated beautifully, "We may sense that the river of black struggle is people, but it is also the hope, the movement, the transformative power that humans create and that create them, us, and makes them, us, new persons. So we black people are the river; the river is us."[14] Stephen Henderson's work on the Black aesthetic was pioneering in its critical analysis. Even Henry Louis Gates Jr. recognized that Henderson's schematic for a Black aesthetic was "seminal," though perhaps flawed.[15] Sylvia Wynter's early analysis of Black Studies and her theory of the human emerge from her work at the IBW.[16] In total, the IBW was a great example of what historian Manning Marable describes as "transformative Black Studies," or "the collective efforts of black people neither to integrate or self-segregate but to transform the existing power relationships and the racist institutions of the state, economy, and society." This perspective accounts for structural racism embedded in the political economy and as an ideology.[17] Throughout the IBW's decade-long existence, associates used Black Studies as a theoretical and institutional foundation to rethink the world.

A Black Political Agenda

By defining itself as an activist think tank, any evaluation of the IBW's legacy must address its influence on public policy. The IBW's attempts at policy development faltered because of internal weaknesses, but also revealed larger issues relating to Black politics. Internally, the IBW's attempts at policy development were diminished by financial instability. The inability of the IBW to maintain the BAN meant policy research was reliant on larger outside structures like the National Black Political Assembly, the organizational apparatus of the Gary Convention. As the assembly fell apart over disagreements about strategies and ideologies, the IBW had no outlet for policy development nor the money to complete the work itself.

The IBW's struggles to influence public policy stood in contrast to the growing power of conservative think tanks like the Heritage Foundation, revealing the difficulty that progressive ideas had in gaining stable financial support in the battle of ideas. The Heritage Foundation, for example, promoted free market economics, thus obtaining financial support from big business. Joseph Coors, beer company owner, donated $250,000, and Richard Scaife, heir to the Mellon fortune, donated $3.8 million to the conservative think tank over its first eight years. The IBW's redistributionist economics naturally did not gain it allies among big business.[18]

The IBW's progressive policies—which addressed structural racism and the need to gain equality in results, not simply in opportunity—exposed points of convergence between aspects of conservatism and liberalism, as both prioritized individualism. Some conservatives emphasized a libertarian individualism and an unfettered free market economy, while some liberals believed the government needed to protect equal opportunity and partially regulate the economy. Liberalism was extremely successful as the basis for the civil rights movement, but in the 1970s and beyond, the civil rights liberal perspective struggled to address systemic issues of poverty that disproportionately affected Black communities. Conservatism could no longer explicitly support racism, but it could argue that racially divergent results were the natural workings of the market. The IBW's progressive politics attempted to counter both the limits of liberalism and conservative ascendancy during the long seventies. Political scientist David Caroll Cochran aptly describes the limitations of liberalism: "The American language of politics has a great deal of difficulty identifying and making sense of *deeper sources of power* in civil society. . . . By focusing almost exclusively on the 'individual-state-market grid,' American political discourse misses the importance of cultural and communal forces to both an individual's identity and to his or her prospects in life."[19] The IBW's progressive politics, led by Harding and Strickland, were beyond "the general horizon of understanding," and therefore impossible to support under the normal political paradigms.[20]

The IBW's work with Maynard Jackson also reveals an early example of the limitations facing BEOs. Scholar J. Phillip Thompson's *Double Trouble* identifies two problems that plagued Black mayors—the structural limitations of cities in relation to wider local and state politics, and the lack of empowerment of Black civic organizations. Structurally, cities with Black mayors faced a declining tax base, as middle-class Whites (and later Blacks) fled to the suburbs. Moreover, cities faced tremendous deindustrialization because multinational corporations moved jobs to Sunbelt states, then to developing countries. Middle-class flight and the loss of jobs left many cities predominately Black, poor, fiscally constrained, and chronically underemployed. The IBW's structural analysis identified many of these issues, but this analysis was often lost in the euphoria of having BEOs. In addition, since the 1970s, few politicians have wanted to be linked with progressives, reflecting the rightward trajectory of American politics. Thompson describes the "dirty little secret" of Black politics as the way in which BEOs mobilize the Black electorate, often with race-based appeals, to win elections, then remain unaccountable to this population while governing. The IBW's experiences with developing a Black political agenda provide an early example of an organization trying to address the issues Thompson identifies.[21] The IBW's weaknesses in policy development reflect larger problems in progressive politics since the 1970s.

Collective Scholarship

The IBW's use of collective scholarship functioned to balance radical analysis with pragmatic outcomes. This organizational methodology allowed the IBW to navigate the different phases of Black activism during the seventies. Moreover, the IBW's collective scholarship served as a model for future organizations. Two organizations in the late twentieth and early twenty-first century used the IBW as an example of a progressive organization needed in the modern era. In 1997, thirty-five activist-intellectuals, including former IBW associates Strickland, Alkalimat, and Manning Marable, met in Chicago to discuss the meager state of the Black Left. The activists called for a national meeting the following year. With echoes of the Gary Convention, two thousand activists, intellectuals, and concerned citizens arrived in Chicago to establish the Black Radical Congress (BRC) and to revive a progressive political agenda for the coming twenty-first century.[22]

The BRC convened with the principle of unity based on a "center without walls." The planning committee recognized the "diverse historical tendencies in the Black radical tradition including revolutionary nationalism, feminism, and socialism." Remembering the lack of gender analysis and dissension during the long seventies, the BRC planning committee asserted, "Gender and sexuality can no longer be viewed solely as personal issues but must be a basic part of our analyses, politics and struggle," and the organization must make "room for constructive criticism" and "honest dissent." The BRC document echoed IBW's Gary Convention "Preamble." "We know that America's capitalist economy has completely failed us." The diverse activists came together collectively to develop a "Freedom Agenda," which called for human rights, political democracy, quality public education, a healthy environment, an end to police brutality, and gender equality among other issues. The BRC sought to resurrect the collective scholarship that the IBW practiced two decades earlier.[23]

Despite having learned from the lessons of the 1960s and 1970s, familiar problems plagued the BRC activists. Scholars have described how, by 2000, the BRC "lacked a coordinated strategy for implementing any practical program" and devolved into "a hodgepodge of countervailing activities."[24] The BRC was disrupted by issues of fund-raising and personality politics as well. The larger issue was the difficulty of accommodating a wide array of views. Despite the weaknesses and the ultimate closure of the BRC, its brief history demonstrates how the former IBW associates carried the idea of collective scholarship (and activism) into the twenty-first century.

Another organization was created in the months after the horrific events of September 11, this time paying homage to the IBW by using its name. Long-time activist Ron Daniels, who actively participated in the Gary Convention, organized the State of the Black World Conference in December 2001. The conference attracted over two thousand participants, including California congresswomen Maxine Waters, Jesse Jackson, and Al Sharpton. At the conference's conclusion, participants recognized the need for an Institute of the Black World for the twenty-first century. At the following conference in April 2002, during a workshop on the mission of the IBW 21st Century, Dr. Jemardari Kamara stated, "I see the institute as a vehicle for the reconstruction of a movement . . . there is too much individualism. We need a more collective outlook and in the process to link up the Black world. We need a research of resistance . . . and we need to be prepared to make a sacrifice."[25] Although the original IBW senior associates were not actively involved in Daniels's IBW 21st Century, several staff members, including William Dorsey, were at the founding conference. The IBW 21st Century attempts to continue the IBW's tradition of research, policy, and advocacy. After the devastating 2009 earthquake in Haiti, for instance, the IBW 21st Century started a Haitian relief fund.

The Black Radical Tradition

The BRC and the IBW 21st Century have been modeled on the IBW because the Harding-led organization created analyses that moved beyond liberals' representations of racial progress and embodied the Black radical tradition. As Cedric J. Robinson observed, Black radicalism "is not a variant of Western radicalism whose proponents happen to be Black. Rather, it is a specifically African response to an oppression emergent from the immediate determinants of European development in the modern era and framed by orders of human exploitation woven into the interstices of European social life from the inception of Western civilization."[26] He adds that the radical tradition is "the continuing development of a collective consciousness informed by the historical struggles for liberation and motivated by the shared sense of obligation to preserve the collective being, the ontological totality."[27] The IBW, more than any other organization, exemplified the Black radical tradition during the long seventies.

Though the IBW officially closed its doors in 1983, it had been a shell of its former self for the last six years.[28] Still, the IBW's activities during its early years—from Black Studies, to a Black political agenda, to radical analysis—demonstrated the institute's role as the premier location for radical Black intellectual work in the seventies. The IBW opposed racial liberalism, recognizing that any attempt at Black liberation must include new ideas about history, economics, and humanity; in essence, its associates and supporters tried to rethink the post–civil rights world. This was the challenge of Blackness after the civil rights movement.

Throughout the IBW's existence, it tried to forge a hard-earned, issue-based consensus through pragmatic nationalism. The IBW associates prioritized analysis over ideology by using the organizational methodology of collective scholarship. Under Harding and Strickland's leadership, the IBW contributed to the Black radical tradition through its research and analyses, reconnecting a Black radical network of intellectuals, activists, and scholars from across the diaspora. Unfortunately, the IBW's radicalism made survival difficult and providing an alternative to the conservative ascendency impossible. Aspects of the IBW's experiences reflected larger problems in the Black Freedom Struggle during the seventies. In particular, troubles in generating consensus, maintaining financial stability, and withstanding police infiltration beset all Black organizations regardless of their ideology. The loss of the IBW's intellectual space and the reduction of its radical analyses proved traumatic, as conservatives and neoconservatives began to control the definition of civil rights and limited the political possibilities. Scholar Robert C. Smith has argued that the closing of the IBW meant, "the radical wing of the black movement was unable to sustain what it critically needed and needs, a gathering place for critical research and thinking."[29]

Despite the IBW's underfinanced operation, during its heyday it generated tremendous intellectual production through collective scholarship, it influenced a generation of intellectuals, and its associates took the ideal of radical intellectualism with them when they moved back into the university. As professors at various universities nationwide, the IBW's former associates passed on the importance of intellectual work, collective scholarship, and radical analysis to a new generation of students, introducing them to critical examination of the American system and its inequalities. Harding's *There Is a River* describes the meaning of history and the purpose of intellectual work as well as summing up the IBW's influence and goals.

> Indeed . . . such persistent probes toward meaning are absolutely necessary, not primarily as a source of psychic comfort or as diversionary, apolitical spiritualizing, but because there is no truly human history with them. For just as each of us at one time or another is fiercely driven to seek coherence and purpose in the deciphering of our own personal histories, so it is in this *collective* venture toward wholeness. A sense of meaning—which we surely create out of our particular responses to the "facts" of experience—is crucial if we are to join ourselves to the past and the future, to commune with the ancestors as well as the coming children. . . . Without the search for meaning, the quest for vision, there can be no authentic movement toward liberation, no true identity or radical integration for an individual or a people. Above all, where there is no vision we lose the sense of our great power to transcend history and create a new future for ourselves with others, and we perish utterly in hopelessness, mutual terror, and despair. Therefore the quest is not a luxury; life demands it.[30]

The Institute of the Black World's history demonstrates the hopes and possibilities of radical, unflinching racial analysis. The institute's story also points out the obstacles to creating and developing such analyses. Despite the potential difficulties and problems, the next generation of activist-intellectuals must continue the IBW's analytical thrust in order to transform America. Echoing Frantz Fanon, this is not a luxury, but our mission. The struggle must continue.

Appendix

IBW Membership, Conferences, and Symposium Lists

The Institute of the Black World Governing Council—1969

Margaret Walker Alexander
Walter F. Anderson
Lerone Bennett Jr.
Horace Mann Bond
Robert S. Browne
John Henrik Clarke
Dorothy Cotton
Ossie Davis
St. Clair Drake
Katherine Dunham
Freddye Henderson
Vivian Henderson
Tobe Johnson
Julius Lester
Frances Lucas
Jesse Noel
Rene Piquion
Eleo Pomare
Pearl Primus
Benjamin Quarles
Bernice Reagon
William Strickland
Councill Taylor
E. U. Essien-Udom

C. T. Vivian
Charles White
Hosea Williams

Library Documentation Project Advisory Council

Ralph Abernathy
Harry Belafonte
Randolph Blackwell
Horace Mann Bond
Julian Bond
John Hope Franklin
Vincent Harding (director)
Miles Jackson
Slater King
C. Eric Lincoln
John D. Maguire (chairman)
Albert E. Manley
L. D. Reddick
James Tanis
Marian Wright
Andrew Young

LDP Staff Members Fired or Released in 1970

James Allen—student
Willie P. Berrien
Wilson Brown
Darryl Chandler—student
Debra Cheeks—student
Pearl Cleage
Louis Dunbar—student and/or summer employee
Louise Gray
Alvin Griggs—student
Marylyn Henry—student
Lois Johnson—student
Keith Jones—student
Ora Dee Jones—student
Eloise Joyner
Arlon Kennedy
Dorie Ladner

Sylvia Murrell—student
William Porter
Farrel Thomas—transferred to IBW
Robert Todd—student
Leah Wise

IBW Administrative Staff in 1969–70

Judy Barton
Jill Douglass
Brenda Gregory
Tina Harriford
Mamie Jackson
Barbara Knight
Colia LaFayette
Daulton Lewis
Laura Luster
Mayme Mitcham
Ojeda Penn
LaSayde Potter

IBW Staff Fall 1969

Lerone Bennett Jr.: senior editor, *Ebony*; visiting professor, History Department Northwestern University, fall seminar: Black Reconstruction in America

Christine Coleman: B.A. Clark College; Mississippi high school teacher; Southern Education intern; Child Education Task Force

Robert S. Browne: economist (based at the Black Economic Research Center, NYC)

Chester Davis: assistant professor of education, Sir George Williams University, Montreal (Black Studies and the Building of Public School Curriculum; Black Studies and the Training of Teachers); Fall seminar: Building Black Curriculum in the Public Schools

Lonetta Gaines: B.A. Fisk University, New Haven, Connecticut; teacher; Southern Education Foundation intern; Childhood Education Task Force

Vincent Harding: chairman, History Department, Spelman College; director of Martin Luther King Library Documentation Project (Black Radicalism and Black Religion)

Stephen Henderson: chairman, English Department, Morehouse College (The Poetry of the Blues, Modern Black Writers); Fall Seminar: Blues, Soul and the Black Identity

Joyce Ladner: assistant professor, Sociology, University of Southern Illinois (Black Women and the Ghetto; Black Student Protest; The Black Family); Fall Seminar: The Socialization of the Black Child

Daulton Lewis: B.A. sociology, Wesleyan University; Southern Education Foundation intern

William Strickland: consultant, CBS; lecturer, Department of History, Columbia University (Political History of Racism; Politics and the Black Urban Community); Fall Seminar: Racism and American Social Analysis

Sterling Stuckey: Ph.D. candidate, assistant professor, Northwestern University (The Slave Experience; Black Americans and Africans)

Black Studies Directors Conference, Partial Attendee List

Vincent Harding (IBW)
Lerone Bennett Jr. (IBW and *Ebony*)
Andrew Billingsley (University of California)
Robert S. Browne (IBW and Black Economic Research Center)
Chester Davis (IBW)
Stephen Henderson (IBW)
Robert Johnson (University of Indiana)
Joyce Ladner (IBW and University of Southern Illinois)
Basil Matthews (Talladega College)
Kwame McDonald (Livingstone College)
Boniface Obichere (University of Southern California)
Armstead Robinson (Yale University)
William Strickland (IBW)
Sterling Stuckey (IBW)
Michael Thelwell (University of Massachusetts—Amherst)
James Turner (Cornell University)

IBW Staff and Associates December 1970

Georgianna Armour
Judy Barton
Lerone Bennett Jr.
Eulalia Brooks
Chester Davis
Howard Dodson
James Early
Sylvia Ferrell
Jyl Hagler
Vincent Harding (director)

Stephen Henderson
Robert Hill
Melvin Huell
Henry Jackson
Arlon Kennedy
Joyce Ladner
Mayme Mitchem
Bryce Smith
William Strickland
Farrel Thomas
Derek Wheeler
Aljosie Yabura

ASSOCIATES

Clarence Bayne
Mary Frances Berry
Andrew Billingsley
J. Herman Blake
John H. Bracy Jr.
Robert S. Browne
Roy Bryce-LaPorte
Haywood Burns
Lemoine Callendar
John Churchville
Kermit Coleman
Norman Cook
Dorothy Cotton
E. U. Essien-Udom
Marshall Hall
Barbara Jones
Mack Jones
John O. Killens
Julius Lester
Frances Lucas
Carman Moore
William Mackey
Jesse Noel
Alphonso Pinkney
Rene Piquion
Alvin Poussaint
Bernice Reagon

Euguene Redmond
Leslie Rout
Councill Taylor
George B. Thomas
John Williams
William J. Wilson
Lloyd Yabura

October 1970 Black Agenda Network Committee Chairpersons

Communication: Lerone Bennett Jr.
Cultural Definitions and Survival: Stephen Henderson
Economic Development: Robert S. Browne and Robert Vowels (dean, School of
    Business Administration, Atlanta University)
Education: Chester Davis
Health and Welfare: Andrew Billingsley (vice president of Academic Affairs,
    Howard University)
Pan-African History and Relationships: Canute Parris (director of Black Stud-
    ies, Hofstra University) and Robert Hill
Political Organization: William Strickland
Organized Religious Resources: Leon Watts (associate director, National Com-
    mittee of Black Churchmen)

SRS 1971

FULL-TIME PARTICIPANTS

Mary L. Allen, Atlanta
E. J. Brisker, Seattle, WA (Staff volunteer)
Patricia Daly, Livingston College, New Brunswick, NJ (faculty)
Richard Dill, Hofstra University, Garden City, NY
Janet Douglass, Livingston College, New Brunswick (faculty)
Eddy Gouraige, Hofstra University
Sybil R. Griffin, Michigan State University
Leslie I. Hill, Barnard College, NY, NY
Catherine Jackson, University of Chicago
Evans Jacobs, Wesleyan University
Archie D. Sanders, Howard University (faculty)
Hazel L. Symonette, University of Wisconsin
George B. Thomas, Interdenominational Theological Center (faculty)
Vincent G. Yancey, Northeastern University, Boston

PART-TIME PARTICIPANTS

Dwight L. Greene, Wesleyan University (faculty)
Billy Jackson, Seattle, WA (staff volunteer)
Jackie Raab, Seattle (staff volunteer)
Gwendolyn Robinson, Dartmouth College (faculty)
George Stewart, Seattle (staff volunteer)
William H. Wilkinson, Dartmouth College (faculty)

SYMPOSIUM STAFF

Howard Dodson, symposium coordinator
Cheryll Greene, administrative assistant
Derek Wheeler, administrative assistant

IBW RESEARCH STAFF

Howard Dodson
Vincent Harding
Robert Hill
William Strickland

Seminar Lecturers

George Beckford
Edward Braithwaite
St. Clair Drake
Vincent Harding
Robert Hill
C.L.R. James

December 1978 Organizational Structure

Board of Directors

Lerone Bennett Jr.
Haywood Burns
Howard Dodson
St. Clair Drake
Katherine Dunham
Vincent Harding, chairperson
Robert Hill
Mack Jones
William Strickland

C. T. Vivian
Sylvia Wynter

OFFICERS

Vincent Harding, President
William Strickland, Vice President
Farrel Thomas, Secretary
Ruth Harmon, Treasurer
Bernard Parks, Legal Counsel
Howard Dodson, Executive Director

ADVISORY COUNCIL

Chinua Achebe
Robert Allen
George Beckford
Julian Bond
J. Alfred Cannon
Elizabeth Catlett
Chinweiru
Robert Chrisman
John Henrik Clarke
Charles Cobb Sr.
John Conyers
Ossie Davis
Ronald Dellums
Tran Van Dinh
Jualynne Dodson
Adisa Douglass
Janet Douglass
Dewitt Dykes
E. U. Ession-Udom
Norman Girvan
Kenneth Haskins
Stephen Henderson
Robert Holmes
Maynard Jackson
Tobe Johnson
John O. Killians
Lewis M. King
Crystal Kuykendall
Joyce Ladner

Roberto Marquez
Elridge McMillan
Alex Poinsett
Bernice Reagon
Myrian Richmond
Clayton Riley
Walter Rodney
Andrea Rushing
Byron Rushing
Andrew Salkey
Barbara Sizemore
Councill Taylor
George Thomas
James Turner
Margaret Walker
Charles White
Preston Wilcox
Aljosie Yarborough

Notes

Introduction. Where Do We Go From Here? The Long Seventies

1. Peter N. Carroll, *It Seems Like Nothing Happened*. Bruce Schulman, *The Seventies*.

2. Clayborne Carson, *In Struggle*, 215–304.

3. Peniel E. Joseph, "Black Liberation without Apology: Reconceptualizing the Black Power Movement," 8. Joseph provides an excellent historiography of Black Power scholarship in this essay.

4. William Van Deburg, *New Day in Babylon*. Jeffrey O. G. Ogbar, *Black Power*. Peniel E. Joseph, *Waiting 'Til the Midnight Hour*.

5. Timothy B. Tyson, *Radio Free Dixie*. Scot Brown, *Fighting for Us*. Komozi Woodard, *A Nation within a Nation*. Charles E. Jones, ed., *The Black Panther Party: Reconsidered*. Kathleen Cleaver and George Katsiaficas, eds., *Liberation, Imagination, and the Black Panther Party*.

6. Christopher B. Strain, *Pure Fire*. Curtis J. Austin, *Up against the Wall*. John T. McCartney, *Black Power Ideologies*. Dean E. Robinson, *Black Nationalism in American Politics and Thought*. Michael C. Dawson, *Black Visions*. Nikhil Pal Singh, *Black Is a Country*. Devin Fergus, *Liberalism, Black Power, and the Making of American Politics, 1965–1980*.

7. Robert O. Self, *American Babylon*. Matthew J. Countryman, *Up South*. Hasan Kwame Jeffries, *Bloody Lowndes*.

8. James Smethurst, *The Black Arts Movement*. Cedric Johnson, *Revolutionaries to Race Leaders*. Fabio Rojas, *From Black Power to Black Studies*. Amy Bass, *Not the Triumph but the Struggle*.

9. For example, Joseph's *Waiting 'Til the Midnight Hour* stops around 1974.

10. Joseph, *Waiting 'Til the Midnight Hour*, 254.

11. IBW, "Institute of the Black World: Statement of Purpose and Program," *Negro Digest* 19, no. 5 (March 1970): 20.

12. Donald E. Abelson, *Do Think Tanks Matter?*, 31–34.

13. Robert C. Smith, *We Have No Leaders*, 115–22. James Allen Smith, *The Idea Brokers*, 190–239. Donald T. Critchlow, *The Conservative Ascendancy*, 116–22.

14. Brown, *Fighting for Us*, 6.

15. Smethurst, *The Black Arts Movement*, 16.

16. "Addison Gayle: Interviewed by Saundra Towns," in *The Addison Gayle, Jr. Reader*, 378.

17. Louis Menand, *The Metaphysical Club*.

18. William James, in Louis Menand, ed., *Pragmatism*, xiii.

19. Tommie Shelby, *We Who Are Dark*. Eddie S. Glaude Jr., *In a Shade of Blue*. Bill E. Lawson and Donald F. Koch, eds., *Pragmatism and the Problem of Race*.

20. Martin Luther King Jr., *Where Do We Go From Here?*, 4. Carroll, *It Seems Like Nothing Happened*, xxi.

21. Rachel E. Harding and Vincent Harding, "Biography, Democracy and Spirit: An Interview with Vincent Harding," 682–98.

22. "Interview with Vincent Harding," in Henry Abelove et al., eds., *Visions of History*, 229.

23. Harding and Harding, "Biography, Democracy and Spirit," 682–98. "Interview with Vincent Harding," *Visions of History*, 219–44. Civil Rights Documentation Project, Howard University, "Interview with Vincent Harding by Vincent Browne, August 16, 1968." Vincent Harding and Staughton Lynd, "Albany, Georgia," *The Crisis* (February 1963): 69–78. Vincent Harding, "A Beginning in Birmingham," *The Reporter*, June 6, 1963, 13–19. Rose Marie Berger, "I've Known Rivers: The Story of Freedom Movement Leaders Rosemarie Fenny Harding and Vincent Harding," in *Sojourners: Faith, Politics, and Culture*.

24. W.E.B. Du Bois, *The Souls of Black Folk*, 3–14.

25. Vincent Harding, "The Gift of Blackness" (paper presented at the Sixth National Conference of Friends on Race Relations, Black Mountain, North Carolina, July 6–9, 1967).

26. Vincent Harding, "The Uses of the Afro-American Past: Blueprint for National Renewal," *Negro Digest* (February 1968): 4–9, 81–84.

27. *The Holy Bible*, Matthew 25:40 (King James Version).

28. E. Ethelbert Miller, "Stephen E. Henderson: Conversation with a Literary Critic," in Paul Logan, ed., *A Howard Reader*, 317–25. Stephen E. Henderson, "'Survival Motion': a Study of the Black Writer in the Black Revolution in America," in Mercer Cook and Stephen E. Henderson, eds., *The Militant Black Writer in Africa and the United States*, 67.

29. William Strickland, interview with author, February 7, 2003. "William Strickland Resume," William Strickland Series, IBW Papers, Schomburg Center for Research in Black Culture (hereafter referred to as the IBW Papers). The IBW Papers are unprocessed, but I will provide the series when available. "History of the NSM, 1961–1964," box 1, folder 1, Northern Student Movement Papers, Schomburg Center for Research in Black Culture, New York (hereafter cited as NSM Papers). Matthew J. Countryman, *Up South*, 181–89.

30. William Strickland, "The Movement and Mississippi," *Freedomways* 5:2 (Spring 1965): 313.

31. Quoted in Winston A. Grady-Willis, *Challenging US Apartheid*, 154. William Strickland, interview with author, February 7, 2003.

32. Manning Marable, *Race, Reform, and Rebellion*, 96–97.

33. William Strickland, interview with author, February 7, 2003. "William Strickland Resume," IBW Papers. See also William Strickland, *Malcolm X: Make It Plain*. It should be noted that the IBW's lead associates had an alienating military experience that encouraged the desire for alternatives to the American system. James Smethurst notes a similar alienating experience among Black Arts Movement activists, *The Black Arts Movement*, 33.

34. Vincent Harding, "A Long Hard Winter to Endure: Reflection on the Meaning of the 1970s," *The Black Collegian* 10:2 (1979/1980): 95.

35. Benedict Anderson, *Imagined Communities*.

Chapter 1. "The Challenge of Blackness"

1. Lerone Bennett Jr., *The Challenge of Blackness*, 1.

2. Ibid., 2–8.

3. Joseph, *Waiting 'Til the Midnight Hour*, 214–16. Rojas, *From Black Power to Black Studies*, 45–92. Donald Downs, *Cornell '69*.

4. Pero G. Dagbovie, *The Early Black History Movement, Carter G. Woodson, and Lorenzo Johnston Greene*, 1–14.

5. Du Bois, *Black Reconstruction*, 725.

6. Peter Novick, *That Noble Dream*, 111–280. Stephen G. Hall, *A Faithful Account of the Race*, 151–226.

7. Gunnar Myrdal, *An American Dilemma*, 928. Emphasis in original.

8. Lee Rainwater and William L. Yancey, *The Moynihan Report and the Politics of Controversy*, 188–93, 417–26.

9. William Van Deburg, *New Day in Babylon*, 17–18. "A Time Louis Harris Poll: The Black Mood: More Militant, More Hopeful, More Determined," *Time*, April 6, 1970, 29.

10. Rojas, *From Black Power to Black Studies*, 93.

11. One notable exception was Maulana Karenga's *Introduction to Black Studies*. Karenga's work was the one of the first significant attempts to define the boundaries of Black Studies.

12. For a theory of the experience of Blackness see: Sylvia Wynter, "Towards the Sociogenic Principle: Fanon, the Puzzle of Conscious Experience, of 'Identity' and What It's Like to Be 'Black,'" in *National Identity and Sociopolitical Change*, 30–66.

13. Charles V. Hamilton, "The Place of the Black College in the Human Rights Struggle," *Negro Digest* 16, no. 11 (September 1967): 4–10. Emphasis in original.

14. Michael S. Foley, *Confronting the War Machine*, 37–40.

15. "Hershey Forced Off Stage by Students at Howard U," *New York Times*, March 22, 1967, 13. George Q. Flynn, *Lewis B. Hershey, Mr. Selective Service*, 249–50. Robert A. Malson, "The Black Power Rebellion at Howard University," *Negro Digest* 11, no. 2 (1967): 21–30.

16. Quoted in Eddie W. Morris, "The Contemporary Negro College and the Brain Drain," 310.

17. Fabio Rojas, *From Black Power to Black Studies*, 100–29.

18. See Alex Poinsett, "The 'Brain Drain' at Negro Colleges," *Ebony* (October 1970):

74–82. Vincent Harding, "Toward the Black University," *Ebony* (August 1970): 156–59. "Students, Educators Discuss 'Black University,'" *Jet* (November 28, 1968): 26.

19. Clovis E. Semmes, "Foundations in Africana Studies: Revisiting *Negro Digest/Black World*, 1961–1976," 195–201.

20. For example, see: Novick, *That Noble Dream*. Lee D. Baker, *From Savage to Negro*. Mills, *The Racial Contract*.

21. Jonathan Scott Holloway and Ben Keppel, "Introduction: Segregated Social Science and Its Legacy," 25–26.

22. Wlad Godzich quoted in Sylvia Wynter, "On How We Mistook the Map for the Territory, and Re-Imprisoned Ourselves in Our Unbearable Wrongness of Being, of *Désêtre*: Black Studies toward the Human Project," 113. Wlad Godzich, "Forward: The Further Possibility of Knowledge," in *Heterologies*, x.

23. Baker, *From Savage to Negro*. Daryl Scott, *Contempt and Pity*. Lawrence Levine, *Highbrow/Lowbrow*. Joyce Ladner, ed., *The Death of White Sociology*.

24. Alice O'Connor, *Poverty Knowledge*, 94–98.

25. Gerald McWorter, "The Nature and Needs of the Black University," *Negro Digest* 17, no. 5 (March 1968): 4–13.

26. Vincent Harding, "For Our People—Everywhere: Some International Implications of the Black University," *Negro Digest* 17, no. 5 (1968): 32–39.

27. Woodson, *The Mis-Education of the Negro*, 7.

28. Hoyt Fuller, "Editor's Notes," *Negro Digest* 18, no. 5 (March 1969): 4.

29. McWorter, "The Nature and Needs of the Black University," 8–11.

30. Vincent Harding, "For Our People—Everywhere: Some International Implications of the Black University," 32–39.

31. McWorter, "The Nature and Needs of the Black University," 9. James D Anderson, *The Education of Blacks in the South, 1860–1935*. William H. Watkins, *The White Architects of Black Education*. Joy Ann Williamson, *Radicalizing the Ebony Tower*.

32. "Student Statement," box 573, folder 5, T. D. Jarrett Records 1939–1979, Archives and Special Collections, Robert W. Woodruff Library, Atlanta University Center, Atlanta (hereafter referred to as the T. D. Jarrett Papers).

33. Henderson, "The Black University: Towards Its Realization," *Negro Digest* 17, no. 5 (1968): 21–26, 80–83.

34. Scott, *Contempt and Pity*. Godzich, "Forward: The Further Possibility of Knowledge." Mills, *The Racial Contract*. Jason E. Glenn, "A Second Failed Reconstruction?: The Counter Reformation of African American Studies, a Treason on Black Studies," 119–71.

35. Fred M. Hechinger, "The Negro Colleges: Victims of Progress," *New York Times*, October 6, 1969, 46.

36. James W. Bryant, *A Survey of Black American Doctorates*, 11.

37. Hechinger, "The Negro Colleges: Victims of Progress," 46. Morris, "The Contemporary Negro College and the Brain Drain," 309–19.

38. Harding, "New Creation or Familiar Death: An Open Letter to Black Students in the North," *Negro Digest* 18, no. 5 (1969): 5–15.

39. Martin Kilson Jr., "Anatomy of the Black Studies Movement," the *Massachusetts Review* 10, no. 4 (1969): 718–25.

40. "The Black University Concept: Educators Respond," *Negro Digest* 18, no. 5 (1969): 66–77, 96–98.

41. Rojas, *From Black Power to Black Studies*, 108–16.

42. Ronald Coleman, "Student Power," *Clark College Panther*, November 12, 1968.

43. Ibid.

44. "Flyer," box 573, folder 6, T. D. Jarrett Papers.

45. Coleman, "Student Power."

46. Raymond Wolters, *The New Negro on Campus*. Harry G. Lefever, *Undaunted by the Fight*. Grady-Willis, *Challenging US Apartheid*, 3–55. Cynthia Griggs Fleming, *Soon We Will Not Cry*. "Spelman Women Lead Atlanta," *Jet*, November 28, 1968, 24–25. Albert E. Manley, *A Legacy Continues*, 44–55.

47. Atlanta University and Clark College merged in 1988 to form Clark Atlanta University. "Department of History Self-Study, 1968," box 6, folder 10, Vincent Harding Papers, Special Collections and Archives, Robert W. Woodruff Library, Emory University, Atlanta (hereafter referred to as the Vincent Harding Papers).

48. "Proposal for the creation of: *The W.E.B. Du Bois Institute for Advanced Afro-American Studies*," IBW at King Center Series—IBW Papers

49. Du Bois' Atlanta University research can be found at Special Collections & University Archives, W.E.B. Du Bois Library, University of Massachusetts—Amherst. http://www.library.umass.edu/spcoll/dubois/?tag=atlantastudies. Accessed January 6, 2010. For analysis of Du Bois' Atlanta University research, see Fancille Rusan Wilson, *The Segregated Scholars*, 9–39.

50. "Proposal for the creation of: *The W.E.B. Du Bois Institute for Advanced Afro-American Studies*." "Administrative Structure and Lines of Authority, proposed, 30 May 1969," box 13, folder 2, Vincent Harding Papers. "Models of Relationship to the Institute of the Black World," box 13, folder 4, Vincent Harding Papers.

51. Ibid.

52. "Institute of the Black World Seminars in Black Studies—Fall 1969," box 26, folder 3, Vincent Harding Papers.

53. Harding and Harding, "Biography, Democracy and Spirit," 691. Harding, "Introduction," in *IBW and Education for Liberation* (Chicago: Third World Press/Institute of the Black World, 1973), vi.

54. Harding, "Introduction," vi.

55. Coretta Scott King, "Announcement of the Martin Luther King Memorial Center," January 15, 1969. IBW Vertical File—1969, Robert W. Woodruff Library, Atlanta University Center.

56. Quoted in Robert L. Terrell, "Black Awareness Versus Negro Traditions: Atlanta University Center," *New South* (Winter 1969): 31. Box 573, folder 5, T. D. Jarrett Papers.

57. "Statement on Students Rights and Freedoms," box 573, folder 5, T. D. Jarrett Papers. Manley, *A Legacy Continues*, 49–50. Terrell, "Black Awareness Versus Negro Traditions," 29–30. "Spelman Women Lead Atlanta," 25.

58. Nick Aaron Ford, *Black Studies*. Ford found that many Black colleges, such as Fisk University in Nashville, Tennessee, had provided some courses on Black life as early as 1921, yet after the demands for Black Studies, many colleges drastically increased their

offerings. See also Amiri YaSin Al-Hadid, "Africana Studies at Tennessee State University: Traditions and Diversity," 93–114. Al-Hadid points out that because of the incorporation of Black Studies-type classes into the general curriculum, a department was not established until the late 1980s, after the merger with the predominately White University of Tennessee—Nashville threatened the identity of the Black college. For a detailed examination of the "second curriculum," see Jelani Manu-Gowon Favors, "Shelter in a Time of Storm: Black Colleges and the Rise of Student Activism in Jackson, Mississippi" (Ph.D. dissertation, The Ohio State University, 2006).

59. Manley, *A Legacy Continues*, 49. "Introduction to Curriculum Task Force and Appendix," box 6, folder 12, Vincent Harding Papers. The members of the task force were: Edgar Becham—Wesleyan University, William Bulware—Wesleyan, Theresa Chandler—Spelman College, Prentis Cook—Clark College, Beulah Farmer—Morris Brown College, Dwight Greene—Wesleyan University, Stephen Henderson—Morehouse College, Linda Housch—Spelman College, Douglas Johnson—Wesleyan University, Harvey Smith—Morehouse College, Christine Thomas—Morris Brown College, Russell Williams—Spelman College.

60. Williamson, *Radicalizing the Ebony Tower*. Watkins, *The White Architects of Black Education*.

61. "Department of History Self-Study—Spelman College, 1968," box 6, folder 10, Vincent Harding Papers. Terrell, "Black Awareness Versus Negro Traditions," 33–36. Grady-Willis, *Challenging US Apartheid*, 143–68.

62. Williamson, *Radicalizing the Ebony Tower*, 6.

63. *The Atlanta University Black Paper* and "An Open Letter from A. B. Spellman," box 8, folder 5, Vincent Harding Papers.

64. Smethurst, *Black Arts Movement*, 39.

65. Grady-Willis, *Challenging US Apartheid*, 144. Cleveland Sellers and Robert Terrell, *The River of No Return*, 250–60.

66. Benjamin E. Mays, *Born to Rebel*, 312.

67. "April 16, 1969 Letter to the Board of Trustees AUC from Spelman students," box 573, folder 1, and "April 19, 1969 Letter" box 573, folder 5, T. D. Jarrett Papers. Mays, *Born to Rebel*, 312–15. Manley, *A Legacy Continues*, 50–51. "Students in Atlanta Free Trustees," *New York Times*, April 20, 1969, 77. "Atlanta University Faculty Statement on Campus Unrest," box 6, folder 17, Vincent Harding Papers. "Memo to Mr. James W. Armsey, from John J. Scanlon: April 29, 1969," Institute of the Black World File—Grant 700–0089, Ford Foundation Archives, New York (hereafter referred to as the Ford Foundation Papers).

68. Harding, "Introduction," vi. Correspondence with Abdul Alkalimat by author, August 21, 2002, and August 24, 2005. Harding and Harding, "Biography, Democracy and Spirit," 691. "King Center Board of Directors as of January 1, 1970," box 11, folder 9, Vincent Harding Papers.

69. The administrative staff in 1969–70 included: Judy Barton, Jill Douglass, Brenda Gregory, Tina Harriford, Mamie Jackson, Barbara Knight, Colia LaFayette, Daulton Lewis, Laura Luster, Mayme Mitcham, Ojeda Penn, and LaSayde Potter.

70. IBW, *IBW: The First Year, 1969–1970*, 13–15. See Appendix A.

71. Harding, "Introduction," vi. See Appendix A.

72. Ibid., vi–vii.

73. IBW, "The Institute of the Black World: Statement of Purpose and Program," (1969). Versions of the "Statement of Purpose" appeared in the *Massachusetts Review* 10, no. 4 (1969): 713–17 and *Negro Digest* (March 1970): 20–23.

74. Harding, "Introduction," vii. "An Approach To Black Studies: Statement of the Planning Staff," IBW Papers. Alex Poinsett, "Think Tank for Black Scholars: Institute of the Black World Serves Liberation Movement," *Ebony* (February 1970): 46–54.

75. Francis Ward, "Black Meeting Mired in Factional Dispute," *Los Angeles Times*, September 1, 1969, B12.

76. IBW, "Preliminary Report of a Summer Workshop on Black Studies," box 26, folder 7, Vincent Harding Papers.

77. "Kweli," in *The Perspectives Gained*.

78. Abdul Alkalimat, interview with author, April 7, 2006.

79. See www.eblackstudies.org. Accessed March 3, 2009.

80. Poinsett, "Think Tank for Black Scholars," 46–54. "Black Studies Directors Program," box 22, folder 15, Vincent Harding Papers.

81. Harding, "Introduction," iii.

82. IBW, *Institute of the Black World Directors Seminar*.

83. Ibid.

84. IBW, "Report on Black Studies Directors Seminar," IBW Papers, Reorganization Series.

85. Harding, "Toward the Black University," 156–59.

86. Miller, "Stephen E. Henderson: Conversation with a Literary Critic," 320.

Chapter 2. "Liberated Grounds"

1. "December 6, 1969 Memo," box 22, folder 3, Vincent Harding Papers. "Black Institute Beginning Shows Enthusiasm Here," *Atlanta Voice*, January 25, 1970, 1. "Black World Institute in Operation At A.U." *Atlanta Daily World*, January 20, 1970, 1. IBW, "The Institute of the Black World: Statement of Purpose and Program," (1969).

2. "Dr. M. L. King Jr.'s Body Brought Home to Auburn Ave.," *Atlanta Daily World*, January 15, 1970, 1.

3. "Discussion," in *Black Consciousness and Higher Education*, 8, 9.

4. IBW, *IBW: The First Year, 1969–1970*, 1–24.

5. Gary Daynes, *Making Villains, Making Heroes*, 47–82. W. Fitzhugh Brundage, *The Southern Past*, 1–11.

6. Harding, *Martin Luther King*, 87.

7. Harding, "The Vocation of the Black Scholar and the Struggles of the Black Community," in *Education and Black Struggle*, 25. Derrick E. White, "'Liberated Grounds': The Institute of the Black World and Black Intellectual Space," in *"We Shall Independent Be,"* 167–84.

8. IBW, "Institute of the Black World: Statement of Purpose and Program," *Negro Digest* 19, no. 5 (1970): 19–23. IBW, *IBW: The First Year, 1969–1970*.

9. Stephen Ward, "'Scholarship in the Context of Struggle': Activist Intellectuals, the

Institute of the Black World (IBW), and the Contours of Black Power Radicalism," *Black Scholar* 31, nos. 3/4 (2001): 48.

10. Harding, *Beyond Chaos*, 7, 16, 21.

11. Quoted in Grady-Willis, *Challenging US Apartheid*, 155. Ladner, *Tomorrow's Tomorrow*.

12. Ladner, *Tomorrow's Tomorrow*, xii.

13. Ibid., xix, xxiii, 271.

14. Henderson, ed., *Understanding Black Poetry*, 1–69.

15. FBI, "Institute of the Black World," March 17, 1970, file #: 157–4032, FBI Archive.

16. James, *Black Jacobins*. Hill, ed., *The Marcus Garvey and Universal Negro Improvement Association Papers*. Drake and Cayton, *Black Metropolis*. Alexander, *Jubilee*. Brisbane, *The Black Vanguard* and *Black Activism*.

17. IBW, "Statement of Purpose and Program."

18. Harding, "Toward the Black University," 156. Devin Fergus, *Liberalism, Black Power, and the Making of American Politics, 1965–1980*, 74–90.

19. See FBI, Institute of the Black World," December 1, 1969, file #: 157–4032-3, FBI Archive. This file describes the IBW as an "affiliate of the Malcolm X University" that opened in Atlanta. It seems that the FBI could not initially differentiate between Black Power educational organizations. This was resolved by December 29, 1969, see file#: 157–4032-10.

20. FBI, "Institute of the Black World: Racial Matters," February 12, 1970, file #: 157–4032-27, FBI Archive. Daynes, *Making Villians, Making Heroes*, 47–82. FBI, "Coretta Scott King," File #: 62–108052, FBI Archive. Some of the files can be accessed at: http://foia.fbi.gov/kingcorettascott/kingcorettascott4.pdf. Accessed March 10, 2009. FBI, "Stanley Levinson," file #: 100–392-452-339, FBI Archive. Some of Levinson's file can be accessed at: http://foia.fbi.gov/foiaindex/levison.htm. Accessed March 10, 2009.

21. Carmichael and Hamilton, *Black Power: The Politics of Liberation in America*. Joseph, *Waiting 'Til the Midnight Hour*, 198–201.

22. Stokely Carmichael and Ekwueme Michael Thelwell, *Ready for Revolution*, 659–76. Carson, *In Struggle*, 272–93. Ethel N. Minor, "Editor Notes," in *Stokely Speaks*, ix–xvii. "Stokely Carmichael Returns from Africa," *New York Amsterdam News*, March 28, 1970, 1.

23. Marybeth Gasman, *Envisioning Black Colleges*, 119–37.

24. Bill Montgomery, "Stokely Carmichael Here, Press Barred From Talk," *Atlanta Journal-Constitution*, April 15, 1970, 2A. FBI, "Stokely Carmichael," April 16, 1970, File #: 100–5812 and File #157–4032-36. FBI, "Stokely Carmichael: Racial Matter Black Nationalist," April 21, 1970, File #: 157–4032-38. FBI, "Institute of the Black World: Racial Matters," May 11, 1970, File #: 157–4032-46.

25. Stokely Carmichael, *Stokely Speaks*, 184.

26. Ibid., 189.

27. Ibid. It must be said that Carmichael's public attempts at reconciliation differed from his private conversations. In a letter from William Strickland to the Student Organization of Black Unity, which had been organizing under revolutionary Pan-Africanist ideology, Strickland noted that, during his visit, Carmichael made "attacks on SNCC

and other movement people." Although this was a personal letter encouraging SOBU not to become trapped in ideological pettiness, it also suggests that Carmichael's public discussion of unity differed from his private actions. See "Letter to SOBU," IBW Papers.

28. FBI, "Stokely Carmichael, Racial Matters Black Nationalist," April 16, 1970, 3. For an examination of Carmichael's shift towards Pan-Africanism, see Kwame Ture, "Afterword, 1992," in *Black Power*, 187–200; Carmichael, *Ready for Revolution*, 680–728.

29. IBW, "Black World without End. Amen," *Renewal* (October–November 1970): 3.

30. Von Eschen, *Race against Empire*, 112.

31. Ibid., 167–84. Grace Lee Boggs, "C.L.R. James: Organizing in the U.S., 1938–1952," in *C.L.R. James*, 163–72. Scott McLemee, *C. L. R. James on The "Negro Question."*

32. Here I somewhat disagree with Von Eschen. She argues that activists of the 1960s were cut off from earlier generations and forced to "reinvent the wheel" in developing their own critique of capitalism and imperialism (187). I think that the IBW modifies her conclusion, and believe that the interactions between James, Cayton, and Drake nurtured the analysis of young activists such as Rodney, Hill, Wynter, and Harding. While there was indeed some reinventing, there was a great deal of sharing between activists of different generations. James Smethurst and Peniel E. Joseph both identify how Black Power advocates maintained links with radicals from the 1940s. Von Eschen, *Race Against Empire*, 187. Smethurst, *Black Arts Movement*, 22–56. Joseph, *Waiting 'Til the Midnight Hour*, 9–67.

33. Walter Rodney and Robert Hill, "Statement on the Jamaican Situation," in *Grounding with My Brothers*, 12–15.

34. Clinton Chisholm, "The Rasta-Selassie-Ethiopian Connections," in *Chanting Down Babylon*, 166–77. Nathaniel Samuel Murrell and Burchell K. Taylor, "Rastafari's Messianic Ideology and Caribbean Theology of Liberation," in *Chanting Down Babylon*, 390–414.

35. Michel Foucault, *Archaeology of Knowledge and the Discourse on Language*, 217.

36. Bogues, *Black Heretics, Black Prophets*, 154. Ralph Gonsalves, "The Rodney Affair and Its Aftermath," *Caribbean Quarterly* 25, no. 3 (1979). Michael O. West, "Seeing Darkly: Guyana, Black Power, and Walter Rodney's Expulsion from Jamaica," *Small Axe* 25 (February 2008): 93–104. Robert A. Hill, "From *New World* to *Abeng*: George Beckford and the Horn of Black Power in Jamaica, 1968–1970," *Small Axe* 24 (October 2007): 1–15. Rupert Lewis, *Walter Rodney's Intellectual and Political Thought*, 85–123.

37. Quoted in Hill, "From *New World* to *Abeng*," 6.

38. "Institute of the Black World Seminar," *Small Axe* Conference on African American Studies, April 7–8, 2005. Tape recording in author's possession. Walter Rodney, *Grounding with My Brothers*.

39. "Institute of the Black World Seminar," *Small Axe* Conference. Ula Yvette Taylor, *The Veiled Garvey*.

40. "Robert Hill Speaks at I.T.C.," *Atlanta Daily World*, May 3, 1970, 2.

41. The Institute of the Black World Session at *Small Axe* Conference, April 7, 2005. *Inside the Black World*, 1.1 (April 1971). David Scott, "The Archaeology of Black Memory: An Interview with Robert A. Hill," *Small Axe* 5 (March 1999): 80–150. FBI, "Institute of the Black World: Racial Matter," August 12, 1971, file #: 157–403–92.

42. "Vincent Harding Notes August 1, 1970," box 10, folder 10, Vincent Harding Papers.

43. Taylor Branch, *Pillar of Fire*, 197. Taylor Branch, *At Canaan's Edge*, 595–97.

44. "Operating Budget: Institute of the Black World, 1969–1970," box 21, folder 28, Vincent Harding Papers. "Proposal to Fund the Library-Documentation Project, July 1, 1969–June 30, 1970," box 12, folder 14, Vincent Harding Papers.

45. "Report of the Library-Documentation Project of the Martin Luther King Jr. Memorial Center," May 12, 1970, box 12, folder 16, Vincent Harding Papers.

46. "The Martin Luther King Library Documentation Project: A Report and Recommendations to the Board of Directors From the Evaluation Panel," box 12, folder 22, Vincent Harding Papers.

47. Ibid.

48. For Harry Wachtel's role in SCLC, see Adam Fairclough, *To Redeem the Soul of America*, 97–99.

49. "Actions of the Board of the Directors of the Martin Luther King Jr. Memorial Center Regarding the Library-Documentation Project," box 12, folder 22, Vincent Harding Papers. Meetings attendees were as follows: Benjamin Mays, Harry Wachtel, John Maguire, Stanley Levinson, Edythe Bagley, Joseph Lowery, Andrew Young, Vincent Harding, Isaac Farris, Coretta Scott King.

50. "Plan of Implementation Prepared by the Library-Documentation Project's Governing Council," July 27, 1970, box 12, folder 22, Vincent Harding Papers.

51. "Response to "Actions of the Board of Directors of the MLK Jr. Memorial Center Regarding the LDP," box 12, folder 23, Vincent Harding Papers.

52. "Plan of Implementation Prepared by the Library-Documentation Project's Governing Council, July 27, 1970," box 12, folder 20, Vincent Harding Papers.

53. Ibid.

54. "Vincent Harding Notes—August 1, 1970," box 13, folder 5, Vincent Harding Papers.

55. "Board of Directors Meeting, Martin Luther King Memorial Center, July 27, 1970," box 11, folder 9, Vincent Harding Papers.

56. "Board of Directors Meeting, Martin Luther King Memorial Center, July 27, 1970," box 11, folder 9, Vincent Harding Papers. "LDP Protesters Press Release," box 13, folder 5, Vincent Harding Papers. Boyd Lewis, "MLK Memorial in Money Trouble?" *Atlanta Voice*, August 9, 1970, 1. Bill Montgomery, "Prospects of King Center Shrunken by Tight Budget," *Atlanta Journal and Constitution*, August 16, 1970, 2A.

57. Gailey, "Ousted Workers Picket King Widow at Center," *Atlanta Constitution*, August 5, 1970, 6A.

58. "LDP Protesters Press Release," box 12, folder 19, Vincent Harding Papers.

59. "LDP Demands," box 12, folder 19, Vincent Harding Papers.

60. Gailey, "Ousted Workers Picket King Widow at Center," 2A.

61. Thomas F. Jackson, *From Civil Rights to Human Rights*.

62. "Notes on a phone conversation with Stanley Levinson, 11 August 1970," box 13, folder 5, Vincent Harding Papers.

63. "Fund Shortages and Dissension Plague King Memorial Center," *New York Times*, August 9, 1970, 44.

64. "Vincent Harding Notes—August 1, 1970," box 13, folder 5, Vincent Harding Papers.

65. William Strickland to Vincent Harding, July 16, 1969, IBW at King Center Series—IBW Papers.

66. Joyce Ladner to Vincent Harding, August 23, 1970, box 14, folder 5, Vincent Harding Papers. "Board of Directors Meeting, Martin Luther King Memorial Center minutes, July 27, 1970," box 11, folder 9, Vincent Harding Papers.

67. "Report of the Committee Appointed to Evaluate the Institute of the Black World," box 21, folder 14, Vincent Harding Papers.

68. Ibid.

69. "Letter To Our Friends, Associates and Companions in the Struggle: A Letter on Behalf of the Institute of the Black World Regarding the Current Crisis in the Martin Luther King Jr. Memorial Center," August 14, 1970, IBW at King Center Series—IBW Papers.

70. Ibid., 2.

71. Harding, "Vocation of the Black Scholar," 10.

72. "Memorandum of Understanding," box 15, folder 2, Vincent Harding Papers.

73. King, *Where Do We Go from Here.*

74. Jackson, *From Civil Rights to Human Rights.* Michael K. Honey, *Going Down Jericho Road.*

75. Martin Luther King Jr., *The Trumpet of Conscience*, 16–17.

76. IBW, *IBW: The First Year, 1969–1970.*

77. "Gala Star Fete Raises $60,000 Plus for MLK Memorial," *Los Angeles Sentinel*, December 4, 1969, 1A.

78. "Board of Directors Meeting, Martin Luther King Memorial Center minutes, July 27, 1970," box 11, folder 9, Vincent Harding Papers. "Proposal to Fund the Library-Documentation Project, July 1, 1969–June 30, 1970," April 1, 1969, box 12, folder 14, Vincent Harding Papers. "Institute of the Black World Audit Report," July 27, 1970, box 21, folder 28, Vincent Harding Papers. "Letter To Our Friends, Associates and Companions in the Struggle," 4.

79. Lerone Bennett Jr., "January 20, 1970 Memo" IBW Papers.

80. Ibid., 2.

81. Sterling Stuckey, "4 February 1970, Letter of Resignation," box 14, folder 2, Vincent Harding Papers.

82. Ibid., 1–2.

83. Strickland, "From Liberalism to Organization," box 13, folder 8, Vincent Harding Papers.

84. Rojas, *From Black Power to Black Studies*, 133.

85. Ibid., 151–53. Also see Noliwe Rooks, *White Money/ Black Power*, 1–29, 93–121.

86. "Income For the Institute of the Black World: (July, 1969–May, 1970)," box 21, folder 28, Vincent Harding Papers. Jeffrey L. Cruikshank and David B. Scilia, *The Engine That Could*, 322–24.

87. Richard J. Margolis, "The Two Nations at Wesleyan University," the *New York Times Magazine*, January 18, 1969, 48–60.

88. Vincent Harding, "May 4, 1971 Letter from Alfred Minor, Dartmouth College." IBW Papers, General Correspondence, April–June 1971.

89. "Two Black Programs Receive Grants," *Atlanta Voice*, February 22, 1970, 3. Joyce Ladner to Vincent Harding, August 23, 1970, box 14, folder 5, Vincent Harding Papers.

90. "Memo from William Strickland to IBW Negotiating Committee," August 28, 1970. IBW Papers—IBW at King Center Series.

91. "Memorandum of Understanding," box 15, folder 2, Vincent Harding Papers.

92. "To Our Friends, Associates and Companions in the Struggle: A Letter on Behalf of the Institute of the Black World Regarding the Current Crisis in the Martin Luther King Jr. Memorial Center," 5, IBW Papers—IBW at King Center Series.

93. Ronald W. Walters to IBW, February 10, 1971. Council Taylor to IBW, February 17, 1971. IBW Papers.

94. William Strickland, "Beginning Again," box 13, folder 8, Vincent Harding Papers.

95. William Strickland, "Critik: The Institute of the Black World (IBW), the Political Legacy of Martin Luther King, and the Intellectual Struggle to Rethink America's Racial Meaning," in *Radicalism in the South since Reconstruction*, 174–76.

96. William Strickland, "Reorganization Reconsidered: Stage One and a Half," box 13, folder 9, Vincent Harding Papers.

97. Strickland, "From Liberalism to Organization," box 13, folder 8, Vincent Harding Papers.

98. William Strickland, "Reflections on the Staff Reorganization," box 13, folder 10, Vincent Harding Papers.

99. See Cornel West, "The Paradox of the African American Rebellion," Adolph Reed Jr., "Black Particularity Reconsidered," and Wahneema Lubiano, "Standing in for the State: Black Nationalism and 'Writing' the Black Subject," in Eddie S. Glaude, ed., *Is It Nation Time?*, 22–38, 39–66, 156–64.

100. William Strickland, "Notes from Jamaica," box 13, folder 8, Vincent Harding Papers.

101. The scholarship on the IBW reinforces this perspective as well. See Ward, "Scholarship in the Context of Struggle,"42–53. Peniel E. Joseph, "Dashikis and Democracy: Black Studies, Student Activism, and the Black Power Movement," *Journal of African American History* 88, no. 2 (2003): 182–203. Grady-Willis, *Challenging US Apartheid*, 143–68. Rojas, *From Black Power to Black Studies*.

102. Miller, "Stephen E. Henderson: Conversation with a Literary Critic," 317–25.

103. *Inside the Black World*1, no. 1 (April 1971): 4. *IBW Monthly Report* (June 1971), 2. *IBW Monthly Report* (July 1971), 2. Rachel Harding, "Biography, Democracy, and Spirit," 692. Harding, "May 4, 1971 Letter from Alfred Minor, Dartmouth College." Strickland, "Notes from Jamaica." Brisbane, *Black Activism*, 240. Miller, "Stephen E. Henderson: Conversation with a Literary Critic," 317–25.

104. Strickland, "Notes from Jamaica."

105. "Black World Symposium Underway," *Chicago Defender*, June 26, 1971, 10.

106. William Strickland examined the work of James Boggs and the political ideas

of Amilcar Cabral, see "The Evolution of Revolution: James Boggs and American Social Analysis" and "The Evolution of Revolution: The Contribution of Amilcar Cabral," IBW Papers—Summer Research Symposia 1971 Series.

107. William Strickland, "Some Reflections and Recommendations on Research for Summer Research Symposium," IBW Papers—Summer Research Symposia 1971 Series.

108. Ibid.

109. "Institute of the Black World Summer Research Symposium 1971—Official Report," IBW Papers—Summer Research Symposia 1971 Series.

110. William Strickland, "Some Reflections and Recommendations on Research for Summer Research Symposium." For additional details on the SRS '71, see Robert A. Hill, "Preface: The C.L.R. James Lectures," *Small Axe* 8 (September 2000): 61–64. George Beckford did not arrive until the last week of the symposium; he could not receive a visa because of his activism in Jamaica. Institute of the Black World, *Monthly Report* (June 1971). Scott, "The Archaeology of Black Memory: An Interview with Robert A. Hill," *Small Axe* (March 1999), 80–150. See Appendix A for a list of participants.

111. C.L.R. James, "The Role of the Black Scholar," 23, IBW Papers. James, "Lectures on the Black Jacobins," in *Small Axe* (September 2000): 78.

112. St. Clair Drake, "The Black University and the American Social Order," *Daedalus* 100 (1971): 889–92.

113. St. Clair Drake, "In the Mirror of Black Scholarship: W. Allison Davis and *Deep South*," in *Education and Black Struggle*, ed. IBW (Cambridge: Harvard Educational Review, 1974), 42.

114. Institute of the Black World Summer Research Symposium 1971—Official Report," IBW Papers. George Beckford, "The Role of the Black Intellectual and the Struggles of the Black Community: Public Lecture 27 July 1971," 18. IBW Papers. George L. Beckford, *Persistent Poverty*. IBW, *Monthly Report* (June 1971). Sylvia Wynter, "On Disenchanting Discourse: 'Minority' Literary Criticism and Beyond," in *The Nature and Context of Minority Discourse*, 432–71. J.G.A. Pocock, *Politics, Language, and Time*, 6. James, "African Independence and the Myth of African Inferiority," in *Education and Black Struggle: Notes from the Colonized World*, 34.

115. Hazel V. Carby, *Race Men*.

116. "Memo: June 28, 1972 from Leslie Hill to SRS Committee," box 26, folder 5, Vincent Harding Papers.

117. "Excerpts from Participants' Evaluations of the 1971 SRS," box 26, folder 6, Vincent Harding Papers.

118. "Black (Studies) Vatican," *Newsweek*, August 11, 1969, 38.

119. Strickland, "From Liberalism to Organization." Emphasis in original.

120. Strickland, "Beginning Again," box 13, folder 8, Vincent Harding Papers.

121. Robnett, *How Long? How Long?*, 19–23.

122. "Note on the Document," box 13, folder 8, Vincent Harding Papers. Sharon Bourke, personal correspondence, November 1, 2006. IBW Executive Committee, "Minutes of Meetings—April 21–22, 1971," box 20, folder 15, Vincent Harding Papers.

123. "July 18, 1971 Memo to Executive Committee, from Sharon Bourke," IBW Papers.

124. Jualynne Dodson, interview with author, April 6, 2006.

125. IBW, "IBW Reconsidered: Moving to a Higher Stage," IBW Papers—Administrative series.

126. Ibid., 198–205. Bourke, personal correspondence.

127. Jualynne Dodson, "Memo to Executive Committee," box 13, folder 9, Vincent Harding Papers. Jualynne Dodson, interview with author, April 4, 2006. For additional examples of Black women's response to the masculine tendencies in the Black Power era, see: Stephen Ward, "The Third World Women's Alliance: Black Feminist Radicalism and Black Power Politics," in *The Black Power Movement*, 119–44; Kimberly Springer, *Living for the Revolution*.

128. Stephen E. Henderson, "On Reorganization Reconsidered—May 5/6, 1971," IBW Papers—Reorganization Series.

129. "The Truth of IBW—Notes from Staff Education Meeting 8/31/1971," IBW Papers. Staff Caucus, "Reorganization Begun, but Incomplete," IBW Papers—Reorganization Series.

130. "Memo: Interim and Long-range Organizational Consolidation from Vincent Harding, April 24, 1972," IBW Papers—Reorganization Series. "Memo: Vincent Harding to William Strickland, May 20, 1972," IBW Papers—Reorganization Series.

131. "Memo to Planning Committee from Janet Douglass," July 22, 1972, IBW Papers—Reorganization Series.

132. Ibid. See her criticism of the IBW, "Memo: Leadership and Organization from Janet Douglass, April 23, 1972," IBW Papers—Reorganization Series.

133. Quoted in Grady-Willis, *Challenging US Apartheid*, 198.

134. Ibid.

135. William Strickland, "Reflections on the Staff Reorganization Documents," IBW Papers.

136. Vincent Harding, "Response to: 'Reorganization Begun, But Incomplete,'" IBW Papers.

137. "Summary of the Minutes, IBW Reorganization Meeting, November 19, 1971," box 13, folder 13, Vincent Harding Papers.

138. Bettina Aptheker, *The Morning Breaks*.

139. "Mrs. King Blames Financial Situation in Firing of 12," *Atlanta Daily World*, August 6, 1970, 1

140. Vincent Harding, "Towards the Black Agenda," box 21, folder 6, Hoyt Fuller Collection, Archives and Special Collections, Robert W. Woodruff Library, Atlanta University Center (hereafter referred to as the Hoyt Fuller Papers).

Chapter 3. "Toward a Black Agenda"

1. "The Gary Declaration: Black Politics at the Crossroads," *IBW Monthly Report* (February 1972): 1–3. Ibid., 1–5. Smith, *We Have No Leaders*, 46, 300–47. Thomas A. Johnson mistakenly attributes the "Preamble" to Congressman Walter Fauntroy and Illinois State senator Richard Newhouse. Thomas A. Johnson, "N.A.A.C.P. Aide Opposes Draft of Black Preamble," *New York Times*, March 10, 1972, 20. The preamble was introduced through a panel chaired by Fauntroy and Newhouse. Jerry Gafio Watts repeats this mistake; see Jerry Gafio Watts, *Amiri Baraka*, 408.

2. *National Black Political Agenda*, (Washington, D.C.: National Black Political Convention, 1972).

3. *National Black Political Agenda*, 1–4.

4. Thomas Kuhn, *The Structure of Scientific Revolutions*, 11.

5. William Julius Wilson, *More Than Just Race*, 95–100. Wilson describes the Black perspective as "racial chauvinism" and "black glorification."

6. William Strickland, "Toward a Statement of Position," box 13, folder 6, Vincent Harding Papers.

7. Andrew Grant-Thomas and john a. powell, "Toward a Structural Racism Framework," *Poverty and Race* 15, no. 6 (2006): 5. Emphasis in original. See also Bonilla-Silva, "Rethinking Racism: Toward a Structural Interpretation," *American Sociological Review* 62 (1996): 465–80.

8. Ibid., 6.

9. IBW, "The Institute of the Black World: Statement of Purpose and Program," (1969), 4. Vincent Harding, "Towards the Black Agenda." Emphasis in original.

10. Ronald W. Walters, *Black Presidential Politics in America*, 31–38.

11. David A. Bositis, *Black Elected Officials*, 17. In 1970 there were a total of 1,469 BEOs, in 1972 there were 2,264, and by 2000 there were 9,040.

12. The Congressional Black Caucus Web site, http://www.thecongressionalblackcaucus.com/. Accessed April 10, 2008.

13. Bayard Rustin, "From Protest to Politics: The Future of the Civil Rights Movement," *Commentary* 39, no. 1 (1965): 25–31.

14. Smith, *The Idea Brokers*, 196–202.

15. Frank Kusch, *Battleground Chicago: The Police and the 1968 Democratic National Convention*, 69–115.

16. Quoted in Carroll, *It Seemed Like Nothing Happened*, 72.

17. Adolph Reed Jr., "Black Particularity Reconsidered," in *Is It Nation Time?*, 51.

18. William Strickland, "Notes from Jamaica," IBW Papers—Administrative Series.

19. Woodard, *A Nation within a Nation*, 1–45. Brown, *Fighting for Us*, 1–6, 74–107.

20. William Strickland, "Politics and Black Liberation," box 36, folder 1, Larry Neal Papers, Schomburg Center for Research in Black Culture, New York (hereafter referred to as the Larry Neal Papers).

21. Stephen Henderson, "Black Art and Culture: The 70s," box 22, folder 8, Vincent Harding Papers.

22. See also Rooks, *White Money/Black Power*.

23. Chester Davis, "Black Pre-College Education: Notes on an Agenda for the 70s," box 22, folder 8, Vincent Harding Papers.

24. Robert S. Browne and Bill Strickland, "Black Economic Development: Some Considerations," box 36, folder 1, Larry Neal Papers.

25. Bill Strickland, "Suppress Your Local Police," box 36, folder 1, Larry Neal Papers.

26. Addison Gayle to Vincent Harding, Re: BAN articles. Mack Jones to Vincent Harding, July 24, 1970. "Comments by Julius Lester on the Black Agenda Working Papers," IBW Papers—Activities and Projects—Black Agenda Network Series. Ronald J. Stephens, *Idlewild*.

27. "Proposal for Funding Black Agenda Network," December 18, 1970, box 22, folder 7, Vincent Harding Papers. See Appendix for a list of BAN chairpersons.

28. Ibid., 4–6.

29. "Report of Political Organizing Task Force," 1–6. Emphasis in original. IBW Papers—Activities and Projects—Black Agenda Network Series. This committee included: William Strickland, chairman; Ella Baker; Robert Chapman, Department of Social Justice, National Council of Churches; Mack Jones, political scientist; Mayme Mitcham, IBW staff; Alex Poinsett, *Ebony* magazine; Bryant Rollins, H. Carl McCall Associates; Nehaz Rogers, Black Consultants, representing offices of the mayor of Gary, Indiana; Stanley Smith, dean, Fisk University; Charles Turner, Black United Front, Boston; James Turner, chair of Africana Studies, Cornell University; and Leon Watts, associate director, National Committee of Black Churchmen.

30. Vincent Harding and William Strickland, "For a Black Political Agenda," *New York Times,* December 23, 1970, 27.

31. Ibid.

32. "Proposal for Funding Black Agenda Network," December 18, 1970, box 22, folder 7, Vincent Harding Papers.

33. "4 February 1971 Memo: To Executive Committee; From Black Agenda Network Committee, Aljosie Yabura; Re. Proposed revisions in BAN Structure." IBW Papers—Activities and Projects—Black Agenda Network Series. *IBW Monthly Report*, December 3, 1971.

34. Other meetings were held in Washington, D.C., and Greensboro, North Carolina. The central figures at the meetings were Jesse Jackson, Cleveland mayor Carl Stokes, Gary mayor Richard Hatcher, Detroit congressman John Conyers, Percy Sutton, Julian Bond, Michigan congressman Charles Diggs, Coretta King, California state legislators Willie Brown and Mervyn Dymally, Texas state senator Barbara Jordan, the Urban League's Vernon Jordan, California congressman Augustus Hawkins, District of Columbia congressman Walter Fauntroy, Clarence Mitchell of the Washington, D.C., NAACP, New York politician Basil Patterson, Roy Innis of CORE, and Amiri Baraka. Smith, *We Have No Leaders*, 39–40. Woodard, A *Nation within a Nation*, 184–203.

35. Quoted in Shirley Chisholm, *The Good Fight*, 29.

36. Imamu Amiri Baraka, "Toward the Creation of Political Institutions for All African People," *Black World* 21, no. 12 (1972): 54–78. Smith, *We Have No Leaders*, 41–43. For an examination of the Black electoral theories, see Walters, *Black Presidential Politics in America*, 1–84.

37. William L. Clay, *Just Permanent Interests*, 192–99. Smith, *We Have No Leaders*, 41–42.

38. Bennett quoted in Clay, *Just Permanent Interests*, 200–201. Emphasis mine.

39. Quoted in Johnson, "N.A.A.C.P. Aide Opposes Draft of Black Preamble," *New York Times*, March 10, 1972, 20.

40. Ibid.

41. Harold Cruse will link the NAACP's position to its long-standing ideology of noneconomic liberalism. According to Cruse, this perspective led to impressive victories during the civil rights phase of the Black Freedom Struggle, but by the 1970s, with the

advancement of BEOs, their program became "obsolete." Harold Cruse, *Plural but Equal*, 341–370.

42. *IBW Monthly Report* (March 1972): 1.

43. Ibid., 1–4.

44. Ibid., 2–3.

45. Ibid., 3. For minimum wage data, see U.S. Department of Labor Web site, http://www.dol.gov/esa/minwage/chart.pdf. Accessed February 6, 2008. For poverty data, see U.S. Census Bureau Web site, http://www.census.gov/hhes/www/poverty/histpov/hst-pov1.html. Accessed February 6, 2008. For a discussion of Nixon's Family Assistance Plan, see Daniel P. Moynihan, *The Politics of a Guaranteed Income*. Gareth Davies describes the Family Assistance Plan as the zenith of liberal entitlement; Gareth Davies, *From Opportunity to Entitlement*, 211–34. It should also be noted that Martin Luther King Jr. promoted a guaranteed income aimed at the median American income, not just above the poverty line. The IBW's proposal is in line with King's suggestion. This must have been ironic to Harding and other associates, who had been accused by the King Center of not following King's philosophy. King, *Where Do We Go from Here*, 170–75.

46. *IBW Monthly Report* (March 1972): 4.

47. Ibid., 4. Vincent Harding, *There Is a River*.

48. Henry and Steve Fayer Hampton, eds., *Voices of Freedom*, 573.

49. Woodard, *A Nation within a Nation*, 204–7.

50. Ibid., 207–10. Thomas A. Johnson, "Blacks Divided on Basic Role in Politics," *New York Times*, March 12, 1972, 1.

51. William Strickland, "Notes on Gary," IBW Papers—William Strickland Series.

52. Quoted in Smith, *We Have No Leaders*, 50–51.

53. Coleman Young and Lonnie Wheeler, *Hard Stuff*, 190–91.

54. Smith, *We Have No Leaders*, 49–52, 302–72.

55. Johnson, "Blacks Divided on Basic Role in Politics," *New York Times*, March 12, 1972, 1. Thomas A. Johnson, "Parley Shows Complexity and Vitality in Black America," *New York Times*, March 14, 1972, 31. William Strickland, "Memo on Gary: From Bill; To: Vincent/Sharon," IBW Papers—William Strickland Series.

56. William Strickland, "Notes on Gary," IBW Papers—William Strickland Series.

57. William Strickland, "Notes on Gary." William Strickland, "Memo on Gary." William Strickland, "Notes on Carbon." William Strickland, "Bill Strickland at the Black Political Science Association: On Gary and the Politics of 1972, May 4, 1972." IBW Papers—William Strickland Series.

58. William Strickland, "Notes on Gary." William Strickland, "The Gary Convention and the Crisis of American Politics," *Black World* 12, no. 2 (1972): 18–26.

59. William Strickland, "Notes on Carbon." William Strickland, "Memo on Gary." William Strickland, "7 April 1972 Memo to Alex Poinsett."

60. William Strickland, "Notes on Carbon." William Strickland, "Memo on Gary." William Strickland, "7 April 1972 Memo to Alex Poinsett." The IBW sought to attach a "coupon" with the broadside encouraging people to send it back if they agreed with the principles of the preamble. They realized that trying to include the concerns of "30 million people in one document" was impossible.

61. *National Black Political Agenda*, 6–8.

62. Ibid., 9–10.

63. Strickland, "The Gary Convention and the Crisis of American Politics," *Negro Digest* 21:12 (October 1972), 20.

64. Ibid., 22–23.

65. Vincent Harding, *The Other American Revolution*, 217. Clay, *Just Permanent Interests*, 215–18. Walters, *Black Presidential Politics in America*, 92–93.

66. Smith, *We Have No Leaders*, 78.

67. Smith, *We Have No Leaders*, 75–85. For another detailed examination of political ideologies in Black communities, see Michael C. Dawson, *Black Visions*.

68. Cedric Johnson, *Revolutionaries to Race Leaders*, 129.

69. J. Phillip Thompson, *Double Trouble*, 39–72.

70. William Strickland, "Gary and the Politics of 1972 at the Black Political Science Association Conference," May 4, 1972. See also Strickland, "The Gary Convention and the Crisis of American Politics."

71. Thomas J. Sugrue, *The Origins of the Urban Crisis*. Thompson, *Double Trouble*. William E. Nelson and Philip J. Meranto, *Electing Black Mayors*. Leonard N. Moore, *Carl B. Stokes and the Rise of Black Political Power*. Woodard, *A Nation within a Nation*.

72. Clarence N. Stone, *Regime Politics*, 29.

73. Grady-Willis, *Challenging US Apartheid*, 3–55.

74. Ibid., 79–113.

75. Ibid., 79–113. Mack H. Jones, "Black Political Empowerment in Atlanta: Myth and Reality," *Annals of the American Academy of Political and Social Science* 439 (1978): 90–117. Kevin Kruse, *White Flight*, 19–41. Ronald H. Bayor, *Race and the Shaping of Twentieth-Century Atlanta*.

76. James T. Wooten, "Mayor Enlivens Atlanta Contest," the *New York Times*, October 20, 1969, 30. Peter H. Prugh, "Atlanta: Black-White Coalition Fades," *Wall Street Journal*, October 6, 1969, 22.

77. Mack Jones, "Black Political Empowerment in Atlanta," *Annals of the American Academy of Political and Social Science* 439 (1978), 99. Bayor, *Race and the Shaping of Twentieth-Century Atlanta*, 41–48.

78. "Memo from William Strickland to Vincent Harding, Re: Black Leadership in Atlanta," IBW Papers—Georgia Politics Series. "Memo to James Cheek, President and Andrew Billingsley, Vice-President Howard University, from Vincent Harding, Re: Conversation with Mayor Gibson and Imamu Baraka," June 12, 1971, IBW Papers—Administrative Series.

79. IBW, "Drafted Statement in Response to Attica and Governor Carter's Redistricting," IBW Papers—Georgia Politics Series. See Duane Riner, "Carter Okays Redistricting," *Atlanta Constitution*, September 13, 1971, 7a.

80. *National Black Political Agenda*, 1.

81. Maynard Jackson, "Announcement of Candidacy for Mayor," March 28, 1973. Maynard Jackson Papers—Speeches Series, Robert W. Woodruff Library, Atlanta University Center, (hereafter referred to as the Maynard Jackson Papers—Speeches Series).

82. Vincent Harding and Bill Strickland to Maynard Jackson, Re: The Speech, June

15, 1973; "Atlanta in the Best and Worst of Times," both in IBW Papers—Georgia Politics Series.

83. R. T. Roland, "Editorial," *Atlanta Fraternal Order of Police Newsletter*, IBW Papers—Georgia Politics series.

84. Jones, "Black Political Empowerment in Atlanta," 107–8. Bayor, *Race and the Shaping of Twentieth-Century Atlanta*. Kruse, *White Flight*.

85. Jones, "Black Political Empowerment in Atlanta." Stone, *Regime Politics*, 85–89.

86. Stone, *Regime Politics*, 91.

87. Jones, "Black Political Empowerment in Atlanta," 113–15. Stone, *Regime Politics*, 89–91. "Striking Sanitation Workers Fired after Refusal to Work," *Atlanta Daily World*, April 3, 1977, 1.

Chapter 4. "Collective Scholarship"

1. Harding, "The Vocation of the Black Scholar and the Struggles of the Black Community," in *Education and Black Struggle*, 1–29.

2. Quoted in Johnson, *Revolutionaries to Race Leaders*, 139.

3. Ibid., 142.

4. Cedric Johnson, "From Popular Anti-Imperialism to Sectarianism: The African Liberation Support Committee and Black Power Radicals," *New Political Science* 25:4 (December 2003): 477–507. Joseph, *Waiting 'Til the Midnight Hour*, 289–93. Marable, *Race, Reform, and Rebellion*, 132–37. Imamu Amiri Baraka, "Why I Changed My Ideology," *Black World* 24, no. 9 (July 1975): 30–42.

5. Abelson, *Do Think Tanks Matter?*, 20, 31.

6. IBW, "Appendix," in *Education and Black Struggle*. Bennett, *The Challenge of Blackness*. Harding, *Beyond Chaos*. Margaret Walker, *How I Wrote Jubilee*. St. Clair Drake, *The Redemption of Africa and Black Religion*. "IBW Needs Your Help and We All Need IBW," *IBW Monthly Report* (May/June 1979): 7.

7. IBW, "Appendix." *IBW Monthly Report* (May 1974).

8. Ibid. Vincent Harding to Hoyt Fuller, June 3, 1971, box 21, folder 17, Hoyt Fuller Papers. Claude A. Clegg, *An Original Man*, 160.

9. IBW, "The Meaning of Malcolm for the 70s," in *Black Analysis for Seventies*. All of the columns from 1971–72 were published together in *Black Analysis for the Seventies*.

10. Joseph Lelyveld "Friends Bid Louis Armstrong a Nostalgic Farewell at Simple Service: Friends Bid Louis Armstrong Farewell," *New York Times*, July 10, 1971, 1.

11. IBW, "The King of Jazz Is Ours," in *Black Analysis for the Seventies*, 17–20. Emphasis in original.

12. IBW, "Agnew in Africa: What Is the Real Deal?," in *Black Analysis for the Seventies*, 21–23.

13. Eric Cummings, *The Rise and Fall of California's Radical Prison Movement*.

14. George Jackson, *Soledad Brother*, 225. Emphasis in original.

15. Marable, *Race, Reform, and Rebellion*, 128–30. Joseph, *Waiting 'Til the Midnight Hour*, 268–75. Bettina Aptheker, *The Morning Breaks*. Michel Foucault, Catharine von Bülow, and Daniel Defert, "The Masked Assassination," in Joy James, ed., *Warfare in the American Homeland*, 140–58. Bob Dylan, "George Jackson," 1971.

16. Clayborne Carson, David J. Garrow, Gerald Gill, Vincent Harding, Darlene Clarke Hine, eds., *The Eyes on the Prize Reader*, 557–90. Marable, *Race, Reform, and Rebellion*, 128–30.

17. Grady-Willis, *Challenging US Apartheid*, 186–87. "Attica: Troopers Surround Meeting of Students and Legislators," *Atlanta Voice*, October 2, 1971, 1. FBI File # 157–4032–95, October 12, 1971. Harmon Perry, "Dissatisfied Blacks March to Capitol," *Atlanta Journal*.

18. *IBW Monthly Report* (September 1971). *IBW Monthly Report* (October 1971). IBW, "Attica: The Revolution That Was/ the Revolution That Is to Be," in *Black Analysis for the Seventies*, 6–8. Harmon Perry, "Dissatisfied Blacks March to Capitol," *Atlanta Journal*. 10. FBI, file #: 157–4032–94, October 7, 1971, FBI Archive.

19. IBW, "The American State Vs. Black People," in *Black Analysis for the Seventies*, 25–27. Edwin L. Dale Jr., "Inflation Linked to Jobless Level: More Economic Pressures Found in Present Decade If Employment Is Low," *New York Times*, February 15, 1971, 2.

20. IBW, "Black Reflections on 1971," in *Black Analysis for the Seventies*, 35–39.

21. Amy Jacques Garvey to Vincent Harding, April 13, 1971, box 15, folder 7, Vincent Harding Papers.

22. IBW, "From Gary to McGovern: Black Politics—Lost, Strayed, and Betrayed," *IBW Monthly Report* (September 1972).

23. IBW, "The Crisis and Challenge of Black Politics—Part One," *IBW Monthly Report* (March 1973).

24. IBW, "The Crisis and Challenge of Black Politics—Part Two: Towards a Politics of Self-Reliance," *IBW Monthly Report* (April 1973).

25. Frantz Fanon, *The Wretched of the Earth*, 311–16. Fanon said, "For Europe, for ourselves, and for humanity, comrades, we must turn over a new leaf, we must work out new concepts, and try to set afoot a new man."

26. IBW, "Activities and Publications," *An IBW Special Report* (July 1975): 5. A current review of the WorldCat database shows that approximately two hundred libraries own *Education and Black Struggle*, nearly four times as many as possess Lerone Bennett Jr.'s *IBW and Education for Liberation*.

27. IBW, ed., *Education and Black Struggle*, 113–26.

28. IBW, "Racism and Black Depression," *Monthly Report* (November 1972).

29. Ibid. Adam Smith, *An Inquiry into the Nature and Causes of the Wealth of Nations*, 198–221. Karl Marx, "Economic and Philosophical Manuscripts of 1844," in *The Marx-Engels Reader*, 66–125.

30. "IBW—SRS '74 Draft Report," IBW Papers—SRS '74 Series. Institute of the Black World, "Summer 1974," *IBW Monthly Report* (Summer 1974). Walter Rodney, *How Europe Underdeveloped Africa*. Amilcar Cabral, *Return to the Source*.

31. William Strickland to Walter Rodney, May 2, 1974, IBW Papers—William Strickland Series. "29 May 1974, Official Letter of Invitation from Vincent Harding," IBW Papers.

32. Rodney, *Walter Rodney Speaks*, 16.

33. Rodney, *Grounding with My Brothers*, 63.

34. Horace Campbell, *Rasta and Resistance*. Lewis, *Walter Rodney's Intellectual and Political Thought*.

35. Rodney, "African History in the Service of the Black Liberation," *Small Axe* 5, no. 2 (2001): 66–80.

36. Vincent Harding, Robert Hill, and William Strickland, "Introduction," in *How Europe Underdeveloped Africa*, xvi. For a brief history of AHSA, see John Henrik Clarke, "The African Heritage Studies Association (AHSA): Some Notes on the Conflict with the African Studies Association (ASA) and the Fight to Reclaim African History," *Issue: A Journal of Opinion* 6, nos. 2/3 (1976): 5–11.

37. Lewis, *Walter Rodney's Intellectual and Political Thought*, xvii.

38. Rodney, *How Europe Underdeveloped Africa*, 4. See also Colin Leys, *The Rise and Fall of Development Theory*; Lewis, *Walter Rodney's Intellectual and Political Thought*, xvi–xvii, 111–12.

39. Rodney, *How Europe Underdeveloped Africa*, 27–28.

40. Walter Rodney, "'Labour' as a Conceptual Framework for Pan-African Studies," IBW Papers—Walter Rodney Series. For an example of the increasing prevalence of dogmatic Marxists and Nationalists, see Johnson, *Revolutionaries to Race Leaders*, 131–72.

41. Walter Rodney, "Politics of the African Ruling Class," *Black World View* 1:7 (1976), 12–17.

42. Ibid., 4, 10. William Strickland and Walter Rodney, "Racism and Capitalism in American National Development: America—the Problem of Theory—SRS '74," IBW Papers—SRS '74 Series.

43. Vincent Harding, Robert Hill, and William Strickland, "Introduction," *How Europe Underdeveloped Africa*, (Washington, DC: Howard University Press, 1981), xviii.

44. Howard Dodson, "Introduction," in *Walter Rodney Speaks*, ix.

45. Marable, *Race, Reform, and Rebellion*, 134.

46. Dodson, "Introduction." William Strickland to Walter Rodney, June 5, 1975, box 4, correspondence with William Strickland, Walter Rodney Papers, Robert W. Woodruff Library, Atlanta University Center, (hereafter referred to as the Walter Rodney Papers). The Rodney Papers were not processed at the time of research.

47. IBW, "An Afternoon with the Institute of the Black World," *An IBW Special Report* (July 1975).

48. IBW, "American in Crisis: Aspects and Dimensions," *An IBW Special Report* (July 1975).

49. Dodson, "Introduction," xii.

50. Stephen G. Rabe, *U. S. Intervention in British Guiana*.

51. Dodson, "Introduction," xii. Vincent Harding, Robert Hill, and William Strickland, "Introduction," in *How Europe Underdeveloped Africa*.

52. Rodney, *Walter Rodney Speaks*, 1–79. Sections of the roundtable discussion appeared in IBW, "Parties, Ideologies, and Political Development: A Conversation with Walter Rodney," *Black World View* 1, no. 2 (1976), 8–9, 15. "The Politicization of Race in Guyana: A Conversation with Walter Rodney," *Black World View* 1, no. 8 (1976), 8–10.

53. Ibid., 81–110.

54. Ibid., 110–22.

55. C.L.R. James, Raya Dunayevskaya and Grace Lee, *State Capitalism and World Revolution*.

56. Stephen Michael Ward, "'Ours Too Was a Struggle for a Better World': Activist Intellectuals and the Radical Promise of the Black Power Movement, 1962–1972," (Ph.D. dissertation, The University of Texas at Austin, 2002), 36. Grace Lee Boggs, *Living for Change*, 50–75.

57. Boggs, *Living for Change*.

58. Boggs, *Racism and Class Struggle*, 26–32. Joseph, *Waiting 'Til the Midnight Hour*, 68–94.

59. Boggs, *The American Revolution*. Boggs, *Racism and Class Struggle*.

60. William Strickland, SRS '71 Lectures, "The Evolution of Revolution: James Boggs and American Social Analysis," IBW Papers—SRS '71 Series.

61. William Strickland, interview with author, February 7, 2003.

62. Grace Lee Boggs, "Education: The Great Obsession," in *Education and Black Struggle*, 61–81.

63. Grace Lee Boggs, "Education to Build a New America," *Black World View* 1, no. 4 (1976).

64. Yvonne Shinhoster, "Role of Education in America Scrutinized," *Atlanta Daily World*, February 3, 1976, 3.

65. Abelove et al., eds., *Visions of History*, 233.

66. "Roundtable with James and Grace Boggs and Lerone Bennett," IBW Papers—Lerone Bennett Series. IBW, "An Afternoon with the Institute of the Black World," *An IBW Special Report* (July 1975).

67. Xavier Nicholas, *Questions of the American Revolution*.

68. Ibid.

69. Ibid.

70. Ibid. Emphasis in original.

71. Ibid. IBW 1976–1979 Vertical File, Robert W. Woodruff Library, Atlanta University Center. Schedule for "Role Alternatives for Black Women: Where to from Here in the Black Freedom Struggle," December 9–10, 1977. See also "Key Women Participate In Workshop At JFK," *Atlanta Daily World*, December 15, 1977, 2.

72. Johnson, *Revolutionaries to Race Leaders*, 163.

73. Nicholas, *Questions of the American Revolution*.

74. David R. Roediger, *The Wages of Whiteness*.

75. IBW, "America in Crisis: Aspects and Dimensions, *IBW Special Report* (July 1975): 1–2, 4, 7.

76. Lerone Bennett Jr., *IBW and Education for Liberation*, vi. "Interview: Vincent Harding's Black World," *The Black Collegian* (September/October 1971): 30.

77. Abelove et al., eds., *Visions of History*, 232.

Chapter 5. "The Tapes Were the Heart of the Matter"

1. "Memo of Burglary," IBW Papers—IBW Under Attack Series. "Watergate-Type Break-In At IBW: Challenge and Response, March 16, 1975" IBW Press Release, Michigan State University, East Lansing, Urban Affairs Vertical File.

2. James T. Patterson, *Grand Expectations*, 783–90. Carroll, *It Seemed Like Nothing Happened*, 126–35.

3. Carroll, *It Seemed Like Nothing Happened*, 126–35.

4. J. Craig Jenkins and Craig M. Eckert, "Channeling Black Insurgency Elite Patronage and Professional Social Movement Organizations in the Development of the Black Movement," *American Sociological Review* 51:6 (Dec 1986): 812–29. Herbert H. Haines, "Black Radicalism and the Funding of Civil Rights," *Social Problems* 32:1 (October 1984): 31–43.

5. Devin Fergus, *Liberalism, Black Power, and the Making of American Politics, 1965–1980*, 196–231. Christopher Strain, "Soul City, North Carolina: Black Power, Utopia, and the African American Dream," *Journal of African American History* 89:1 (Winter 2004): 57–74.

6. David Cunningham, *There's Something Happening Here*, 35–36.

7. David Garrow, *The FBI and Martin Luther King, Jr.* Excerpt in Glick, *War at Home*, 78–79.

8. Marable, *Race, Reform, and Rebellion*, 111–12. Grady-Willis, "Black Panther Party: State Repression and Political Prisoners," in *Black Panther Party Reconsidered*, 363–90.

9. Tom Wells, *Wild Man*, 1–31. David Rudenstein, *The Day the Presses Stopped*.

10. Glick, *War at Home*. Patterson, *Grand Expectations*, 771–78.

11. "Suit Charges Bias by Atlanta Police," *New York Times*, April 28, 1973, 18.

12. Glick, *War at Home*. FBI, "Institute of the Black World Racial Matters," file #: 157-4032-27, FBI Archive. Cunningham, *There's Something Happening Here*, 181–90.

13. Cummings, *The Rise and Fall of California's Radical Prison Movement*, 222–51.

14. Garner, "The Stormy Reign of John Inman," the *Atlanta Journal-Constitution*, August 25, 1974, 7, 42–43. Grady-Willis, *Challenging US Apartheid*, 173–86.

15. Brenda J. Wright, "Policewoman Planted on VOICE Staff," *Atlanta Voice*, May 11, 1974, 1. "Police Press Spy Probe Asked," *Atlanta Constitution*, May 16, 1974, 1. Brenda Wright, "Inman Confesses to Undercover Agent at VOICE," *Atlanta Voice*, May 18, 1974, 1.

16. Ibid. Gregg Mathis, "'Terrorist' Story a Big Fabrication," *Atlanta Voice*, May 25, 1974, 1. For a typology of COINTELPRO actions, see Cunningham, *There's Something Happening Here*, 233–50.

17. Jim Stewart, "Terrorist Fear Put Spy at 'Voice," *Atlanta Constitution*, May 18, 1974, 1A, 13A. Melanie Finny and Adolph Reed, "Symbionese Liberation Army," *Atlanta Voice*, February 23, 1974, 1. Adolph Reed Jr. is currently a professor in the Department of Political Science at New School University in New York City.

18. Strickland, "Watergate and the Restoration of Black Struggle," *Black World View* no. 8 (November 1973), 1–5. Tom Shick Papers, Box 1, the State of Wisconsin Historical Society. Also printed as William Strickland, "Watergate: Its Meaning for Black America," *Black World* 23:2 (December 1973): 4–14.

19. Ibid.

20. Ibid. Peter Hernon, *A Terrible Thunder*. Kent B. Germany, *New Orleans after the Promises*, 287–95.

21. "Letter to Reg Murphy, editor of the *Atlanta Constitution*, from Mack Jones," May 21, 1974, box 18, folder 3, Vincent Harding Papers.

22. "Letter to The Editor, *The Atlanta Constitution*," May 21, 1974, box 41, folder 23, Vincent Harding Papers.

23. "May 21, 1974 Letter from IBW Staff," box 29, folder 1, Black Economic Research Center Papers, Schomburg Center for Research in Black Culture, New York (hereafter referred to as the BERC Papers). Jim Merriner, "1,000 March for Inman's Ouster," *Atlanta Constitution*, May 28, 1974, 6A.

24. "Watergate-Type Break-In At IBW: Challenge and Response, March 16, 1975," IBW Press Release. Cunningham, *There's Something Happening Here*, 25, 333, note 106. Mark Felt and John O'Conner, *A G-Man's Life*, 261–81.

25. Quoted in Stephen Sandweiss, "Spying on Solidarity: The FBI's Investigations of the Venceremos Brigade and CISPES" (MA thesis, San Francisco State University, 1990), 42.

26. All the notes contained misspelled words, improper punctuation, and poor grammar. They are quoted with these errors.

27. "Watergate-Type Break-In At IBW: Challenge and Response, March 16, 1975," IBW Press Release. "Chronology of Harassment," IBW Papers—IBW Under Attack Series.

28. "March 28, 1975 Letter from Vincent Harding," box 29, folder 1, BERC Papers. "Chronology of Harassment," IBW Papers—IBW Under Attack Series. "Racists Attack Institute of Black World: B.P.P. Demands Investigation, Protection," *Black Panther* 13, no. 16 (April 28, 1975): 1–28.

29. "Attacks on IBW Escalate: A Third Burglary," IBW press release, April 18, 1975, box 29, folder 1, BERC Papers.

30. "May 21, 1975, Letter to Vigilance Committee Members, from Vincent Harding—Copy of threatening note," box 29, folder 1, BERC Papers.

31 "Attacks on IBW Escalate: A Third Burglary," IBW press release, April 18, 1975. "Three Burglaries and Bomb Threats Plague IBW," *IBW Special Report* (July 1975). Alexis Scott Reeves, "IBW Says Attacks Political," *Atlanta Constitution*, April 17, 1975, 7K. Institute of the Black World Vertical File 1974–1979, Robert W. Woodruff Library, The Atlanta University Center. Jim Merriner, "Bond Asks Probe in Terror Report," *Atlanta Constitution*, July 17, 1975, 2C. McDonald was also chair of the John Birch Society and was known as the one of the most conservative members of congress.

32. Cunningham, *There's Something Happening Here*, 233–51.

33. "Joseph Lewis Confession—Atlanta Police Department," June 25, 1975, IBW Papers—IBW Under Attack Series. "Threats and Harassments Subside at IBW," *IBW Special Report* (October 1975).

34. John Elliston, ed., *Psywar on Cuba*.

35. Rabe, *U. S. Intervention in British Guiana*.

36. William Strickland, interview with author, February 7, 2003. Mark Mazzetti and Tim Weiner, "Files on Illegal Spying Show C.I.A. Skeletons From Cold War," the *New York Times*, June 27, 2007, 1A.

37. Carroll, *It Seemed Like Nothing Happened*, 116–35.

38. "Income for the Institute of the Black World, 1969–1970," box 21, folder 28, Vincent Harding Papers.

39. Charles L. Betsey, "A Brief Biography of Robert S. Browne," *Review of Black Political Economy* 35, nos. 2–3 (2008): 57–60.

40. Ibid. Robert S. Browne, "The African American as Scholar, Economist and Activist," in *A Different Vision*, 49–65. Robert S. Browne, "The Origin, Birth, and Adolescence Of 'The Review of Black Political Economy' And the Black Economic Research Center," *Review of Black Political Economy* 21, no. 3 (1993): 9–23. Bernard E. Anderson, "A Tribute to Robert S. Browne," *Review of Black Political Economy* 21, no. 3 (1993): 5–8. Judy Tzu-Chun Wu, "An African-Vietnamese American: Robert S. Browne, the Antiwar Movement, and the Personal/Political Dimensions of Black Internationalism," the *Journal of African American History* 92, no. 4 (2007): 492–515. John W. Handy, "The Emergence of the Black Economic Research Center and the Review of Black Political Economy: 1969–1972," *Review of Black Political Economy* 35, nos. 2–3 (2008): 75–89.

41. Browne, "The Origin, Birth, and Adolescence Of 'The Review of Black Political Economy' And the Black Economic Research Center," 14, 17.

42. "Report on Meeting of Representatives of ISER, IBW, and BERC Held at the Institute of the Black World, Atlanta, GA July 1971," box 28, folder 13, BERC Papers. IBW, *Institute of the Black World Directors Seminar*.

43. "Atlanta Meeting: Committee on Priorities of the Association of the Black Foundation Executives," IBW Papers—Administrative Series. William Strickland to Harriet Michel, November 5, 1971, box 15, folder 3, Vincent Harding Papers. Vincent Harding to Robert Browne, June 9, 1976, box 29, folder 1, BERC Papers. Cruikshank and Scilia, *The Engine That Could*, 322–25.

44. DJB Foundation, *Report of the DJB Foundation*.

45. "On the Black Mission in White Foundation," box 21, folder 16, Vincent Harding Papers.

46. "Memo from Chet Davis for Economic Support Group, February 15, 1971," box 19, folder 5, Vincent Harding Papers. "Fund Development Office: IBW's Fund Raising History," box 21, folder 23, Vincent Harding Papers.

47. "Fund Development Office: IBW's Fund Raising History." "Donation Lists," box 21, folder 29, Vincent Harding Papers. "Fund Appeal," *Monthly Report* (May 1974). Elizabeth Catlett, "Portfolio Advertisement," Institute of the Black World Vertical File, University of Michigan, Special Collections Labidie Collection, Ann Arbor, Michigan.

48. William Strickland, interview with author, February 7, 2003.

49. "Response of the Executive Committee of IBW to Howard Dodson's 'Towards Defining the Black Experience from a Black Perspective,'" box 19, folder 5, Vincent Harding Papers.

50. Vincent Harding to Howard Dodson, October 26, 1975, IBW Papers—Reorganization Series.

51. "November 10, 1975 Memo to IBW Staff from Howard Dodson," IBW Papers—Reorganization Series.

52. IBW, *Quality Education and the Black Community*.

53. Abelove et al., eds., *Visions of History*, 232.

54. "Report to the Board of Directors of the Institute of the Black World, February 25–27, 1977," box 49, folder 28, St. Clair Drake Papers, Schomburg Center for Research in Black Culture, New York.

55. Marable, *Race, Reform, and Rebellion*, 149–84.

56. Derrick E. White, "'Blacks Who Had Not Themselves Personally Suffered Illegal Discrimination:' The Symbolic Incorporation of the Black Middle Class," in *Race and the Foundations of Knowledge*, 197–210.

Epilogue

1. Strickland, "The Rise and Fall of Black Political Culture: Or How Blacks Became a Minority," *IBW Monthly Report* (May/June 1979).

2. Rozell Clark, "Atlanta's Institute of the Black World Holding Birthday Fete," *Atlanta Daily World*, June 5, 1980, 3.

3. Rojas, *From Black Power to Black Studies*, 100–104.

4. Harding, "A Long Hard Winter to Endure," 96.

5. "IBW Project to Engage Scholars in Behalf of Black Studies," the *Journal of Negro History* 66, no. 2 (1981): 177.

6. IBW, "Black Studies Curriculum Development Course Evaluations: Conference II: Culture and Social Analysis: February 12–14, 1982" (paper presented at the Black Studies curriculum development course evaluations in Atlanta, 1982), c22.

7. Grace Lee Boggs, "Education: The Great Obsession," in *Education and Black Struggle*, 61–81.

8. IBW, "Black Studies Curriculum Development Course Evaluations: Conference II: Culture and Social Analysis: February 12–14, 1982," c25.

9. IBW, "Black Studies Curriculum Development Course Evaluations: Conference II: Culture and Social Analysis: February 12–14, 1982," f3.

10. Perry Hall, *In the Vineyard*, 72–73. "Proposal for Black Studies Curriculum Development Project," box 13, folder 7, 21st Century Foundation Papers, Schomburg Center for Research in Black Culture, New York.

11. Wynter, "On Disenchanting Discourse: 'Minority' Literary Criticism and Beyond," 441–42.

12. Gloria T. Hull, Patricia Bell Scott, and Barbara Smith, eds., *All the Women Are White, All the Blacks Are Men, but Some of Us Are Brave*.

13. IBW, "Black Studies Curriculum Development Course Evaluations: Conference II: Culture and Social Analysis: February 12–14, 1982."

14. Harding, *There is a River*, xix.

15. Henry Louis Gates Jr., *Figures in Black*, 32–35.

16. Sylvia Wynter, "Black Metamorphosis," (unpublished essay), IBW Papers-Sylvia Wynter Series. Wynter, "On How We Mistook the Map for the Territory, and Re-Imprisoned Ourselves in Our Unbearable Wrongness of Being, of *Désêtre*: Black Studies toward the Human Project," in *Not Only the Master's Tools*, 107–69. Derrick E. White,

"Black Metamorphosis: A Prelude to Sylvia Wynter's Theory of the Human," *C.L.R. James Journal* 16:1 (Fall 2010): 127–48.

17. Marable, "Introduction: Black Studies and the Racial Mountain," in *Dispatches from the Ebony Tower*, 19–23.

18. Critchlow, *The Conservative Ascendancy*, 121–22.

19. Cochran, *The Color of Freedom*, 55. Emphasis mine.

20. Paul Ricoeur, "Ideology and Utopia," in *From Text to Action*, 316. Thomas Kuhn, *The Structure of Scientific Revolutions*, 37.

21. Thompson, *Double Trouble*, 2–15, 54–62.

22. Marable, "Toward the Black Radical Congress," in *Race and Resistance*, ed. Herb Boyd, 137–42.

23. "Black Radical Congress," in *Let Nobody Turn Us Around*, eds. Manning Marable and Leith Mullings, 592–99.

24. Jennifer Hamer and Clarence Lang, "Black Radicalism, Reinvented: The Promise of the Black Radical Congress," in *Race and Resistance*, ed. Herb Boyd, 118.

25. Quoted in Herb Boyd, "Institute of the Black World Formally Launched," the *Black World Today*, April 30, 2002. I also attended the conference.

26. Robinson, *Black Marxism: The Making of the Black Radical Tradition*, 72–73.

27. Ibid., 171.

28. Howard Dodson accepted a position at the Schomburg Center for Research in Black Culture in the New York Public Library System in 1983. He also brought with him the IBW's files that form the core of my research. There are no references to a specific date of closing—like many organizations, the IBW faded away more than it emphatically closed.

29. Smith, *We Have No Leaders*, 117.

30. Harding, *There Is a River*, xii–xiii.

Bibliography

Manuscript Collections

Archives and Special Collections, Robert W. Woodruff Library, Atlanta University Center. Atlanta University Presidential Records, T. D. Jarrett Records 1939–1978. *Clark College Panther* File. Hoyt Fuller Papers. Institute of the Black World Vertical Files. Maynard Jackson Papers. Walter Rodney Papers.

Archives, the Wisconsin Historical Society. Tom W. Shick Papers.

Ford Foundation Archives. Ford Foundation Headquarters, New York.

Labadie Collection, The University of Michigan. The Institute of the Black World Vertical File.

Manuscripts, Archives, and Rare Books Division, Schomburg Center for Research in Black Culture. New York Public Library. Black Economic Research Center Papers. The Institute of the Black World Papers. Larry Neal Papers. St. Clair Drake Collection. 21st Century Foundation Papers.

Manuscript, Archives, and Rare Book Library, Robert W. Woodruff Library, Emory University. Vincent Harding Papers.

Special Collections Divisions, Michigan State University, American Radicalism Collection. The Institute of the Black World Vertical File.

Interviews

Alkalimat, Abdul. Interviewed by Derrick E. White, April 7, 2006, in East Lansing, Michigan. In possession of author.

Dodson, Jualynne. Interviewed by Derrick E. White, April 6, 2006, in East Lansing, Michigan. In possession of author.

Vincent Harding, Robert Hill, and William Strickland. The Institute of the Black World session, Small Axe Conference at Brown University, April 7, 2005. In possession of author.

Strickland, William. Interviewed by Derrick E. White, February 7, 2003, in New York City. In possession of author.

IBW Publications

Monthly Report, April 1971–October 1979.

The *Black World View*, 1976–79.

Bennett Jr., Lerone. *The Challenge of Blackness*. Atlanta: Institute of the Black World, 1970.

———. *IBW and Education for Liberation*. Chicago: Third World Press/Institute of the Black World, 1973.

Drake, St. Clair. *The Redemption of Africa and Black Religion*. Edited by IBW. Chicago: Third World Press, 1970.

Girvan, Norman. *Aspects of the Political Economy of Race in the Caribbean and the Americas: A Preliminary Interpretation*. Atlanta: Institute of the Black World, 1975.

Harding, Vincent. *Beyond Chaos: Black History and the Search for New Land*. Atlanta: The Institute of the Black World, 1970.

IBW. *Black Analysis for the Seventies, 1971–1972*. Atlanta: IBW Press, 1973.

———, ed. *Black Studies Curriculum Development Course Evaluations: Conference I: History and Political Economy: October 1–3, 1981*. Atlanta: Institute of the Black World, 1982.

———, ed. *Black Studies Curriculum Development Course Evaluation Conference II: Culture and Social analysis: February 12–14, 1982*. Atlanta: Institute of the Black World, 1982.

———, ed. *Education and Black Struggle: Notes from the Colonized World*. Cambridge: Harvard Educational Review, 1974.

———. *Institute of the Black World Directors Seminar*. Atlanta: Institute of the Black World, 1969.

———. *Quality Education and the Black Community*. Atlanta: IBW, 1977.

Walker, Margaret. *How I Wrote Jubilee*. Edited by IBW, *Black Paper*. Chicago: Third World Press, 1972.

Secondary Sources

Abelove, Henry, Betsy Blackmar, Peter Dimock, and Johnathan Scheer, eds. *Visions of History*. New York: Pantheon Books, 1984.

Abelson, Donald E. *Do Think Tanks Matter?: Assessing the Impact of Public Policy Institutes*. Montreal: McGill-Queen's University Press, 2002.

Al-Hadid, Amiri YaSin. "Africana Studies at Tennessee State University: Traditions and Diversity." In *Out of the Revolution: The Development of Africana Studies*, edited by Delores P. and Carlene Young Aldridge, 93–114. Lanham, Maryland: Lexington Books, 2003.

Alexander, Margaret Walker. *Jubilee*. New York: Mariner Books, 1966, 1999.

Alkalimat, Abdul. "Africana Studies in the US." (2007), http://eblackstudies.org/su/complete.pdf.

Anderson, Benedict. *Imagined Communities: Reflections on the Origins and Spread of Nationalism*. New York: Verso Books, 1991.

Anderson, Bernard E. "A Tribute to Robert S. Browne." *Review of Black Political Economy* 21, no. 3 (1993): 5–8.

Anderson, James D. *The Education of Blacks in the South, 1860–1935.* Chapel Hill: University of North Carolina Press, 1988.

Aptheker, Bettina. *The Morning Breaks: The Trial of Angela Davis.* 2nd ed. Ithaca: Cornell University Press, 1975, 1999.

Austin, Curtis J. *Up against the Wall: Violence in the Making and Unmaking of the Black Panther Party.* Fayetteville: University of Arkansas Press, 2006.

Baker, Lee D. *From Savage to Negro: Anthropology and the Construction of Race, 1896–1954.* Berkeley: University of California Press, 1998.

Baldwin, James. *The Fire Next Time.* New York: Vintage, 1963, 1992.

Bass, Amy. *Not the Triumph but the Struggle: The 1968 Olympics and the Making of the Black Athlete.* Minneapolis: University of Minnesota Press, 2002.

Bayor, Ronald H. *Race and the Shaping of Twentieth-Century Atlanta.* Chapel Hill: University of North Carolina Press, 1996.

Beckford, George L. *Persistent Poverty: Underdevelopment in Plantation Economies of the Third World.* New York: Oxford University Press, 1972.

Boggs, Grace Lee. "C.L.R. James: Organizing in the U.S., 1938–1952." In *C.L.R. James: His Intellectual Legacies,* edited by Selwyn Cudjoe and William E. Cain, 163–72. Amherst: University of Massachusetts Press, 1995.

——. *Living for Change: An Autobiography.* Minneapolis: University of Minnesota Press, 1998.

Boggs, James. *The American Revolution: Pages from a Negro Worker's Notebook.* New York: Monthly Review, 1963.

——. *Racism and Class Struggle: Further Pages of a Black Worker's Notebook.* New York: Monthly Review Press, 1970.

Bogues, Anthony. *Black Heretics, Black Prophets: Radical Political Intellectuals.* New York: Routledge, 2003.

Bonilla-Silva, Eduardo. "Rethinking Racism: Toward a Structural Interpretation." *American Sociological Review* 62 (1996): 465–80.

Bositis, David A. *Black Elected Officials: A Statistical Summary 2000.* Washington, D.C.: Joint Center for Political and Economic Studies, 2002.

Branch, Taylor. *Pillar of Fire: America in the King Years, 1963–65.* New York: Simon & Schuster Press, 1998.

——. *At Canaan's Edge: America in the King Years, 1965–68.* New York: Simon and Schuster, 2006.

Brisbane, Robert H. *Black Activism: Racial Revolution in the United States, 1954–1970.* Valley Forge, Penn.: Judson Press, 1973.

——. *The Black Vanguard: Origins of the Negro Social Revolution, 1900–1960.* Valley Forge, Penn.: Judson Press, 1969.

Brown, Scot. *Fighting for Us: Maulana Karenga, the Us Organization, and Black Cultural Nationalism.* New York: New York University Press, 2003.

Browne, Robert S. "The African American as Scholar, Economist and Activist." In *A*

Different Vision: African American Economic Thought, edited by Thomas D. Boston, 49–65. New York: Routledge, 1997.

———. "The Origin, Birth, and Adolescence of 'The Review of Black Political Economy' and the Black Economic Research Center." *Review of Black Political Economy* 21, no. 3 (1993): 9–23.

Brundage, W. Fitzhugh. *The Southern Past: A Clash of Race and Memory*. Cambridge: The Belknap Press, 2005.

Bryant, James W. *A Survey of Black American Doctorates*. New York: Ford Foundation, 1970.

Cabral, Amilcar. *Return to the Source: Selected Speeches of Amilcar Cabral*. New York: African Information Service and African Party for the Independence of Guinea and the Cape Verde Islands (PAIGC), 1973.

Campbell, Horace. *Rasta and Resistance: From Marcus Garvey to Walter Rodney*. Trenton: African World Press, 1987.

Carby, Hazel V. *Race Men*. Cambridge: Harvard University Press, 1998.

Carmichael, Stokely. *Stokely Speaks: Black Power Back to Pan-Africanism*. New York: Random House, 1971.

Carmichael, Stokely, and Ekwueme Michael Thelwell. *Ready for Revolution: The Life and Struggles of Stokely Carmichael (Kwame Ture)*. New York: Scribner, 2003.

Carmichael, Stokely (Kwame Ture), and Charles V. Hamilton. *Black Power: The Politics of Liberation in America*. New York: Random House, 1967.

Carroll, Peter N. *It Seemed Like Nothing Happened: America in the 1970s*. New Brunswick: Rutgers University Press, 1990.

Carson, Clayborne. *In Struggle: SNCC and the Black Awakening of the 1960s*. Cambridge: Harvard University Press, 1981, 1996.

Carson, Clayborne, David J. Garrow, Gerald Gill, Vincent Harding, and Darlene Clarke Hine, eds. *The Eyes on the Prize Reader: Documents, Speeches, and Firsthand Accounts from the Black Freedom Struggle, 1954–1990*. New York: Penguin Books, 1991.

Chisholm, Clinton. "The Rasta-Selassie-Ethiopian Connections." In *Chanting Down Babylon: The Rastafari Reader*, edited by Nathaniel Murrell, William David Spence, and Adrian Anthony McFarlane, 166–77. Philadelphia: Temple University Press, 1998.

Chisholm, Shirley. *The Good Fight*. New York: Harper & Row, 1973.

The Church Society for College Work. *Black Consciousness in Higher Education*. Cambridge: Church Society for College Work, 1968.

Clarke, John Henrik. "The African Heritage Studies Association (AHSA): Some Notes on the Conflict with the African Studies Association (ASA) and the Fight to Reclaim African History." *Issue: A Journal of Opinion* 6, nos. 2/3 (1976): 5–11.

Clay, William L. *Just Permanent Interests: Black Americans in Congress, 1870–1992*. New York: Amistad Press, 1993.

Cleaver, Kathleen, and George Katsiaficas, eds. *Liberation, Imagination, and the Black Panther Party: A New Look at the Panthers and Their Legacy*. New York: Routledge, 2001.

Clegg, Claude A. *An Original Man: The Life and Times of Elijah Muhammad*. New York: St. Martin's Press, 1997.

Cochran, David Carroll. *The Color of Freedom: Race and Contemporary American Liberalism*. Albany: State University of New York Press, 1999.

Countryman, Matthew J. *Up South: Civil Rights and Black Power in Philadelphia, Politics and Culture in Modern America*. Philadelphia: University of Pennsylvania Press, 2006.

Critchlow, Donald T. *The Conservative Ascendancy: How the GOP Right Made Political History*. Cambridge: Harvard University Press, 2007.

Cruikshank, Jeffrey L., and David B. Scilia. *The Engine That Could: Seventy-Five Years of Values-Driven Change at Cummins Engine Company*. Boston: Harvard Business School Press, 1997.

Cruse, Harold. *The Crisis of the Negro Intellectual: A Historical Analysis of the Failure of Black Leadership*. New York: Quill, 1967, 1984.

———. *Plural but Equal: A Critical Study of Blacks and Minorities and America's Plural Society*. New York: William Morrow, 1987.

———. *Rebellion or Revolution?* New York: William Morrow, 1968.

Cummings, Eric. *The Rise and Fall of California's Radical Prison Movement*. Palo Alto: Stanford University Press, 1994.

Cunningham, David. *There's Something Happening Here: The New Left, the Klan, and FBI Counterintelligence*. Berkeley: University of California Press, 2004.

Dagbovie, Pero Gaglo. *The Early Black History Movement, Carter G. Woodson, and Lorenzo Johnston Greene*. Urbana: University of Illinois Press, 2007.

Davies, Gareth. *From Opportunity to Entitlement: The Transformation of and Decline of Great Society Liberalism*. Lawrence: University of Kansas Press, 1996.

Davis, Allison. *Deep South: A Social Anthropological Study of Caste and Class*. Chicago: University of Chicago Press, 1941.

Dawson, Michael C. *Black Visions: The Roots of Contemporary African-American Political Ideologies*. Chicago: University of Chicago Press, 2003.

Daynes, Gary. *Making Villains, Making Heroes: Joseph R. McCarthy, Martin Luther King, Jr. and the Politics of American Memory*. New York: Garland Publishing, 1997.

DJB Foundation. *Report of the DJB Foundation*. Scarsdale, New York: DJB Foundation, 1975.

Downs, Donald. *Cornell '69: Liberalism and the Crisis of the American University*. Ithaca: Cornell University Press, 1999.

Drake, St. Clair. "The Black University and the American Social Order." *Daedalus* 100 (1971): 833–97.

Drake, St. Clair, and Horace Cayton Jr. *Black Metropolis: A Study of Negro Life in a Northern City*. New York: Harcourt, Brace and Company, 1945.

Du Bois, W.E.B. *The Souls of Black Folk*. Boston: Bedford/St. Martin's Books, 1903, 1997.

———. *Black Reconstruction in America, 1860–1880*. New York: Touchstone, 1935, 1995.

Edwards, Harry. *The Revolt of the Black Athlete*. New York: Free Press, 1969.

Elliston, John, ed. *Psywar on Cuba: The Declassified History of U.S. Anti-Castro Propaganda*. New York: Ocean Press, 1999.

Fairclough, Adam. *Martin Luther King Jr.* Athens: University of Georgia Press, 1995.

———. *To Redeem the Soul of America: The Southern Christian Leadership Conference and Martin Luther King, Jr.* Athens: University of Georgia Press, 1987, 2001.

Fanon, Frantz. *The Wretched of the Earth.* New York: Grove Press, 1963.

Favors, Jelani Manu-Gowon. "Shelter in a Time of Storm: Black Colleges and the Rise of Student Activism in Jackson, Mississippi." Ph.D. dissertation, The Ohio State University, 2006.

Felt, Mark, and John O'Conner. *A G-Man's Life: The FBI, Being 'Deep Throat,' and the Struggle for Honor in Washington.* New York: Public Affairs, 2006.

Fergus, Devin. *Liberalism, Black Power, and the Making of American Politics, 1965–1980.* Athens: University of Georgia Press, 2009.

Fleming, Cynthia Griggs. *Soon We Will Not Cry: The Liberation of Ruby Doris Smith Robinson.* Lanham, Maryland: Rowman & Littlefield, 1998.

Flynn, George Q. *Lewis B. Hershey, Mr. Selective Service.* Chapel Hill: University of North Carolina Press, 1985.

Foley, Michael S. *Confronting the War Machine: Draft Resistance During the Vietnam War.* Chapel Hill: University of North Carolina Press, 2003.

Foner, Philip S., ed. *The Black Panthers Speak.* New York: De Capo Press, 1970, 1995.

Ford, Nick Aaron. *Black Studies: Threat or Challenge.* Port Washington, New York: Kennikat Press, 1973.

Forgacs, David, ed. *The Antonio Gramsci Reader.* New York: New York University Press, 2000.

Foucault, Michel. *The Order of Things: An Archaeology of the Human Sciences.* New York: Vintage Press, 1970.

Foucault, Michel, Catharine von Bülow, and Daniel Defert. "The Masked Assassination." In *Warfare in the American Homeland,* edited by Joy James, 140–58. Durham: Duke University Press, 2009.

Fuller, Hoyt, and Dudley Randall. *Homage to Hoyt Fuller.* Detroit: Broadside Press, 1984.

Garrow, David. *The FBI and Martin Luther King, Jr.* New York: W. W. Norton, 1981.

Gasman, Marybeth. *Envisioning Black Colleges: A History of the United Negro College Fund.* Baltimore: Johns Hopkins University Press, 2007.

Gates Jr., Henry Louis. "Preface to Blackness: Text and Pretext." In *Afro-American Literature: The Reconstruction of Instruction,* edited by Dexter Fisher and Robert B. Stepto, 44–71. Chicago: MLA, 1978.

Germany, Kent B. *New Orleans after the Promises: Poverty, Citizenship, and the Search for the Great Society.* Athens: University of Georgia Press, 2007.

Glaude Jr., Eddie S., ed. *Is It Nation Time? Contemporary Essays on Black Power and Black Nationalism.* Chicago: University of Chicago Press, 2006.

———. *In a Shade of Blue: Pragmatism and the Politics of Black America.* Chicago: University of Chicago Press, 2007.

Glazer, Nathan, and Daniel Patrick Moynihan. *Beyond the Melting Pot: The Negroes, Puerto Ricans, Jews, Italians, and Irish of New York.* Cambridge: M.I.T. Press, 1963.

Glenn, Jason E. "A Second Failed Reconstruction?: The Counter Reformation of African American Studies, a Treason on Black Studies." *Journal of West Indian Literature* 10, nos. 1 & 2 (2001): 119–71.

Glick, Brian. *War at Home: Covert Action against U.S. Activists and What We Can Do About It.* Cambridge: South End Press, 1989.

Godzich, Wlad. "Forward: The Further Possibility of Knowledge." In *Herterologies,* edited by Michael de Ceerteau and Brian Massumi, vii–xxi. Minneapolis: University of Minnesota Press, 1986.

Grady-Willis, Winston A. *Challenging US Apartheid: Atlanta and Black Struggles for Human Rights, 1960–1977.* Durham: Duke University Press, 2006.

Grant-Thomas, Andrew, and john a. powell. "Toward a Structural Racism Framework." *Poverty and Race* 15, no. 6 (2006): 3–6.

Haines, Herbert H. "Black Radicalism and the Funding of Civil Rights." *Social Problems* 32, no. 1 (October 1984): 31–43.

Hall, Perry. *In the Vineyard: Working in African American Studies.* Knoxville: University of Tennessee Press, 1999.

Hall, Stephen G. *A Faithful Account of the Race: African American Historical Writing in Nineteenth-Century America.* Chapel Hill: University of North Carolina Press, 2009.

Hamer, Jennifer, and Clarence Lang. "Black Radicalism, Reinvented: The Promise of the Black Radical Congress." In *Race and Resistance: African Americans in the 21st Century,* edited by Herb Boyd, 109–36. Cambridge: South End Press, 2002.

Hampton, Henry, and Steve Fayer, eds. *Voices of Freedom: An Oral History of the Civil Rights Movement from the 1950s through the 1980s.* New York: Bantam Books, 1990.

Harding, Rachel E., and Vincent Harding. "Biography, Democracy and Spirit: An Interview with Vincent Harding." *Callaloo* 20, no. 3 (1997): 682–98.

Harding, Vincent. *The Other American Revolution.* Los Angeles: Center for Afro-American Studies, UCLA, 1980.

———. *There Is a River: Black Struggle in America.* New York: Harcourt Brace Jovanovich, 1981.

———. *Martin Luther King: The Inconvenient Hero.* Maryknoll, New York: Orbis Books, 1996.

Henderson, Stephen E. "'Survival Motion': A Study of the Black Writer in the Black Revolution in America." In *The Militant Black Writer in Africa and the United States,* edited by Mercer Cook and Stephen E. Henderson, 65–129. Madison: University of Wisconsin Press, 1969.

———, ed. *Understanding Black Poetry: Black Speech and Black Music as Poetic Reference.* New York: William and Morrow, 1973.

Hernon, Petter. *A Terrible Thunder: The Story of the New Orleans Sniper.* New Orleans: Garrett County Press, 1978, 2002.

Hill, Robert, ed. *The Marcus Garvey and Universal Negro Improvement Association Papers: 1826–1919.* Berkeley: University of California Press, 1983.

Hill, Robert A. "Preface: The C.L.R. James Lectures." *Small Axe* 8 (September 2000): 61–64.

———. "From *New World* to *Abeng*: George Beckford and the Horn of Black Power in Jamaica, 1968–1970." *Small Axe* 24 (October 2007): 1–15.

Holloway, Jonathan Scott. *Confronting the Veil: Abram Harris Jr., E. Franklin Frazier, and Ralph Bunche, 1919–1941.* Chapel Hill: University of North Carolina Press, 2002.

Holloway, Jonathan Scott, and Ben Keppel. "Introduction: Segregated Social Science and Its Legacy." In *Black Scholars on the Line: Race, Social Science, and American Thought in the Twentieth Century*, edited by Jonathan Scott Holloway and Ben Keppel, 1–37. Notre Dame: University of Notre Dame Press, 2007.

Honey, Michael K. *Going Down Jericho Road: The Memphis Strike, Martin Luther King's Last Campaign.* New York: W. W. Norton, 2007.

Horne, Gerald. *Race Woman: The Lives of Shirley Graham Du Bois.* New York: New York University Press, 2000.

Hull, Gloria T., Patricia Bell Scott, and Barbara Smith, eds. *All the Women Are White, All the Blacks Are Men, but Some of Us Are Brave: Black Women's Studies.* Old Westbury, New York: The Feminist Press, 1982.

Jackson, George. *Soledad Brother: The Prison Letters of George Jackson.* Chicago: Lawrence Hill Books, 1970, 1994.

Jackson, Thomas F. *From Civil Rights to Human Rights: Martin Luther King, Jr., and the Struggle for Economic Justice.* Philadelphia: University of Pennsylvania Press, 2006.

James, C.L.R. *Black Jacobins: Toussaint L'ouverture and the San Domingo Revolution.* 2nd ed. New York: Vintage Press, 1938, 1962.

James, C.L.R., Raya Dunayevskaya, and Grace Lee. *State Capitalism and World Revolution.* Chicago: Charles H. Kerr, 1986.

Jeffries, Hasan Kwame. *Bloody Lowndes: Civil Rights and Black Power in Alabama's Black Belt.* New York: New York University Press, 2009.

Jeffries, Judson L., ed. *Black Power in the Belly of the Beast.* Urbana: University of Illinois Press, 2006.

———. *Huey P. Newton: The Radical Theorist.* Jackson: University Press of Mississippi, 2002.

Jenkins, J. Craig, and Craig M. Eckert. "Channeling Black Insurgency Elite Patronage and Professional Social Movement Organizations in the Development of the Black Movement." *American Sociological Review* 51, no. 6 (December 1986): 812–29.

Johnson, Cedric. *Revolutionaries to Race Leaders: Black Power and the Making of African American Politics.* Minneapolis: University of Minnesota Press, 2007.

Jones, Charles E., ed. *The Black Panther Party: Reconsidered.* Baltimore: Black Classic Press, 1998.

Jones, Mack H. "Black Political Empowerment in Atlanta: Myth and Reality." *Annals of the American Academy of Political and Social Science* 439 (1978): 90–117.

Joseph, Peniel E. "Black Liberation without Apology: Reconceptualizing the Black Power Movement." *Black Scholar* 31, nos. 3/4 (2001): 2.

———. "Dashikis and Democracy: Black Studies, Student Activism, and the Black Power Movement." *Journal of African American History* 88, no. 2 (2003): 182–203.

———. *Waiting 'Til the Midnight Hour: A Narrative History of Black Power in America.* New York: Henry Holt, 2006.

Karenga, Maulana. *Introduction to Black Studies.* Los Angeles: University of Sankore Press, 1979, 1993.

Kilson, Martin. "Anatomy of the Black Studies Movement." the *Massachusetts Review* 10, no. 4 (1969): 718–25.

King, Martin Luther Jr. *Where Do We Go from Here: Chaos or Community?* Boston: Beacon Press, 1968, 2010.

———. *The Trumpet of Conscience.* New York: Random House, 1968.

Kruse, Kevin. *White Flight: Atlanta and the Making of Modern Conservatism.* Princeton: Princeton University Press, 2005.

Kuhn, Thomas. *The Structure of Scientific Revolutions.* 3rd ed. Chicago: University of Chicago Press, 1962, 1996.

Kusch, Frank. *Battleground Chicago: The Police and the 1968 Democratic National Convention.* Chicago: University of Chicago Press, 2008.

"Kweli." In *The Perspectives Gained: Findings of a Five Day Black University*, edited by M. Lee Montgomery. New York: National Association for African American Education, 1970.

Ladner, Joyce, ed. *The Death of White Sociology: Essays on Race and Culture.* Baltimore: Black Classic Press, 1973, 1998.

Ladner, Joyce. *Tomorrow's Tomorrow: The Black Woman.* Garden City, New York: Doubleday, 1971.

Lawson, Bill E., and Donald F. Koch, eds. *Pragmatism and the Problem of Race.* Bloomington: Indiana University Press, 2004.

Lawson, Steven F. "Freedom Then, Freedom Now: The Historiography of the Civil Rights Movement." the *American Historical Review* 96, no. 2 (1991): 456–71.

Lawson, Steven F., and Charles Payne, eds. *Debating the Civil Rights Movement, 1945–1968.* Lanham, Marlyand: Rowman and Littlefield, 1998.

Lefever, Harry G. *Undaunted by the Fight: Spelman College and the Civil Rights Movement, 1957–1967.* Macon, Georgia: Mercer University Press, 2005.

Levine, Lawrence. *Highbrow/Lowbrow: The Emergence of Cultural Hierarchy in America.* Cambridge: Harvard University Press, 1988.

Lewis, Rupert. *Walter Rodney's Intellectual and Political Thought.* Detroit: Wayne State University Press, 1998.

Leys, Colin. *The Rise and Fall of Development Theory.* Bloomington: Indiana University Press, 1996.

Lucas, Christopher J. *American Higher Education: A History.* New York: Macmillian, 1994.

Manley, Albert E. *A Legacy Continues: The Manley Years at Spelman College, 1953–1976.* Lanham, Maryland: University Press of America, 1995.

Marable, Manning, ed. *Dispatches from the Ebony Tower: Intellectuals Confront the African American Experience.* New York: Columbia University Press, 2000.

Marable, Manning. *Race, Reform, and Rebellion: The Second Reconstruction in Black America, 1945–1990.* 2nd ed. Oxford: University of Mississippi Press, 1991.

———. "Towards the Black Radical Congress." In *Race and Resistance: African Americans in The 21st Century*, edited by Herb Boyd, 137–42. Cambridge: South End Press, 2002.

Marable, Manning, and Leith Mullings, eds. *Let Nobody Turn Us Around: An African American Anthology.* 2nd ed. Lanham, Maryland: Rowman & Littlefield, 2009.

Mays, Benjamin E. *Born to Rebel.* New York: Charles Scibner's Sons, 1971.

McCartney, John T. *Black Power Ideologies: An Essay in African-American Political Thought.* Philadelphia: Temple University, 1992.

McLemee, Scott. *C.L.R. James on the "Negro Question."* Jackson: University Press of Mississippi, 1996.

Menand, Louis. *The Metaphysical Club: A Story of Ideas in America.* New York: Farrar, Straus and Giroux, 2001.

———, ed. *Pragmatism: A Reader.* New York: Vintage Books, 1997.

Miller, E. Ethelbert. "Stephen E. Henderson: Conversation with a Literary Critic." In *A Howard Reader: An Intellectual Cultural Quilt of the African-American Experience,* edited by Paul E. Logan, 317–25. Boston: Houghton Mifflin, 1997.

Mills, Charles. *The Racial Contract.* Ithaca: Cornell University Press, 1997.

Moore, Leonard N. *Carl B. Stokes and the Rise of Black Political Power.* Champaign: University of Illinois Press, 2003.

Morris, Eddie W. "The Contemporary Negro College and the Brain Drain." the *Journal of Negro Education* 41, no. 4 (1972): 309–19.

Moynihan, Daniel P. *The Politics of a Guaranteed Income: The Nixon Administration and the Family Assistance Plan.* New York: Vintage, 1973.

Murrell, Nathaniel Samuel, and Burchell K. Taylor. "Rastafari's Messianic Ideology and Caribbean Theology of Liberation." In *Chanting Down Babylon: The Rastafari Reader,* edited by Nathaniel Murrell, William David Spence, and Adrian Anthony McFarlane, 390–414. Philadelphia: Temple University Press, 1998.

Myrdal, Gunnar. *An American Dilemma: The Negro Problem and Modern Democracy.* New York: Harper and Brothers Publishers, 1944.

National Black Political Agenda. Washington, D.C.: National Black Political Convention, 1972.

Nelson, William E., and Philip J. Meranto. *Electing Black Mayors: Political Action in the Black Community.* Columbus: Ohio State University Press, 1977.

Norment Jr., Nathaniel, ed. *The Addison Gayle Jr. Reader.* Urbana: University of Illinois Press, 2009.

Novick, Peter. *That Noble Dream: The 'Objectivity Question' and the American Historical Profession.* Cambridge: Cambridge University Press, 1988.

O'Conner, Alice. *Poverty Knowledge: Social Science, Social Policy, and the Poor in Twentieth Century U.S. History.* Princeton: Princeton University Press, 2001.

Ogbar, Jeffrey O. G. *Black Power: Radical Politics and African American Identity.* Baltimore: Johns Hopkins University Press, 2004.

Payne, Charles M. *I've Got the Light of Freedom: The Organizing Tradition and the Mississippi Freedom Struggle.* Berkeley: University of California Press, 1996.

Pocock, J.G.A. *Virtue, Commerce, and History: Essays on Political Thought and History Chiefly in the Eighteenth Century.* Cambridge: Cambridge University Press, 1985.

———. *Politics, Language, and Time: Essays on Political Thought and History.* Chicago: University of Chicago Press, 1989.

Rabe, Stephen G. *U. S. Intervention in British Guiana: A Cold War Story.* Chapel Hill: University of North Carolina Press, 2005.

Rainwater, Lee, and William L. Yancey. *The Moynihan Report and the Politics of Controversy*. Cambridge: M.I.T. Press, 1967.

Reed Jr., Adolph. "Black Particularity Reconsidered." In *Is It Nation Time? Contemporary Essays on Black Power and Black Nationalism*, edited by Eddie S. Glaude Jr., 39–66. Chicago: University of Chicago Press, 2002.

Ricoeur, Paul. "Ideology and Utopia." In *From Text to Action: Essays in Hermeneutics, II*, translated by Kathleen Blamey and John B. Thompson, 308–24. Evanston: Northwestern University Press, 1991.

Robinson, Armstead L., Craig C. Foster, and Donald H. Ogilvie, eds. *Black Studies in the University*. New Haven: Yale University Press, 1969.

Robinson, Cedric J. *Black Marxism: The Making of the Black Radical Tradition*. Chapel Hill: University of North Carolina Press, 2000, 1983.

Robinson, Dean E. *Black Nationalism in American Politics and Thought*. Cambridge: Cambridge University Press, 2001.

Robnett, Belinda. *How Long? How Long? African-American Women in the Struggle for Civil Rights*. New York: Oxford University Press, 1997.

Rodney, Walter. *Grounding with My Brothers*. London: Bogle-L'Ouverture Press, 1969.

———. *How Europe Underdeveloped Africa*. Washington, D.C.: Howard University Press, 1972, 1981.

———. *Walter Rodney Speaks: Making of an African Intellectual*. Edited by Robert Hill. Trenton: Third World Press, 1990.

———. "African History in the Service of the Black Liberation." *Small Axe* 5, no. 2 (2001): 66–80.

Roediger, David R. *The Wages of Whiteness: Race and the Making of the American Working Class*. London: Verso, 1991.

Rojas, Fabio. *From Black Power to Black Studies: How a Radical Social Movement Became an Academic Discipline*. Baltimore: Johns Hopkins University Press, 2007.

Rooks, Noliwe. *White Money/ Black Power: The Surprising History of African American Studies and the Crisis of Race in Higher Education*. Boston: Beacon Press, 2006.

Rustin, Bayard. "From Protest to Politics: The Future of the Civil Rights Movement." *Commentary* 39, no. 2 (1965): 25–31.

Sandweiss, Stephen. "Spying on Solidarity: The FBI's Investigations of the Venceremos Brigade and CISPES." MA thesis, San Francisco State University, 1990.

Schulman, Bruce. *The Seventies: The Great Shift in American Culture*. Cambridge: Da Capo Press, 2002.

Scott, Daryl. *Contempt and Pity: Social Policy and the Image of the Damaged Black Psyche, 1880–1996*. Chapel Hill: University of North Carolina Press, 1997.

Scott, David. "The Archaeology of Black Memory: An Interview with Robert A. Hill." *Small Axe* 5 (March 1999): 80–150.

Self, Robert O. *American Babylon: Race and the Struggle for Postwar Oakland*. Princeton: Princeton University Press, 2003.

Sellers, Cleveland, and Robert Terrell. *The River of No Return: The Autobiography of a Black Militant and the Life and Death of SNCC*. Jackson: University Press of Mississippi, 1990, 1973.

Semmes, Clovis E. "Foundations in Africana Studies: Revisiting *Negro Digest/Black World*, 1961–1976." *Western Journal of Black Studies* 25, no. 4 (2001): 195–201.

Shelby, Tommy. *We Who are Dark: The Philosophical Foundations of Black Solidarity*. Cambridge: Harvard University Press, 2005.

Singh, Nikhil Pal. *Black Is a Country: Race and the Unfinished Struggle for Democracy*. Cambridge: Harvard University Press, 2005.

Smethurst, James Edward. *The Black Arts Movement: Literary Nationalism in the 1960s and 1970s*. Chapel Hill: University of North Carolina Press, 2005.

Smith, Adam. *An Inquiry into the Nature and Causes of the Wealth of Nations*. Abridged ed. New York: The Modern Library, 1776, 1985.

Smith, James A. *The Idea Brokers: Think Tanks and the New Policy Elites*. New York: Free Press, 1991.

Smith, Robert C. *We Have No Leaders: African Americans in the Post-Civil Rights Era*. Albany: SUNY Press, 1996.

Springer, Kimberly. *Living for the Revolution: Black Feminist Organizations, 1968–1980*. Durham: Duke University Press, 2005.

Stephens, Ronald J. *Idlewild: The Black Eden of Michigan*. Charleston, South Carolina: Arcadia, 2001.

Stone, Clarence N. *Regime Politics: Governing Atlanta, 1946–1988*. Lawrence: University of Kansas, 1989.

Strain, Christopher B. "Soul City, North Carolina: Black Power, Utopia, and the African American Dream," *Journal of African American History* 89, no. 1 (Winter 2004), 57–74.

———. *Pure Fire: Self-Defense as Activism in the Civil Rights Era*. Athens: University of Georgia Press, 2005.

Strickland, William. *Malcolm X: Make It Plain*. New York: Viking, 1994.

———. "Critik: The Institute of the Black World (IBW), the Political Legacy of Martin Luther King, and the Intellectual Struggle to Rethink America's Racial Meaning." In *Radicalism in the South since Reconstruction*, edited by Chris Green, Rachel Rubin, and James Smethurst, 167–79. New York: Palgrave, 2006.

———. "The Movement and Mississippi." *Freedomways* 5, no. 2 (Spring 1965): 310–13.

Sugrue, Thomas J. *The Origins of the Urban Crisis: Race and Inequality in Postwar Detroit*. Princeton: Princeton University Press, 1996.

Taylor, Ula Yvette. *The Veiled Garvey: The Life and Times of Amy Jacques Garvey*. Chapel Hill: University of North Carolina Press, 2002.

Terrell, Robert L. "Black Awareness Versus Negro Traditions: Atlanta University Center." *New South* (Winter 1969):29–40.

Thompson, J. Phillip. *Double Trouble: Black Mayors, Black Communities, and the Call for a Deep Democracy*. New York: Oxford University Press, 2006.

Tucker, Robert C., Karl Marx, and Robert Engels, eds. *The Marx-Engels Reader*. New York: W. W. Norton, 1978.

Tyson, Timothy B. *Radio Free Dixie: Robert F. Williams and the Roots of Black Power*. Chapel Hill: University of North Carolina Press, 1999.

Van Deburg, William. *New Day in Babylon: The Black Power Movement and American Culture, 1965–1975*. Chicago: University of Chicago Press, 1992.

Von Eschen, Penny M. *Race against Empire: Black Americans and Anticolonialism, 1937–1957*. Ithaca: Cornell University Press, 1997.

Walters, Ronald W. *Black Presidential Politics in America: A Strategic Approach*. Albany: SUNY Press, 1988.

Ward, Stephen. "'Scholarship in the Context of Struggle': Activist Intellectuals, the Institute of the Black World (IBW), and the Contours of Black Power Radicalism." *Black Scholar* 31, nos. 3/4 (2001): 42–53.

———. "The Third World Women's Alliance: Black Feminist Radicalism and Black Power Politics." In *The Black Power Movement: Rethinking the Civil Rights–Black Power Era*, edited by Peniel E. Joseph, 119–44. New York: Routledge, 2006.

Watkins, William H. *The White Architects of Black Education: Ideology and Power in America, 1865–1954*. New York: Teacher's College Press, 2001.

Watts, Jerry Gafio. *Amiri Baraka: The Politics and the Art of a Black Intellectual*. New York: New York University Press, 2001.

———, ed. *Harold Cruse's* The Crisis of the Negro Intellectual *Reconsidered*. New York: Routledge, 2004.

Webb, Clive, ed. *Massive Resistance: Southern Opposition to the Second Reconstruction*. New York: Oxford University Press, 2005.

Wendt, Simon. *The Spirit and the Shotgun: Armed Resistance and the Struggle for Civil Rights*. Gainesville: University Press of Florida, 2007.

West, Michael O. "Seeing Darkly: Guyana, Black Power, and Walter Rodney's Expulsion from Jamaica." *Small Axe* 25 (February 2008): 93–104.

White, Derrick E. "'Blacks Who Had Not Themselves Personally Suffered Illegal Discrimination': The Symbolic Incorporation of the Black Middle Class." In *Race and the Foundations of Knowledge*, edited by Joseph Young and Jana Evans Braziel, 197–210. Urbana: University of Illinois Press, 2006.

———. "Black Metamorphosis: A Prelude to Sylvia Wynter's Theory of the Human." *C.L.R. James Journal* 16, no. 1 (Fall 2010): 127–48.

Williamson, Joy Ann. *Radicalizing the Ebony Tower: Black Colleges and the Black Freedom Struggle in Mississippi*. New York: Teachers College Press, 2008.

Wilson, Francille Rusan. *The Segregated Scholars: Black Social Scientists and the Creation of Black Labor Studies, 1890–1950*. Charlottesville: University of Virginia Press, 2006.

Wilson, William Julius. *More Than Just Race: Being Black and Poor in the Inner City*. New York: W. W. Norton, 2009.

Wolters, Raymond. *The New Negro on Campus: Black College Rebellions of the 1920s*. Princeton: Princeton University Press, 1975.

Woodard, Komozi. *A Nation within a Nation: Amiri Baraka (Leroi Jones) & Black Power Politics*. Chapel Hill: University of North Carolina Press, 1999.

Woodson, Carter G. *The Mis-Education of the Negro*. Washington, D.C.: Associated Publishers, 1972, 1933.

Wu, Judy Tzu-Chun. "An African-Vietnamese American: Robert S. Browne, the Anti-

War Movement, and the Personal/Political Dimensions of Black Internationalism." the *Journal of African American History* 92, no. 4 (2007): 492–515.

Wynter, Sylvia. "'No Humans Involved': An Open Letter to My Colleagues." *Forum N.H.I.: Knowledge for the 21st Century* 1, no. 1 (1994): 42–69.

———. "On Disenchanting Discourse: 'Minority' Literary Criticism and Beyond." In *The Nature and Context of Minority Discourse*, edited by Abdul R. JanMohamed and David Lloyd, 432–71. New York: Oxford University Press, 1990.

———. "Towards the Sociogenic Principle: Fanon, the Puzzle of Conscious Experience, of 'Identity' and What It's Like to Be 'Black.'" In *National Identity and Sociopolitical Change: Latin America between Marginalization and Integration*, edited by Mercedes and Antonio Gómez-Moriana Durán-Cogan, 30–66. New York: Routledge Press, 2001.

———. "Unsettling the Coloniality of Being/Power/Truth/Freedom: Towards the Human, after Man, Its Overrepresentation—An Argument." *New Centennial Review* 3, no. 3 (2003): 257–337.

———. "On How We Mistook the Map for the Territory, and Re-Imprisoned Ourselves in Our Unbearable Wrongness of Being of Désêtre." In *Not Only the Master's Tools: African-American Studies in Theory and Practice*, edited by Lewis B. Gordon and Jane Anna Gordon, 107–69. Boulder, Col.: Paradigm, 2005.

X, Malcolm. *Malcolm X Speaks: Selected Speeches and Statements.* Edited by George Breitman. New York: Grove Press, 1965, 1994.

Young, Coleman, and Lonnie Wheeler. *Hard Stuff: The Autobiography of Coleman Young.* New York: Viking, 1994.

Index

Associate professor of history at Florida Atlantic University, Derrick E. White is a contributor to *"We Shall Independent Be": African American Place-Making and the Struggle to Claim Space in the United States* and has published articles in the *Journal of African American History*, the *C.L.R. James Journal*, and the *Florida Historical Quarterly*.

SOUTHERN DISSENT
Edited by Stanley Harrold and Randall M. Miller

The Other South: Southern Dissenters in the Nineteenth Century, by Carl N. Degler, with a new preface (2000)

Crowds and Soldiers in Revolutionary North Carolina: The Culture of Violence in Riot and War, by Wayne E. Lee (2001)

"Lord, We're Just Trying to Save Your Water": Environmental Activism and Dissent in the Appalachian South, by Suzanne Marshall (2002)

The Changing South of Gene Patterson: Journalism and Civil Rights, 1960–1968, edited by Roy Peter Clark and Raymond Arsenault (2002)

Gendered Freedoms: Race, Rights, and the Politics of Household in the Delta, 1861–1875, by Nancy D. Bercaw (2003)

Civil War on Race Street: The Civil Rights Movement in Cambridge, Maryland, by Peter B. Levy (2003)

South of the South: Jewish Activists and the Civil Rights Movement in Miami, 1945–1960, by Raymond A. Mohl, with contributions by Matilda "Bobbi" Graff and Shirley M. Zoloth (2004)

Throwing Off the Cloak of Privilege: White Southern Women Activists in the Civil Rights Era, edited by Gail S. Murray (2004)

The Atlanta Riot: Race, Class, and Violence in a New South City, by Gregory Mixon (2004)

Slavery and the Peculiar Solution: A History of the American Colonization Society, by Eric Burin (2005; first paperback edition, 2008)

"I Tremble for My Country": Thomas Jefferson and the Virginia Gentry, by Ronald L. Hatzenbuehler (2006)

From Saint-Domingue to New Orleans: Migration and Influences, by Nathalie Dessens (2007)

Higher Education and the Civil Rights Movement: White Supremacy, Black Southerners, and College Campuses, edited by Peter Wallenstein (2007)

Burning Faith: Church Arson in the American South, by Christopher B. Strain (2008)

Black Power in Dixie: A Political History of African Americans in Atlanta, by Alton Hornsby Jr. (2009)

Looking South: Race, Gender, and the Transformation of Labor from Reconstruction to Globalization, Mary E. Frederickson (2011)

Southern Character: Essays in Honor of Bertram Wyatt-Brown, edited by Lisa Tendrich Frank and Daniel Kilbride (2011)

The Challenge of Blackness: The Institute of the Black World and Political Activism in the 1970s, by Derrick E. White (2011)